Tables For Monthly Mortgages

W9-CEX-846

Covering Interest Rates from 9% to 22%

Copyright © 1980 by Delphi Information
  Sciences Corporation
All rights reserved
Published by Contemporary Books, Inc.
180 North Michigan Avenue, Chicago, Illinois 60601
Manufactured in the United States of America
International Standard Book Number: 0-8092-5709-2

Published simultaneously in Canada by
Beaverbooks, Ltd.
150 Lesmill Road
Don Mills, Ontario M3B 2T5
Canada

This edition published by arrangement with
Delphi Information Sciences Corporation

Contemporary Books, Inc.
Chicago

AMOUNT OF LOAN	NUMBER OF YEARS IN TERM						
	1	2	3	4	5	10	15
$ 25	2.19	1.15	.80	.63	.52	.32	.26
50	4.38	2.29	1.59	1.25	1.04	.64	.51
75	6.56	3.43	2.39	1.87	1.56	.96	.77
100	8.75	4.57	3.18	2.49	2.08	1.27	1.02
200	17.50	9.14	6.36	4.98	4.16	2.54	2.03
300	26.24	13.71	9.54	7.47	6.23	3.81	3.05
400	34.99	18.28	12.72	9.96	8.31	5.07	4.06
500	43.73	22.85	15.90	12.45	10.38	6.34	5.08
600	52.48	27.42	19.08	14.94	12.46	7.61	6.09
700	61.22	31.98	22.26	17.42	14.54	8.87	7.10
800	69.97	36.55	25.44	19.91	16.61	10.14	8.12
900	78.71	41.12	28.62	22.40	18.69	11.41	9.13
1000	87.46	45.69	31.80	24.89	20.76	12.67	10.15
2000	174.91	91.37	63.60	49.78	41.52	25.34	20.29
2500	218.63	114.22	79.50	62.22	51.90	31.67	25.36
3000	262.36	137.06	95.40	74.66	62.28	38.01	30.43
4000	349.81	182.74	127.20	99.55	83.04	50.68	40.58
5000	437.26	228.43	159.00	124.43	103.80	63.34	50.72
6000	524.71	274.11	190.80	149.32	124.56	76.01	60.86
7000	612.17	319.80	222.60	174.20	145.31	88.68	71.00
8000	699.62	365.48	254.40	199.09	166.07	101.35	81.15
9000	787.07	411.17	286.20	223.97	186.83	114.01	91.29
10000	874.52	456.85	318.00	248.86	207.59	126.68	101.43
11000	961.97	502.54	349.80	273.74	228.35	139.35	111.57
12000	1049.42	548.22	381.60	298.63	249.11	152.02	121.72
13000	1136.87	593.91	413.40	323.51	269.86	164.68	131.86
14000	1224.33	639.59	445.20	348.40	290.62	177.35	142.00
15000	1311.78	685.28	477.00	373.28	311.38	190.02	152.14
16000	1399.23	730.96	508.80	398.17	332.14	202.69	162.29
17000	1486.68	776.65	540.60	423.05	352.90	215.35	172.43
18000	1574.13	822.33	572.40	447.94	373.66	228.02	182.57
19000	1661.58	868.02	604.20	472.82	394.41	240.69	192.72
20000	1749.03	913.70	636.00	497.71	415.17	253.36	202.86
21000	1836.49	959.38	667.80	522.59	435.93	266.02	213.00
22000	1923.94	1005.07	699.60	547.48	456.69	278.69	223.14
23000	2011.39	1050.75	731.40	572.36	477.45	291.36	233.29
24000	2098.84	1096.44	763.20	597.25	498.21	304.03	243.43
25000	2186.29	1142.12	795.00	622.13	518.96	316.69	253.57
26000	2273.74	1187.81	826.80	647.02	539.72	329.36	263.71
27000	2361.19	1233.49	858.60	671.90	560.48	342.03	273.86
28000	2448.65	1279.18	890.40	696.79	581.24	354.70	284.00
29000	2536.10	1324.86	922.20	721.67	602.00	367.36	294.14
30000	2623.55	1370.55	954.00	746.56	622.76	380.03	304.28
31000	2711.00	1416.23	985.80	771.44	643.51	392.70	314.43
32000	2798.45	1461.92	1017.60	796.33	664.27	405.37	324.57
33000	2885.90	1507.60	1049.40	821.21	685.03	418.04	334.71
34000	2973.36	1553.29	1081.20	846.10	705.79	430.70	344.86
35000	3060.81	1598.97	1113.00	870.98	726.55	443.37	355.00
36000	3148.26	1644.66	1144.80	895.87	747.31	456.04	365.14
37000	3235.71	1690.34	1176.60	920.75	768.06	468.71	375.28
38000	3323.16	1736.03	1208.39	945.64	788.82	481.37	385.43
39000	3410.61	1781.71	1240.19	970.52	809.58	494.04	395.57
40000	3498.06	1827.39	1271.99	995.41	830.34	506.71	405.71
45000	3935.32	2055.82	1430.99	1119.83	934.13	570.05	456.42
50000	4372.58	2284.24	1589.99	1244.26	1037.92	633.38	507.14
55000	4809.84	2512.67	1748.99	1368.68	1141.71	696.72	557.85
60000	5247.09	2741.09	1907.99	1493.11	1245.51	760.06	608.56
65000	5684.35	2969.51	2066.99	1617.53	1349.30	823.40	659.28
70000	6121.61	3197.94	2225.99	1741.96	1453.09	886.74	709.99
75000	6558.87	3426.36	2384.98	1866.38	1556.88	950.07	760.70
80000	6996.12	3654.78	2543.98	1990.81	1660.67	1013.41	811.42
85000	7433.38	3883.21	2702.98	2115.23	1764.47	1076.75	862.13
90000	7870.64	4111.63	2861.98	2239.66	1868.26	1140.09	912.84
95000	8307.90	4340.06	3020.98	2364.08	1972.05	1203.42	963.56
100000	8745.15	4568.48	3179.98	2488.51	2075.84	1266.76	1014.27

2

MONTHLY AMORTIZING PAYMENTS 9.00%

AMOUNT OF LOAN	NUMBER OF YEARS IN TERM						
	20	25	28	29	30	35	40
$ 25	.23	.21	.21	.21	.21	.20	.20
50	.45	.42	.41	.41	.41	.40	.39
75	.68	.63	.62	.61	.61	.59	.58
100	.90	.84	.82	.82	.81	.79	.78
200	1.80	1.68	1.64	1.63	1.61	1.57	1.55
300	2.70	2.52	2.45	2.44	2.42	2.36	2.32
400	3.60	3.36	3.27	3.25	3.22	3.14	3.09
500	4.50	4.20	4.09	4.06	4.03	3.92	3.86
600	5.40	5.04	4.90	4.87	4.83	4.71	4.63
700	6.30	5.88	5.72	5.68	5.64	5.49	5.40
800	7.20	6.72	6.54	6.49	6.44	6.28	6.18
900	8.10	7.56	7.35	7.30	7.25	7.06	6.95
1000	9.00	8.40	8.17	8.11	8.05	7.84	7.72
2000	18.00	16.79	16.33	16.21	16.10	15.68	15.43
2500	22.50	20.98	20.41	20.26	20.12	19.60	19.29
3000	27.00	25.18	24.49	24.31	24.14	23.52	23.15
4000	35.99	33.57	32.66	32.41	32.19	31.36	30.86
5000	44.99	41.96	40.82	40.51	40.24	39.20	38.57
6000	53.99	50.36	48.98	48.61	48.28	47.04	46.29
7000	62.99	58.75	57.15	56.72	56.33	54.88	54.00
8000	71.98	67.14	65.31	64.82	64.37	62.72	61.71
9000	80.98	75.53	73.47	72.92	72.42	70.56	69.43
10000	89.98	83.92	81.63	81.02	80.47	78.40	77.14
11000	98.97	92.32	89.80	89.12	88.51	86.24	84.85
12000	107.97	100.71	97.96	97.22	96.56	94.08	92.57
13000	116.97	109.10	106.12	105.33	104.61	101.92	100.28
14000	125.97	117.49	114.29	113.43	112.65	109.76	108.00
15000	134.96	125.88	122.45	121.53	120.70	117.60	115.71
16000	143.96	134.28	130.61	129.63	128.74	125.44	123.42
17000	152.96	142.67	138.78	137.73	136.79	133.28	131.14
18000	161.96	151.06	146.94	145.83	144.84	141.12	138.85
19000	170.95	159.45	155.10	153.93	152.88	148.96	146.56
20000	179.95	167.84	163.26	162.04	160.93	156.80	154.28
21000	188.95	176.24	171.43	170.14	168.98	164.64	161.99
22000	197.94	184.63	179.59	178.24	177.02	172.48	169.70
23000	206.94	193.02	187.75	186.34	185.07	180.32	177.42
24000	215.94	201.41	195.92	194.44	193.11	188.16	185.13
25000	224.94	209.80	204.08	202.54	201.16	196.00	192.85
26000	233.93	218.20	212.24	210.65	209.21	203.84	200.56
27000	242.93	226.59	220.41	218.75	217.25	211.68	208.27
28000	251.93	234.98	228.57	226.85	225.30	219.52	215.99
29000	260.93	243.37	236.73	234.95	233.35	227.36	223.70
30000	269.92	251.76	244.89	243.05	241.39	235.20	231.41
31000	278.92	260.16	253.06	251.15	249.44	243.04	239.13
32000	287.92	268.55	261.22	259.26	257.48	250.88	246.84
33000	296.91	276.94	269.38	267.36	265.53	258.72	254.55
34000	305.91	285.33	277.55	275.46	273.58	266.56	262.27
35000	314.91	293.72	285.71	283.56	281.62	274.40	269.98
36000	323.91	302.12	293.87	291.66	289.67	282.24	277.70
37000	332.90	310.51	302.04	299.76	297.72	290.08	285.41
38000	341.90	318.90	310.20	307.86	305.76	297.92	293.12
39000	350.90	327.29	318.36	315.97	313.81	305.76	300.84
40000	359.90	335.68	326.52	324.07	321.85	313.60	308.55
45000	404.88	377.64	367.34	364.58	362.09	352.80	347.12
50000	449.87	419.60	408.15	405.08	402.32	392.00	385.69
55000	494.85	461.56	448.97	445.59	442.55	431.20	424.25
60000	539.84	503.52	489.78	486.10	482.78	470.40	462.82
65000	584.83	545.48	530.60	526.61	523.01	509.60	501.39
70000	629.81	587.44	571.41	567.12	563.24	548.80	539.96
75000	674.80	629.40	612.23	607.62	603.47	588.00	578.53
80000	719.79	671.36	653.04	648.13	643.70	627.20	617.09
85000	764.77	713.32	693.86	688.64	683.93	666.40	655.66
90000	809.76	755.28	734.67	729.15	724.17	705.60	694.23
95000	854.74	797.24	775.49	769.65	764.40	744.80	732.80
100000	899.73	839.20	816.30	810.16	804.63	784.00	771.37

9.25% MONTHLY AMORTIZING PAYMENTS

AMOUNT OF LOAN	NUMBER OF YEARS IN TERM						
	1	2	3	4	5	10	15
$ 25	2.19	1.15	.80	.63	.53	.33	.26
50	4.38	2.29	1.60	1.26	1.05	.65	.52
75	6.57	3.44	2.40	1.88	1.57	.97	.78
100	8.76	4.58	3.20	2.51	2.09	1.29	1.03
200	17.52	9.16	6.39	5.01	4.18	2.57	2.06
300	26.28	13.74	9.58	7.51	6.27	3.85	3.09
400	35.03	18.32	12.77	10.01	8.36	5.13	4.12
500	43.79	22.90	15.96	12.51	10.44	6.41	5.15
600	52.55	27.48	19.15	15.01	12.53	7.69	6.18
700	61.30	32.06	22.35	17.51	14.62	8.97	7.21
800	70.06	36.64	25.54	20.01	16.71	10.25	8.24
900	78.82	41.22	28.73	22.51	18.80	11.53	9.27
1000	87.57	45.80	31.92	25.01	20.88	12.81	10.30
2000	175.14	91.60	63.84	50.01	41.76	25.61	20.59
2500	218.92	114.50	79.80	62.51	52.20	32.01	25.73
3000	262.71	137.40	95.75	75.00	62.64	38.41	30.88
4000	350.27	183.20	127.67	100.00	83.52	51.22	41.17
5000	437.84	229.00	159.59	125.00	104.40	64.02	51.46
6000	525.41	274.80	191.50	150.00	125.28	76.82	61.76
7000	612.98	320.60	223.42	175.00	146.16	89.63	72.05
8000	700.54	366.40	255.33	200.04	167.04	102.43	82.34
9000	788.11	412.20	287.25	225.04	187.92	115.23	92.63
10000	875.68	458.00	319.17	250.00	208.80	128.04	102.92
11000	963.25	503.80	351.08	275.05	229.68	140.84	113.22
12000	1050.81	549.60	383.00	300.05	250.56	153.64	123.51
13000	1138.38	595.40	414.92	325.06	271.44	166.45	133.80
14000	1225.95	641.20	446.83	350.06	292.32	179.25	144.09
15000	1313.52	687.00	478.75	375.06	313.20	192.05	154.38
16000	1401.08	732.80	510.66	400.07	334.08	204.86	164.68
17000	1488.65	778.60	542.58	425.07	354.96	217.66	174.97
18000	1576.22	824.40	574.50	450.08	375.84	230.46	185.26
19000	1663.79	870.20	606.41	475.08	396.72	243.27	195.55
20000	1751.35	916.00	638.33	500.08	417.60	256.07	205.84
21000	1838.92	961.80	670.25	525.09	438.48	268.87	216.14
22000	1926.49	1007.59	702.16	550.09	459.36	281.68	226.43
23000	2014.06	1053.39	734.08	575.10	480.24	294.48	236.72
24000	2101.62	1099.19	765.99	600.10	501.12	307.28	247.01
25000	2189.19	1144.99	797.91	625.10	522.00	320.09	257.30
26000	2276.76	1190.79	829.83	650.11	542.88	332.89	267.59
27000	2364.33	1236.59	861.74	675.11	563.76	345.69	277.89
28000	2451.89	1282.39	893.66	700.11	584.64	358.50	288.18
29000	2539.46	1328.19	925.58	725.12	605.52	371.30	298.47
30000	2627.03	1373.99	957.49	750.12	626.40	384.10	308.76
31000	2714.60	1419.79	989.41	775.13	647.28	396.91	319.05
32000	2802.16	1465.59	1021.32	800.13	668.16	409.71	329.35
33000	2889.73	1511.39	1053.24	825.13	689.04	422.51	339.64
34000	2977.30	1557.19	1085.16	850.14	709.92	435.32	349.93
35000	3064.87	1602.99	1117.07	875.14	730.80	448.12	360.22
36000	3152.43	1648.79	1148.99	900.15	751.68	460.92	370.51
37000	3240.00	1694.59	1180.90	925.15	772.56	473.73	380.81
38000	3327.57	1740.39	1212.82	950.15	793.44	486.53	391.10
39000	3415.14	1786.19	1244.74	975.16	814.32	499.33	401.39
40000	3502.70	1831.99	1276.65	1000.16	835.20	512.14	411.68
45000	3940.54	2060.98	1436.23	1125.18	939.60	576.15	463.14
50000	4378.38	2289.98	1595.82	1250.20	1044.00	640.17	514.60
55000	4816.21	2518.98	1755.40	1375.22	1148.40	704.18	566.06
60000	5254.05	2747.98	1914.98	1500.24	1252.80	768.20	617.52
65000	5691.89	2976.97	2074.56	1625.26	1357.20	832.22	668.98
70000	6129.73	3205.97	2234.14	1750.28	1461.60	896.23	720.44
75000	6567.56	3434.97	2393.72	1875.30	1566.00	960.25	771.90
80000	7005.40	3663.97	2553.30	2000.32	1670.40	1024.27	823.36
85000	7443.24	3892.97	2712.88	2125.34	1774.80	1088.28	874.82
90000	7881.08	4121.96	2872.46	2250.36	1879.20	1152.30	926.28
95000	8318.91	4350.96	3032.05	2375.38	1983.60	1216.32	977.74
100000	8756.75	4579.96	3191.63	2500.40	2087.99	1280.33	1029.20

4

AMOUNT OF LOAN	NUMBER OF YEARS IN TERM						
	20	25	28	29	30	35	40
$ 25	.23	.22	.21	.21	.21	.21	.20
50	.46	.43	.42	.42	.42	.41	.40
75	.69	.65	.63	.63	.62	.61	.60
100	.92	.86	.84	.83	.83	.81	.80
200	1.84	1.72	1.67	1.66	1.65	1.61	1.59
300	2.75	2.57	2.51	2.49	2.47	2.41	2.38
400	3.67	3.43	3.34	3.32	3.30	3.22	3.17
500	4.58	4.29	4.18	4.15	4.12	4.02	3.96
600	5.50	5.14	5.01	4.97	4.94	4.82	4.75
700	6.42	6.00	5.84	5.80	5.76	5.62	5.54
800	7.33	6.86	6.68	6.63	6.59	6.43	6.33
900	8.25	7.71	7.51	7.46	7.41	7.23	7.12
1000	9.16	8.57	8.35	8.29	8.23	8.03	7.91
2000	18.32	17.13	16.69	16.57	16.46	16.06	15.82
2500	22.90	21.41	20.86	20.71	20.57	20.07	19.77
3000	27.48	25.70	25.03	24.85	24.69	24.09	23.72
4000	36.64	34.26	33.37	33.13	32.91	32.11	31.63
5000	45.80	42.82	41.71	41.41	41.14	40.14	39.54
6000	54.96	51.39	50.05	49.69	49.37	48.17	47.44
7000	64.12	59.95	58.39	57.97	57.59	56.20	55.35
8000	73.27	68.52	66.73	66.25	65.82	64.22	63.26
9000	82.43	77.08	75.07	74.53	74.05	72.25	71.16
10000	91.59	85.64	83.41	82.81	82.27	80.28	79.07
11000	100.75	94.21	91.75	91.09	90.50	88.31	86.98
12000	109.91	102.77	100.09	99.37	98.73	96.33	94.88
13000	119.07	111.33	108.43	107.65	106.95	104.36	102.79
14000	128.23	119.90	116.77	115.93	115.18	112.39	110.70
15000	137.39	128.46	125.11	124.21	123.41	120.42	118.60
16000	146.54	137.03	133.45	132.49	131.63	128.44	126.51
17000	155.70	145.59	141.79	140.77	139.86	136.47	134.42
18000	164.86	154.15	150.13	149.05	148.09	144.50	142.32
19000	174.02	162.72	158.47	157.33	156.31	152.53	150.23
20000	183.18	171.28	166.81	165.62	164.54	160.55	158.14
21000	192.34	179.85	175.15	173.90	172.77	168.58	166.04
22000	201.50	188.41	183.49	182.18	180.99	176.61	173.95
23000	210.65	196.97	191.83	190.46	189.22	184.64	181.86
24000	219.81	205.54	200.17	198.74	197.45	192.66	189.76
25000	228.97	214.10	208.51	207.02	205.67	200.69	197.67
26000	238.13	222.66	216.85	215.30	213.90	208.72	205.58
27000	247.29	231.23	225.19	223.58	222.13	216.75	213.48
28000	256.45	239.79	233.53	231.86	230.35	224.77	221.39
29000	265.61	248.36	241.87	240.14	238.58	232.80	229.30
30000	274.77	256.92	250.21	248.42	246.81	240.83	237.20
31000	283.92	265.48	258.55	256.70	255.03	248.86	245.11
32000	293.08	274.05	266.89	264.98	263.26	256.88	253.02
33000	302.24	282.61	275.23	273.26	271.49	264.91	260.92
34000	311.40	291.17	283.57	281.54	279.71	272.94	268.83
35000	320.56	299.74	291.91	289.82	287.94	280.97	276.74
36000	329.72	308.30	300.25	298.11	296.17	288.99	284.64
37000	338.88	316.87	308.59	306.38	304.39	297.02	292.55
38000	348.03	325.43	316.94	314.66	312.62	305.05	300.46
39000	357.19	333.99	325.28	322.94	320.85	313.08	308.36
40000	366.35	342.56	333.62	331.23	329.08	321.10	316.27
45000	412.15	385.38	375.32	372.63	370.21	361.24	355.80
50000	457.94	428.20	417.02	414.03	411.34	401.38	395.34
55000	503.73	471.02	458.72	455.43	452.48	441.51	434.87
60000	549.53	513.83	500.42	496.84	493.61	481.65	474.40
65000	595.32	556.65	542.12	538.24	534.74	521.79	513.93
70000	641.11	599.47	583.82	579.64	575.88	561.93	553.47
75000	686.91	642.29	625.52	621.04	617.01	602.06	593.00
80000	732.70	685.11	667.23	662.45	658.15	642.20	632.53
85000	778.49	727.93	708.93	703.85	699.28	682.34	672.07
90000	824.29	770.75	750.63	745.25	740.41	722.47	711.60
95000	870.08	813.57	792.33	786.65	781.55	762.61	751.13
100000	915.87	856.39	834.03	828.06	822.68	802.75	790.67

9.50% MONTHLY AMORTIZING PAYMENTS

AMOUNT OF LOAN	NUMBER OF YEARS IN TERM						
	1	2	3	4	5	10	15
$ 25	2.20	1.15	.81	.63	.53	.33	.27
50	4.39	2.30	1.61	1.26	1.06	.65	.53
75	6.58	3.45	2.41	1.89	1.58	.98	.79
100	8.77	4.60	3.21	2.52	2.11	1.30	1.05
200	17.54	9.19	6.41	5.03	4.21	2.59	2.09
300	26.31	13.78	9.61	7.54	6.31	3.89	3.14
400	35.08	18.37	12.82	10.05	8.41	5.18	4.18
500	43.85	22.96	16.02	12.57	10.51	6.47	5.23
600	52.62	27.55	19.22	15.08	12.61	7.77	6.27
700	61.38	32.15	22.43	17.59	14.71	9.06	7.31
800	70.15	36.74	25.63	20.10	16.81	10.36	8.36
900	78.92	41.33	28.83	22.62	18.91	11.65	9.40
1000	87.69	45.92	32.04	25.13	21.01	12.94	10.45
2000	175.37	91.83	64.07	50.25	42.01	25.88	20.89
2500	219.21	114.79	80.09	62.81	52.51	32.35	26.11
3000	263.06	137.75	96.10	75.37	63.01	38.82	31.33
4000	350.74	183.66	128.14	100.50	84.01	51.76	41.77
5000	438.42	229.58	160.17	125.62	105.01	64.70	52.22
6000	526.11	275.49	192.20	150.74	126.02	77.64	62.66
7000	613.79	321.41	224.24	175.87	147.02	90.58	73.10
8000	701.47	367.32	256.27	200.99	168.02	103.52	83.54
9000	789.16	413.24	288.30	226.11	189.02	116.46	93.99
10000	876.84	459.15	320.33	251.24	210.02	129.40	104.43
11000	964.52	505.06	352.37	276.36	231.03	142.34	114.87
12000	1052.21	550.98	384.40	301.48	252.03	155.28	125.31
13000	1139.89	596.89	416.43	326.61	273.03	168.22	135.75
14000	1227.57	642.81	448.47	351.73	294.03	181.16	146.20
15000	1315.26	688.72	480.50	376.85	315.03	194.10	156.64
16000	1402.94	734.64	512.53	401.98	336.03	207.04	167.08
17000	1490.62	780.55	544.57	427.10	357.04	219.98	177.52
18000	1578.31	826.47	576.60	452.22	378.04	232.92	187.97
19000	1665.99	872.38	608.63	477.34	399.04	245.86	198.41
20000	1753.68	918.29	640.66	502.47	420.04	258.80	208.85
21000	1841.36	964.21	672.70	527.59	441.04	271.74	219.29
22000	1929.04	1010.12	704.73	552.71	462.05	284.68	229.73
23000	2016.73	1056.04	736.76	577.84	483.05	297.62	240.18
24000	2104.41	1101.95	768.80	602.96	504.05	310.56	250.62
25000	2192.09	1147.87	800.83	628.08	525.05	323.50	261.06
26000	2279.78	1193.78	832.86	653.21	546.05	336.44	271.50
27000	2367.46	1239.70	864.89	678.33	567.06	349.38	281.95
28000	2455.14	1285.61	896.93	703.45	588.06	362.32	292.39
29000	2542.83	1331.53	928.96	728.58	609.06	375.26	302.83
30000	2630.51	1377.44	960.99	753.70	630.06	388.20	313.27
31000	2718.19	1423.35	993.03	778.82	651.06	401.14	323.71
32000	2805.88	1469.27	1025.06	803.95	672.06	414.08	334.16
33000	2893.56	1515.18	1057.09	829.07	693.07	427.02	344.60
34000	2981.24	1561.10	1089.13	854.19	714.07	439.96	355.04
35000	3068.93	1607.01	1121.16	879.31	735.07	452.90	365.48
36000	3156.61	1652.93	1153.19	904.44	756.07	465.84	375.93
37000	3244.29	1698.84	1185.22	929.56	777.07	478.78	386.37
38000	3331.98	1744.76	1217.26	954.68	798.08	491.72	396.81
39000	3419.66	1790.67	1249.29	979.81	819.08	504.66	407.25
40000	3507.35	1836.58	1281.32	1004.93	840.08	517.60	417.69
45000	3945.76	2066.16	1441.49	1130.55	945.09	582.29	469.91
50000	4384.18	2295.73	1601.65	1256.16	1050.10	646.99	522.12
55000	4822.60	2525.30	1761.82	1381.78	1155.11	711.69	574.33
60000	5261.02	2754.87	1921.98	1507.39	1260.12	776.39	626.54
65000	5699.43	2984.45	2082.15	1633.01	1365.13	841.09	678.75
70000	6137.85	3214.02	2242.31	1758.62	1470.14	905.79	730.96
75000	6576.27	3443.59	2402.48	1884.24	1575.14	970.49	783.17
80000	7014.69	3673.16	2562.64	2009.86	1680.15	1035.19	835.38
85000	7453.10	3902.74	2722.81	2135.47	1785.16	1099.88	887.60
90000	7891.52	4132.31	2882.97	2261.09	1890.17	1164.58	939.81
95000	8329.94	4361.88	3043.14	2386.70	1995.18	1229.28	992.02
100000	8768.36	4591.45	3203.30	2512.32	2100.19	1293.98	1044.23

AMOUNT OF LOAN	NUMBER OF YEARS IN TERM						
	20	25	28	29	30	35	40
$ 25	.24	.22	.22	.22	.22	.21	.21
50	.47	.44	.43	.43	.43	.42	.41
75	.70	.66	.64	.64	.64	.62	.61
100	.94	.88	.86	.86	.85	.83	.82
200	1.87	1.75	1.71	1.70	1.69	1.65	1.63
300	2.80	2.63	2.56	2.54	2.53	2.47	2.44
400	3.73	3.50	3.41	3.39	3.37	3.29	3.25
500	4.67	4.37	4.26	4.24	4.21	4.11	4.06
600	5.60	5.25	5.12	5.08	5.05	4.93	4.87
700	6.53	6.12	5.97	5.93	5.89	5.76	5.68
800	7.46	6.99	6.82	6.77	6.73	6.58	6.49
900	8.39	7.87	7.67	7.62	7.57	7.40	7.30
1000	9.33	8.74	8.52	8.47	8.41	8.22	8.11
2000	18.65	17.48	17.04	16.93	16.82	16.44	16.21
2500	23.31	21.85	21.30	21.16	21.03	20.55	20.26
3000	27.97	26.22	25.56	25.39	25.23	24.65	24.31
4000	37.29	34.95	34.08	33.85	33.64	32.87	32.41
5000	46.61	43.69	42.60	42.31	42.05	41.09	40.51
6000	55.93	52.43	51.12	50.77	50.46	49.30	48.61
7000	65.25	61.16	59.64	59.23	58.86	57.52	56.71
8000	74.58	69.90	68.16	67.69	67.27	65.73	64.81
9000	83.90	78.64	76.67	76.15	75.68	73.95	72.91
10000	93.22	87.37	85.19	84.61	84.09	82.17	81.01
11000	102.54	96.11	93.71	93.07	92.50	90.38	89.11
12000	111.86	104.85	102.23	101.53	100.91	98.60	97.21
13000	121.18	113.59	110.75	109.99	109.32	106.81	105.31
14000	130.50	122.32	119.27	118.45	117.72	115.03	113.41
15000	139.82	131.06	127.79	126.92	126.13	123.25	121.51
16000	149.15	139.80	136.31	135.38	134.54	131.46	129.61
17000	158.47	148.53	144.82	143.84	142.95	139.68	137.72
18000	167.79	157.27	153.34	152.30	151.36	147.90	145.82
19000	177.11	166.01	161.86	160.76	159.77	156.11	153.92
20000	186.43	174.74	170.38	169.22	168.18	164.33	162.02
21000	195.75	183.48	178.90	177.68	176.58	172.54	170.12
22000	205.07	192.22	187.42	186.14	184.99	180.76	178.22
23000	214.40	200.96	195.94	194.60	193.40	188.98	186.32
24000	223.72	209.69	204.46	203.06	201.81	197.19	194.42
25000	233.04	218.43	212.98	211.52	210.22	205.41	202.52
26000	242.36	227.17	221.49	219.98	218.63	213.62	210.62
27000	251.68	235.90	230.01	228.44	227.04	221.84	218.72
28000	261.00	244.64	238.53	236.91	235.44	230.06	226.82
29000	270.32	253.38	247.05	245.37	243.85	238.27	234.92
30000	279.64	262.11	255.57	253.83	252.26	246.49	243.02
31000	288.97	270.85	264.09	262.29	260.67	254.70	251.12
32000	298.29	279.59	272.61	270.75	269.08	262.92	259.22
33000	307.61	288.32	281.13	279.21	277.49	271.14	267.33
34000	316.93	297.06	289.64	287.67	285.90	279.35	275.43
35000	326.25	305.80	298.16	296.13	294.30	287.57	283.53
36000	335.57	314.54	306.68	304.59	302.71	295.79	291.63
37000	344.89	323.27	315.20	313.05	311.12	304.00	299.73
38000	354.21	332.01	323.72	321.51	319.53	312.22	307.83
39000	363.54	340.75	332.24	329.97	327.94	320.43	315.93
40000	372.86	349.48	340.76	338.43	336.35	328.65	324.03
45000	419.46	393.17	383.35	380.74	378.39	369.73	364.53
50000	466.07	436.85	425.95	423.04	420.43	410.81	405.04
55000	512.68	480.54	468.54	465.34	462.47	451.89	445.54
60000	559.28	524.22	511.13	507.65	504.52	492.97	486.04
65000	605.89	567.91	553.73	549.95	546.56	534.05	526.55
70000	652.50	611.59	596.32	592.26	588.60	575.13	567.05
75000	699.10	655.28	638.92	634.56	630.65	616.21	607.55
80000	745.71	698.96	681.51	676.86	672.69	657.29	648.05
85000	792.32	742.65	724.10	719.17	714.73	698.37	688.56
90000	838.92	786.33	766.70	761.47	756.77	739.46	729.06
95000	885.53	830.02	809.29	803.77	798.82	780.54	769.56
100000	932.14	873.70	851.89	846.08	840.86	821.62	810.07

AMOUNT OF LOAN	NUMBER OF YEARS IN TERM						
	1	2	3	4	5	10	15
$ 25	2.20	1.16	.81	.64	.53	.33	.27
50	4.39	2.31	1.61	1.27	1.06	.66	.53
75	6.59	3.46	2.42	1.90	1.59	.99	.80
100	8.78	4.61	3.22	2.53	2.12	1.31	1.06
200	17.56	9.21	6.43	5.05	4.23	2.62	2.12
300	26.34	13.81	9.65	7.58	6.34	3.93	3.18
400	35.12	18.42	12.86	10.10	8.45	5.24	4.24
500	43.90	23.02	16.08	12.63	10.57	6.54	5.30
600	52.68	27.62	19.29	15.15	12.68	7.85	6.36
700	61.46	32.23	22.51	17.67	14.79	9.16	7.42
800	70.24	36.83	25.72	20.20	16.90	10.47	8.48
900	79.02	41.43	28.94	22.72	19.02	11.77	9.54
1000	87.80	46.03	32.15	25.25	21.13	13.08	10.60
2000	175.60	92.06	64.30	50.49	42.25	26.16	21.19
2500	219.50	115.08	80.38	63.11	52.82	32.70	26.49
3000	263.40	138.09	96.45	75.73	63.38	39.24	31.79
4000	351.20	184.12	128.60	100.98	84.50	52.31	42.38
5000	439.00	230.15	160.75	126.22	105.63	65.39	52.97
6000	526.80	276.18	192.90	151.46	126.75	78.47	63.57
7000	614.60	322.21	225.05	176.70	147.87	91.54	74.16
8000	702.40	368.24	257.20	201.95	169.00	104.62	84.75
9000	790.20	414.27	289.35	227.19	190.12	117.70	95.35
10000	878.00	460.30	321.50	252.43	211.25	130.78	105.94
11000	965.80	506.33	353.65	277.67	232.37	143.85	116.53
12000	1053.60	552.36	385.80	302.92	253.50	156.93	127.13
13000	1141.40	598.39	417.95	328.16	274.62	170.01	137.72
14000	1229.20	644.42	450.10	353.40	295.74	183.08	148.32
15000	1317.00	690.45	482.25	378.65	316.87	196.16	158.91
16000	1404.80	736.48	514.40	403.89	337.99	209.24	169.50
17000	1492.60	782.51	546.55	429.13	359.12	222.31	180.10
18000	1580.40	828.54	578.70	454.37	380.24	235.39	190.69
19000	1668.20	874.57	610.85	479.62	401.37	248.47	201.28
20000	1756.00	920.60	643.00	504.86	422.49	261.55	211.88
21000	1843.80	966.63	675.15	530.10	443.61	274.62	222.47
22000	1931.60	1012.66	707.30	555.34	464.74	287.70	233.06
23000	2019.40	1058.69	739.45	580.59	485.86	300.78	243.66
24000	2107.20	1104.72	771.60	605.83	506.99	313.85	254.25
25000	2195.00	1150.75	803.75	631.07	528.11	326.93	264.85
26000	2282.80	1196.78	835.90	656.31	549.24	340.01	275.44
27000	2370.60	1242.80	868.05	681.56	570.36	353.08	286.03
28000	2458.40	1288.83	900.20	706.80	591.48	366.16	296.63
29000	2546.20	1334.86	932.35	732.04	612.61	379.24	307.22
30000	2633.99	1380.89	964.50	757.29	633.73	392.32	317.81
31000	2721.79	1426.92	996.65	782.53	654.86	405.39	328.41
32000	2809.59	1472.95	1028.80	807.77	675.98	418.47	339.00
33000	2897.39	1518.98	1060.95	833.01	697.11	431.55	349.59
34000	2985.19	1565.01	1093.10	858.26	718.23	444.62	360.19
35000	3072.99	1611.04	1125.25	883.50	739.35	457.70	370.78
36000	3160.79	1657.07	1157.40	908.74	760.48	470.78	381.38
37000	3248.59	1703.10	1189.55	933.98	781.60	483.85	391.97
38000	3336.39	1749.13	1221.70	959.23	802.73	496.93	402.56
39000	3424.19	1795.16	1253.85	984.47	823.85	510.01	413.16
40000	3511.99	1841.19	1286.00	1009.71	844.97	523.09	423.75
45000	3950.99	2071.34	1446.75	1135.93	950.60	588.47	476.72
50000	4389.99	2301.49	1607.50	1262.14	1056.22	653.86	529.69
55000	4828.99	2531.63	1768.25	1388.35	1161.84	719.24	582.65
60000	5267.99	2761.78	1929.00	1514.57	1267.46	784.63	635.62
65000	5706.98	2991.93	2089.75	1640.78	1373.08	850.01	688.59
70000	6145.98	3222.08	2250.50	1766.99	1478.70	915.40	741.56
75000	6584.98	3452.23	2411.25	1893.21	1584.32	980.78	794.53
80000	7023.98	3682.37	2572.00	2019.42	1689.94	1046.16	847.50
85000	7462.98	3912.52	2732.75	2145.63	1795.57	1111.55	900.46
90000	7901.97	4142.67	2893.50	2271.85	1901.19	1176.94	953.43
95000	8340.97	4372.82	3054.25	2398.06	2006.81	1242.32	1006.40
100000	8779.97	4602.97	3215.00	2524.27	2112.43	1307.71	1059.37

AMOUNT OF LOAN	NUMBER OF YEARS IN TERM						
	20	25	28	29	30	35	40
$ 25	.24	.23	.22	.22	.22	.22	.21
50	.48	.45	.44	.44	.44	.43	.42
75	.72	.67	.66	.65	.65	.64	.63
100	.95	.90	.87	.87	.87	.85	.83
200	1.90	1.79	1.74	1.73	1.72	1.69	1.66
300	2.85	2.68	2.61	2.60	2.58	2.53	2.49
400	3.80	3.57	3.48	3.46	3.44	3.37	3.32
500	4.75	4.46	4.35	4.33	4.30	4.21	4.15
600	5.70	5.35	5.22	5.19	5.16	5.05	4.98
700	6.64	6.24	6.09	6.05	6.02	5.89	5.81
800	7.59	7.13	6.96	6.92	6.88	6.73	6.64
900	8.54	8.03	7.83	7.78	7.74	7.57	7.47
1000	9.49	8.92	8.70	8.65	8.60	8.41	8.30
2000	18.98	17.83	17.40	17.29	17.19	16.82	16.60
2500	23.72	22.28	21.75	21.61	21.48	21.02	20.74
3000	28.46	26.74	26.10	25.93	25.78	25.22	24.89
4000	37.95	35.65	34.80	34.57	34.37	33.63	33.19
5000	47.43	44.56	43.50	43.22	42.96	42.03	41.48
6000	56.92	53.47	52.20	51.86	51.55	50.44	49.78
7000	66.40	62.38	60.90	60.50	60.15	58.85	58.07
8000	75.89	71.30	69.59	69.14	68.74	67.25	66.37
9000	85.37	80.21	78.29	77.78	77.33	75.66	74.67
10000	94.86	89.12	86.99	86.43	85.92	84.06	82.96
11000	104.34	98.03	95.69	95.07	94.51	92.47	91.26
12000	113.83	106.94	104.39	103.71	103.10	100.88	99.55
13000	123.31	115.85	113.09	112.35	111.70	109.28	107.85
14000	132.80	124.76	121.79	121.00	120.29	117.69	116.14
15000	142.28	133.68	130.48	129.64	128.88	126.09	124.44
16000	151.77	142.59	139.18	138.28	137.47	134.50	132.73
17000	161.25	151.50	147.88	146.92	146.06	142.91	141.03
18000	170.74	160.41	156.58	155.56	154.65	151.31	149.33
19000	180.22	169.32	165.28	164.21	163.24	159.72	157.62
20000	189.71	178.23	173.98	172.85	171.84	168.12	165.92
21000	199.19	187.14	182.68	181.49	180.43	176.53	174.21
22000	208.68	196.06	191.37	190.13	189.02	184.93	182.51
23000	218.16	204.97	200.07	198.77	197.61	193.34	190.80
24000	227.65	213.88	208.77	207.42	206.20	201.75	199.10
25000	237.13	222.79	217.47	216.06	214.79	210.15	207.39
26000	246.62	231.70	226.17	224.70	223.39	218.56	215.69
27000	256.10	240.61	234.87	233.34	231.98	226.96	223.99
28000	265.59	249.52	243.57	241.99	240.57	235.37	232.28
29000	275.07	258.43	252.26	250.63	249.16	243.78	240.58
30000	284.56	267.35	260.96	259.27	257.75	252.18	248.87
31000	294.05	276.26	269.66	267.91	266.34	260.59	257.17
32000	303.53	285.17	278.36	276.55	274.93	268.99	265.46
33000	313.02	294.08	287.06	285.20	283.53	277.40	273.76
34000	322.50	302.99	295.76	293.84	292.12	285.81	282.05
35000	331.99	311.90	304.46	302.48	300.71	294.21	290.35
36000	341.47	320.81	313.15	311.12	309.30	302.62	298.65
37000	350.96	329.73	321.85	319.76	317.89	311.02	306.94
38000	360.44	338.64	330.55	328.41	326.48	319.43	315.24
39000	369.93	347.55	339.25	337.05	335.08	327.83	323.53
40000	379.41	356.46	347.95	345.69	343.67	336.24	331.83
45000	426.84	401.02	391.44	388.90	386.62	378.27	373.31
50000	474.26	445.57	434.94	432.11	429.58	420.30	414.78
55000	521.69	490.13	478.43	475.32	472.54	462.33	456.26
60000	569.12	534.69	521.92	518.53	515.50	504.36	497.74
65000	616.54	579.24	565.41	561.74	558.46	546.39	539.22
70000	663.97	623.80	608.91	604.96	601.41	588.42	580.70
75000	711.39	668.36	652.40	648.17	644.37	630.45	622.17
80000	758.82	712.91	695.89	691.38	687.33	672.48	663.65
85000	806.24	757.47	739.39	734.59	730.29	714.51	705.13
90000	853.67	802.03	782.88	777.80	773.24	756.54	746.61
95000	901.10	846.59	826.37	821.01	816.20	798.56	788.09
100000	948.52	891.14	869.87	864.22	859.16	840.59	829.56

10.00% MONTHLY AMORTIZING PAYMENTS

AMOUNT OF LOAN	NUMBER OF YEARS IN TERM						
	1	2	3	4	5	10	15
$ 25	2.20	1.16	.81	.64	.54	.34	.27
50	4.40	2.31	1.62	1.27	1.07	.67	.54
75	6.60	3.47	2.43	1.91	1.60	1.00	.81
100	8.80	4.62	3.23	2.54	2.13	1.33	1.08
200	17.59	9.23	6.46	5.08	4.25	2.65	2.15
300	26.38	13.85	9.69	7.61	6.38	3.97	3.23
400	35.17	18.46	12.91	10.15	8.50	5.29	4.30
500	43.96	23.08	16.14	12.69	10.63	6.61	5.38
600	52.75	27.69	19.37	15.22	12.75	7.93	6.45
700	61.55	32.31	22.59	17.76	14.88	9.26	7.53
800	70.34	36.92	25.82	20.30	17.00	10.58	8.60
900	79.13	41.54	29.05	22.83	19.13	11.90	9.68
1000	87.92	46.15	32.27	25.37	21.25	13.22	10.75
2000	175.84	92.29	64.54	50.73	42.50	26.44	21.50
2500	219.79	115.37	80.67	63.41	53.12	33.04	26.87
3000	263.75	138.44	96.81	76.09	63.75	39.65	32.24
4000	351.67	184.58	129.07	101.46	84.99	52.87	42.99
5000	439.58	230.73	161.34	126.82	106.24	66.08	53.74
6000	527.50	276.87	193.61	152.18	127.49	79.30	64.48
7000	615.42	323.02	225.88	177.54	148.73	92.51	75.23
8000	703.33	369.16	258.14	202.91	169.98	105.73	85.97
9000	791.25	415.31	290.41	228.27	191.23	118.94	96.72
10000	879.16	461.45	322.68	253.63	212.48	132.16	107.47
11000	967.08	507.60	354.94	278.99	233.72	145.37	118.21
12000	1055.00	553.74	387.21	304.36	254.97	158.59	128.96
13000	1142.91	599.89	419.48	329.72	276.22	171.80	139.70
14000	1230.83	646.03	451.75	355.08	297.46	185.02	150.45
15000	1318.74	692.18	484.01	380.44	318.71	198.23	161.20
16000	1406.66	738.32	516.28	405.81	339.96	211.45	171.94
17000	1494.58	784.47	548.55	431.17	361.20	224.66	182.69
18000	1582.49	830.61	580.81	456.53	382.45	237.88	193.43
19000	1670.41	876.76	613.08	481.89	403.70	251.09	204.18
20000	1758.32	922.90	645.35	507.26	424.95	264.31	214.93
21000	1846.24	969.05	677.62	532.62	446.19	277.52	225.67
22000	1934.15	1015.19	709.88	557.98	467.44	290.74	236.42
23000	2022.07	1061.34	742.15	583.34	488.69	303.95	247.16
24000	2109.99	1107.48	774.42	608.71	509.93	317.17	257.91
25000	2197.90	1153.63	806.68	634.07	531.18	330.38	268.66
26000	2285.82	1199.77	838.95	659.43	552.43	343.60	279.40
27000	2373.73	1245.92	871.22	684.79	573.68	356.81	290.15
28000	2461.65	1292.06	903.49	710.16	594.92	370.03	300.89
29000	2549.57	1338.21	935.75	735.52	616.17	383.24	311.64
30000	2637.48	1384.35	968.02	760.88	637.42	396.46	322.39
31000	2725.40	1430.50	1000.29	786.25	658.66	409.67	333.13
32000	2813.31	1476.64	1032.55	811.61	679.91	422.89	343.88
33000	2901.23	1522.79	1064.82	836.97	701.16	436.10	354.62
34000	2989.15	1568.93	1097.09	862.33	722.40	449.32	365.37
35000	3077.06	1615.08	1129.36	887.70	743.65	462.53	376.12
36000	3164.98	1661.22	1161.62	913.06	764.90	475.75	386.86
37000	3252.89	1707.37	1193.89	938.42	786.15	488.96	397.61
38000	3340.81	1753.51	1226.16	963.78	807.39	502.18	408.35
39000	3428.72	1799.66	1258.43	989.15	828.64	515.39	419.10
40000	3516.64	1845.80	1290.69	1014.51	849.89	528.61	429.85
45000	3956.22	2076.53	1452.03	1141.32	956.12	594.68	483.58
50000	4395.80	2307.25	1613.36	1268.13	1062.36	660.76	537.31
55000	4835.38	2537.98	1774.70	1394.95	1168.59	726.83	591.04
60000	5274.96	2768.70	1936.04	1521.76	1274.83	792.91	644.77
65000	5714.54	2999.43	2097.37	1648.57	1381.06	858.98	698.50
70000	6154.12	3230.15	2258.71	1775.39	1487.30	925.06	752.23
75000	6593.70	3460.87	2420.04	1902.20	1593.53	991.14	805.96
80000	7033.38	3691.60	2581.38	2029.01	1699.77	1057.21	859.69
85000	7472.86	3922.32	2742.72	2155.82	1806.00	1123.29	913.42
90000	7912.43	4153.05	2904.05	2282.64	1912.24	1189.36	967.15
95000	8352.01	4383.77	3065.39	2409.45	2018.47	1255.44	1020.88
100000	8791.59	4614.50	3226.72	2536.26	2124.71	1321.51	1074.61

10

MONTHLY AMORTIZING PAYMENTS 10.00%

AMOUNT OF LOAN	NUMBER OF YEARS IN TERM						
	20	25	28	29	30	35	40
$ 25	.25	.23	.23	.23	.22	.22	.22
50	.49	.46	.45	.45	.44	.43	.43
75	.73	.69	.67	.67	.66	.65	.64
100	.97	.91	.89	.89	.88	.86	.85
200	1.94	1.82	1.78	1.77	1.76	1.72	1.70
300	2.90	2.73	2.67	2.65	2.64	2.58	2.55
400	3.87	3.64	3.56	3.53	3.52	3.44	3.40
500	4.83	4.55	4.44	4.42	4.39	4.30	4.25
600	5.80	5.46	5.33	5.30	5.27	5.16	5.10
700	6.76	6.37	6.22	6.18	6.15	6.02	5.95
800	7.73	7.27	7.11	7.06	7.03	6.88	6.80
900	8.69	8.18	8.00	7.95	7.90	7.74	7.65
1000	9.66	9.09	8.88	8.83	8.78	8.60	8.50
2000	19.31	18.18	17.76	17.65	17.56	17.20	16.99
2500	24.13	22.72	22.20	22.07	21.94	21.50	21.23
3000	28.96	27.27	26.64	26.48	26.33	25.80	25.48
4000	38.61	36.35	35.52	35.30	35.11	34.39	33.97
5000	48.26	45.44	44.40	44.13	43.88	42.99	42.46
6000	57.91	54.53	53.28	52.95	52.66	51.59	50.95
7000	67.56	63.61	62.16	61.78	61.44	60.18	59.45
8000	77.21	72.70	71.04	70.60	70.21	68.78	67.94
9000	86.86	81.79	79.92	79.43	78.99	77.38	76.43
10000	96.51	90.88	88.80	88.25	87.76	85.97	84.92
11000	106.16	99.96	97.68	97.08	96.54	94.57	93.41
12000	115.81	109.05	106.56	105.90	105.31	103.17	101.90
13000	125.46	118.14	115.44	114.73	114.09	111.76	110.39
14000	135.11	127.22	124.32	123.55	122.87	120.36	118.89
15000	144.76	136.31	133.20	132.38	131.64	128.96	127.38
16000	154.41	145.40	142.08	141.20	140.42	137.55	135.87
17000	164.06	154.48	150.96	150.03	149.19	146.15	144.36
18000	173.71	163.57	159.84	158.85	157.97	154.75	152.85
19000	183.36	172.66	168.72	167.68	166.74	163.34	161.34
20000	193.01	181.75	177.60	176.50	175.52	171.94	169.83
21000	202.66	190.83	186.48	185.33	184.30	180.54	178.33
22000	212.31	199.92	195.36	194.15	193.07	189.13	186.82
23000	221.96	209.01	204.24	202.97	201.85	197.73	195.31
24000	231.61	218.09	213.12	211.80	210.62	206.33	203.80
25000	241.26	227.18	222.00	220.62	219.40	214.92	212.29
26000	250.91	236.27	230.87	229.45	228.17	223.52	220.78
27000	260.56	245.35	239.75	238.27	236.95	232.12	229.27
28000	270.21	254.44	248.63	247.10	245.73	240.71	237.77
29000	279.86	263.53	257.51	255.92	254.50	249.31	246.26
30000	289.51	272.62	266.39	264.75	263.28	257.91	254.75
31000	299.16	281.70	275.27	273.57	272.05	266.50	263.24
32000	308.81	290.79	284.15	282.40	280.83	275.10	271.73
33000	318.46	299.88	293.03	291.22	289.60	283.70	280.22
34000	328.11	308.96	301.91	300.05	298.38	292.29	288.71
35000	337.76	318.05	310.79	308.87	307.16	300.89	297.21
36000	347.41	327.14	319.67	317.70	315.93	309.49	305.70
37000	357.06	336.22	328.55	326.52	324.71	318.08	314.19
38000	366.71	345.31	337.43	335.35	333.48	326.68	322.68
39000	376.36	354.40	346.31	344.17	342.26	335.28	331.17
40000	386.01	363.49	355.19	353.00	351.03	343.87	339.66
45000	434.26	408.92	399.59	397.12	394.91	386.86	382.12
50000	482.52	454.36	443.99	441.24	438.79	429.84	424.58
55000	530.77	499.79	488.38	485.37	482.67	472.82	467.04
60000	579.02	545.23	532.78	529.49	526.55	515.81	509.49
65000	627.27	590.66	577.18	573.62	570.43	558.79	551.95
70000	675.52	636.10	621.58	617.74	614.31	601.78	594.41
75000	723.77	681.53	665.98	661.86	658.18	644.76	636.86
80000	772.02	726.97	710.38	705.99	702.06	687.74	679.32
85000	820.27	772.40	754.77	750.11	745.94	730.73	721.78
90000	868.52	817.84	799.17	794.23	789.82	773.71	764.24
95000	916.78	863.27	843.57	838.36	833.70	816.69	806.69
100000	965.03	908.71	887.97	882.48	877.58	859.68	849.15

11

10.25% MONTHLY AMORTIZING PAYMENTS

AMOUNT OF LOAN	NUMBER OF YEARS IN TERM						
	1	2	3	4	5	10	15
$ 25	2.21	1.16	.81	.64	.54	.34	.28
50	4.41	2.32	1.62	1.28	1.07	.67	.55
75	6.61	3.47	2.43	1.92	1.61	1.01	.82
100	8.81	4.63	3.24	2.55	2.14	1.34	1.09
200	17.61	9.26	6.48	5.10	4.28	2.68	2.18
300	26.41	13.88	9.72	7.65	6.42	4.01	3.27
400	35.22	18.51	12.96	10.20	8.55	5.35	4.36
500	44.02	23.14	16.20	12.75	10.69	6.68	5.45
600	52.82	27.76	19.44	15.29	12.83	8.02	6.54
700	61.63	32.39	22.67	17.84	14.96	9.35	7.63
800	70.43	37.01	25.91	20.39	17.10	10.69	8.72
900	79.23	41.64	29.15	22.94	19.24	12.02	9.81
1000	88.04	46.27	32.39	25.49	21.38	13.36	10.90
2000	176.07	92.53	64.77	50.97	42.75	26.71	21.80
2500	220.09	115.66	80.97	63.71	53.43	33.39	27.25
3000	264.10	138.79	97.16	76.45	64.12	40.07	32.70
4000	352.13	185.05	129.54	101.94	85.49	53.42	43.60
5000	440.17	231.31	161.93	127.42	106.86	66.77	54.50
6000	528.20	277.57	194.31	152.90	128.23	80.13	65.40
7000	616.23	323.83	226.70	178.38	149.60	93.48	76.30
8000	704.26	370.09	259.08	203.87	170.97	106.84	87.20
9000	792.29	416.35	291.47	229.35	192.34	120.19	98.10
10000	880.33	462.61	323.85	254.83	213.71	133.54	109.00
11000	968.36	508.87	356.24	280.32	235.08	146.90	119.90
12000	1056.39	555.13	388.62	305.80	256.45	160.25	130.80
13000	1144.42	601.39	421.01	331.28	277.82	173.61	141.70
14000	1232.46	647.65	453.39	356.76	299.19	186.96	152.60
15000	1320.49	693.91	485.78	382.25	320.56	200.31	163.50
16000	1408.52	740.17	518.16	407.73	341.93	213.67	174.40
17000	1496.55	786.43	550.54	433.21	363.30	227.02	185.30
18000	1584.58	832.69	582.93	458.70	384.67	240.38	196.20
19000	1672.62	878.95	615.31	484.18	406.04	253.73	207.10
20000	1760.65	925.21	647.70	509.66	427.41	267.08	218.00
21000	1848.68	971.47	680.08	535.14	448.78	280.44	228.89
22000	1936.71	1017.73	712.47	560.63	470.15	293.79	239.79
23000	2024.75	1063.99	744.85	586.11	491.52	307.14	250.69
24000	2112.78	1110.25	777.24	611.59	512.89	320.50	261.59
25000	2200.81	1156.51	809.62	637.08	534.26	333.85	272.49
26000	2288.84	1202.78	842.01	662.56	555.63	347.21	283.39
27000	2376.87	1249.04	874.39	688.04	577.00	360.56	294.29
28000	2464.91	1295.30	906.78	713.52	598.37	373.91	305.19
29000	2552.94	1341.56	939.16	739.01	619.74	387.27	316.09
30000	2640.97	1387.82	971.55	764.49	641.11	400.62	326.99
31000	2729.00	1434.08	1003.93	789.97	662.48	413.98	337.89
32000	2817.04	1480.34	1036.32	815.46	683.85	427.33	348.79
33000	2905.07	1526.60	1068.70	840.94	705.22	440.68	359.69
34000	2993.10	1572.86	1101.08	866.42	726.59	454.04	370.59
35000	3081.13	1619.12	1133.47	891.90	747.96	467.39	381.49
36000	3169.16	1665.38	1165.85	917.39	769.33	480.75	392.39
37000	3257.20	1711.64	1198.24	942.87	790.70	494.10	403.29
38000	3345.23	1757.90	1230.62	968.35	812.08	507.45	414.19
39000	3433.26	1804.16	1263.01	993.83	833.45	520.81	425.09
40000	3521.29	1850.42	1295.39	1019.32	854.82	534.16	435.99
45000	3961.45	2081.72	1457.32	1146.73	961.67	600.93	490.48
50000	4401.62	2313.02	1619.24	1274.15	1068.52	667.70	544.98
55000	4841.78	2544.33	1781.16	1401.56	1175.37	734.47	599.48
60000	5281.94	2775.63	1943.09	1528.99	1282.22	801.24	653.98
65000	5722.10	3006.93	2105.01	1656.39	1389.07	868.01	708.47
70000	6162.26	3238.23	2266.93	1783.80	1495.92	934.78	762.97
75000	6602.42	3469.53	2428.86	1911.22	1602.77	1001.55	817.47
80000	7042.58	3700.84	2590.78	2038.63	1709.63	1068.32	871.97
85000	7482.74	3932.14	2752.70	2166.04	1816.48	1135.09	926.46
90000	7922.90	4163.44	2914.63	2293.46	1923.33	1201.86	980.96
95000	8363.06	4394.74	3076.55	2420.87	2030.18	1268.63	1035.46
100000	8803.23	4626.04	3238.47	2548.29	2137.03	1335.40	1089.96

12

MONTHLY AMORTIZING PAYMENTS 10.25%

AMOUNT OF LOAN	NUMBER OF YEARS IN TERM						
	20	25	28	29	30	35	40
$ 25	.25	.24	.23	.23	.23	.22	.22
50	.50	.47	.46	.46	.45	.44	.44
75	.74	.70	.68	.68	.68	.66	.66
100	.99	.93	.91	.91	.90	.88	.87
200	1.97	1.86	1.82	1.81	1.80	1.76	1.74
300	2.95	2.78	2.72	2.71	2.69	2.64	2.61
400	3.93	3.71	3.63	3.61	3.59	3.52	3.48
500	4.91	4.64	4.54	4.51	4.49	4.40	4.35
600	5.89	5.56	5.44	5.41	5.38	5.28	5.22
700	6.88	6.49	6.35	6.31	6.28	6.16	6.09
800	7.86	7.42	7.25	7.21	7.17	7.04	6.96
900	8.84	8.34	8.16	8.11	8.07	7.91	7.82
1000	9.82	9.27	9.07	9.01	8.97	8.79	8.69
2000	19.64	18.53	18.13	18.02	17.93	17.58	17.38
2500	24.55	23.16	22.66	22.53	22.41	21.98	21.73
3000	29.45	27.80	27.19	27.03	26.89	26.37	26.07
4000	39.27	37.06	36.25	36.04	35.85	35.16	34.76
5000	49.09	46.32	45.31	45.05	44.81	43.95	43.45
6000	58.90	55.59	54.38	54.06	53.77	52.74	52.13
7000	68.72	64.85	63.44	63.06	62.73	61.52	60.82
8000	78.54	74.12	72.50	72.07	71.69	70.31	69.51
9000	88.35	83.38	81.56	81.08	80.65	79.10	78.20
10000	98.17	92.64	90.62	90.09	89.62	87.89	86.89
11000	107.99	101.91	99.68	99.10	98.58	96.68	95.58
12000	117.80	111.17	108.75	108.11	107.54	105.47	104.26
13000	127.62	120.43	117.81	117.12	116.50	114.26	112.95
14000	137.44	129.70	126.87	126.12	125.46	123.04	121.64
15000	147.25	138.96	135.93	135.13	134.42	131.83	130.33
16000	157.07	148.23	144.99	144.14	143.38	140.62	139.02
17000	166.88	157.49	154.05	153.15	152.34	149.41	147.70
18000	176.70	166.75	163.12	162.16	161.30	158.20	156.39
19000	186.52	176.02	172.18	171.17	170.26	166.99	165.08
20000	196.33	185.28	181.24	180.18	179.23	175.78	173.77
21000	206.15	194.55	190.30	189.18	188.19	184.56	182.46
22000	215.97	203.81	199.36	198.19	197.15	193.35	191.15
23000	225.78	213.07	208.43	207.20	206.11	202.14	199.83
24000	235.60	222.34	217.49	216.21	215.07	210.93	208.52
25000	245.42	231.60	226.55	225.22	224.03	219.72	217.21
26000	255.23	240.86	235.61	234.23	232.99	228.51	225.90
27000	265.05	250.13	244.67	243.24	241.95	237.30	234.59
28000	274.87	259.39	253.73	252.24	250.91	246.08	243.27
29000	284.68	268.66	262.80	261.25	259.87	254.87	251.96
30000	294.50	277.92	271.86	270.26	268.84	263.66	260.65
31000	304.31	287.18	280.92	279.27	277.80	272.45	269.34
32000	314.13	296.45	289.98	288.28	286.76	281.24	278.03
33000	323.95	305.71	299.04	297.29	295.72	290.03	286.72
34000	333.76	314.98	308.10	306.30	304.68	298.82	295.40
35000	343.58	324.24	317.17	315.30	313.64	307.60	304.09
36000	353.40	333.50	326.23	324.31	322.60	316.39	312.78
37000	363.21	342.77	335.29	333.32	331.56	325.18	321.47
38000	373.03	352.03	344.35	342.33	340.52	333.97	330.16
39000	382.85	361.29	353.41	351.34	349.48	342.76	338.84
40000	392.66	370.56	362.48	360.35	358.45	351.55	347.53
45000	441.74	416.88	407.78	405.39	403.25	395.49	390.97
50000	490.83	463.20	453.09	450.43	448.06	439.43	434.41
55000	539.91	509.52	498.40	495.47	492.86	483.38	477.86
60000	588.99	555.83	543.71	540.52	537.67	527.32	521.30
65000	638.07	602.15	589.02	585.56	582.47	571.26	564.74
70000	687.16	648.47	634.33	630.60	627.28	615.20	608.18
75000	736.24	694.79	679.64	675.65	672.08	659.15	651.62
80000	785.32	741.11	724.95	720.69	716.89	703.09	695.06
85000	834.40	787.43	770.25	765.73	761.69	747.03	738.50
90000	883.48	833.75	815.56	810.77	806.50	790.98	781.94
95000	932.57	880.07	860.87	855.82	851.30	834.92	825.38
100000	981.65	926.39	906.18	900.86	896.11	878.86	868.82

13

10.50% MONTHLY AMORTIZING PAYMENTS

AMOUNT OF LOAN	NUMBER OF YEARS IN TERM						
	1	2	3	4	5	10	15
$ 25	2.21	1.16	.82	.65	.54	.34	.28
50	4.41	2.32	1.63	1.29	1.08	.68	.56
75	6.62	3.48	2.44	1.93	1.62	1.02	.83
100	8.82	4.64	3.26	2.57	2.15	1.35	1.11
200	17.63	9.28	6.51	5.13	4.30	2.70	2.22
300	26.45	13.92	9.76	7.69	6.45	4.05	3.32
400	35.26	18.56	13.01	10.25	8.60	5.40	4.43
500	44.08	23.19	16.26	12.81	10.75	6.75	5.53
600	52.89	27.83	19.51	15.37	12.90	8.10	6.64
700	61.71	32.47	22.76	17.93	15.05	9.45	7.74
800	70.52	37.11	26.01	20.49	17.20	10.80	8.85
900	79.34	41.74	29.26	23.05	19.35	12.15	9.95
1000	88.15	46.38	32.51	25.61	21.50	13.50	11.06
2000	176.30	92.76	65.01	51.21	42.99	26.99	22.11
2500	220.38	115.95	81.26	64.01	53.74	33.74	27.64
3000	264.45	139.13	97.51	76.82	64.49	40.49	33.17
4000	352.60	185.51	130.01	102.42	85.98	53.98	44.22
5000	440.75	231.89	162.52	128.02	107.47	67.47	55.27
6000	528.90	278.26	195.02	153.63	128.97	80.97	66.33
7000	617.05	324.64	227.52	179.23	150.46	94.46	77.38
8000	705.19	371.01	260.02	204.83	171.96	107.95	88.44
9000	793.34	417.39	292.53	230.44	193.45	121.45	99.49
10000	881.49	463.77	325.03	256.04	214.94	134.94	110.54
11000	969.64	510.14	357.53	281.64	236.44	148.43	121.60
12000	1057.79	556.52	390.03	307.25	257.93	161.93	132.65
13000	1145.94	602.89	422.54	332.85	279.43	175.42	143.71
14000	1234.09	649.27	455.04	358.45	300.92	188.91	154.76
15000	1322.23	695.65	487.54	384.06	322.41	202.41	165.81
16000	1410.38	742.02	520.04	409.66	343.91	215.90	176.87
17000	1498.53	788.40	552.55	435.26	365.40	229.39	187.92
18000	1586.68	834.77	585.05	460.87	386.90	242.89	198.98
19000	1674.83	881.15	617.55	486.47	408.39	256.38	210.03
20000	1762.98	927.53	650.05	512.07	429.88	269.87	221.08
21000	1851.13	973.90	682.56	537.68	451.38	283.37	232.14
22000	1939.27	1020.28	715.06	563.28	472.87	296.86	243.19
23000	2027.42	1066.65	747.56	588.88	494.36	310.36	254.25
24000	2115.57	1113.03	780.06	614.49	515.86	323.85	265.30
25000	2203.72	1159.41	812.57	640.09	537.35	337.34	276.35
26000	2291.87	1205.78	845.07	665.69	558.85	350.84	287.41
27000	2380.02	1252.16	877.57	691.30	580.34	364.33	298.46
28000	2468.17	1298.53	910.07	716.90	601.83	377.82	309.52
29000	2556.31	1344.91	942.58	742.50	623.33	391.32	320.57
30000	2644.46	1391.29	975.08	768.11	644.82	404.81	331.62
31000	2732.61	1437.66	1007.58	793.71	666.32	418.30	342.68
32000	2820.76	1484.04	1040.08	819.31	687.81	431.80	353.73
33000	2908.91	1530.41	1072.59	844.92	709.30	445.29	364.79
34000	2997.06	1576.79	1105.09	870.52	730.80	458.78	375.84
35000	3085.21	1623.17	1137.59	896.12	752.29	472.28	386.89
36000	3173.35	1669.54	1170.09	921.73	773.79	485.77	397.95
37000	3261.50	1715.92	1202.60	947.33	795.28	499.26	409.00
38000	3349.65	1762.29	1235.10	972.93	816.77	512.76	420.06
39000	3437.80	1808.67	1267.60	998.54	838.27	526.25	431.11
40000	3525.95	1855.05	1300.10	1024.14	859.76	539.74	442.16
45000	3966.69	2086.93	1462.61	1152.16	967.23	607.21	497.43
50000	4407.44	2318.81	1625.13	1280.17	1074.70	674.68	552.70
55000	4848.18	2550.69	1787.64	1408.19	1182.17	742.15	607.97
60000	5288.92	2782.57	1950.15	1536.21	1289.64	809.61	663.24
65000	5729.66	3014.45	2112.66	1664.22	1397.11	877.08	718.51
70000	6170.41	3246.33	2275.18	1792.24	1504.58	944.55	773.78
75000	6611.15	3478.21	2437.69	1920.26	1612.05	1012.02	829.05
80000	7051.89	3710.09	2600.20	2048.28	1719.52	1079.48	884.32
85000	7492.60	3941.97	2762.71	2176.29	1826.99	1146.95	939.59
90000	7933.38	4173.85	2925.22	2304.31	1934.46	1214.42	994.86
95000	8374.12	4405.73	3087.74	2432.33	2041.93	1281.89	1050.13
100000	8814.87	4637.61	3250.25	2560.34	2149.40	1349.35	1105.40

14

MONTHLY AMORTIZING PAYMENTS 10.50%

AMOUNT OF LOAN	NUMBER OF YEARS IN TERM						
	20	25	28	29	30	35	40
$ 25	.25	.24	.24	.23	.23	.23	.23
50	.50	.48	.47	.46	.46	.45	.45
75	.75	.71	.70	.69	.69	.68	.67
100	1.00	.95	.93	.92	.92	.90	.89
200	2.00	1.89	1.85	1.84	1.83	1.80	1.78
300	3.00	2.84	2.78	2.76	2.75	2.70	2.67
400	4.00	3.78	3.70	3.68	3.66	3.60	3.56
500	5.00	4.73	4.63	4.60	4.58	4.50	4.45
600	6.00	5.67	5.55	5.52	5.49	5.39	5.34
700	6.99	6.61	6.48	6.44	6.41	6.29	6.22
800	7.99	7.56	7.40	7.36	7.32	7.19	7.11
900	8.99	8.50	8.33	8.28	8.24	8.09	8.00
1000	9.99	9.45	9.25	9.20	9.15	8.99	8.89
2000	19.97	18.89	18.50	18.39	18.30	17.97	17.78
2500	24.96	23.61	23.12	22.99	22.87	22.46	22.22
3000	29.96	28.33	27.74	27.59	27.45	26.95	26.66
4000	39.94	37.77	36.99	36.78	36.59	35.93	35.55
5000	49.92	47.21	46.23	45.97	45.74	44.91	44.43
6000	59.91	56.66	55.48	55.17	54.89	53.89	53.32
7000	69.89	66.10	64.72	64.36	64.04	62.87	62.20
8000	79.88	75.54	73.97	73.55	73.18	71.86	71.09
9000	89.86	84.98	83.21	82.75	82.33	80.84	79.98
10000	99.84	94.42	92.46	91.94	91.48	89.82	88.86
11000	109.83	103.86	101.70	101.13	100.63	98.80	97.75
12000	119.81	113.31	110.95	110.33	109.77	107.78	106.63
13000	129.79	122.75	120.19	119.52	118.92	116.76	115.52
14000	139.78	132.19	129.44	128.71	128.07	125.74	124.40
15000	149.76	141.63	138.68	137.91	137.22	134.73	133.29
16000	159.75	151.07	147.93	147.10	146.36	143.71	142.18
17000	169.73	160.52	157.17	156.29	155.51	152.69	151.06
18000	179.71	169.96	166.42	165.49	164.66	161.67	159.95
19000	189.70	179.40	175.66	174.68	173.81	170.65	168.83
20000	199.68	188.84	184.91	183.87	182.95	179.63	177.72
21000	209.66	198.28	194.15	193.07	192.10	188.61	186.60
22000	219.65	207.72	203.40	202.26	201.25	197.59	195.49
23000	229.63	217.17	212.64	211.45	210.40	206.58	204.38
24000	239.62	226.61	221.89	220.65	219.54	215.56	213.26
25000	249.60	236.05	231.13	229.84	228.69	224.54	222.15
26000	259.58	245.49	240.38	239.03	237.84	233.52	231.03
27000	269.57	254.93	249.62	248.23	246.98	242.50	239.92
28000	279.55	264.38	258.87	257.42	256.13	251.48	248.80
29000	289.54	273.82	268.11	266.61	265.28	260.46	257.69
30000	299.52	283.26	277.36	275.81	274.43	269.45	266.58
31000	309.50	292.70	286.60	285.00	283.57	278.43	275.46
32000	319.49	302.14	295.85	294.19	292.72	287.41	284.35
33000	329.47	311.58	305.09	303.39	301.87	296.39	293.23
34000	339.45	321.03	314.34	312.58	311.02	305.37	302.12
35000	349.44	330.47	323.58	321.77	320.16	314.35	311.00
36000	359.42	339.91	332.83	330.97	329.31	323.33	319.89
37000	369.41	349.35	342.07	340.16	338.46	332.31	328.78
38000	379.39	358.79	351.32	349.35	347.61	341.30	337.66
39000	389.37	368.24	360.56	358.55	356.75	350.28	346.55
40000	399.36	377.68	369.81	367.74	365.90	359.26	355.43
45000	449.28	424.89	416.03	413.71	411.64	404.17	399.86
50000	499.19	472.10	462.26	459.68	457.37	449.07	444.29
55000	549.11	519.30	508.48	505.64	503.11	493.98	488.72
60000	599.03	566.52	554.71	551.61	548.85	538.89	533.15
65000	648.95	613.72	600.93	597.58	594.59	583.79	577.58
70000	698.87	660.93	647.16	643.54	640.32	628.70	622.00
75000	748.79	708.14	693.38	689.51	686.06	673.61	666.43
80000	798.71	755.35	739.61	735.48	731.80	718.51	710.86
85000	848.63	802.56	785.83	781.44	777.53	763.42	755.29
90000	898.55	849.77	832.06	827.41	823.27	808.33	799.72
95000	948.47	896.98	878.28	873.38	869.01	853.23	844.15
100000	998.38	944.19	924.51	919.35	914.74	898.14	888.58

10.75% MONTHLY AMORTIZING PAYMENTS

AMOUNT OF LOAN	NUMBER OF YEARS IN TERM						
	1	2	3	4	5	10	15
$ 25	2.21	1.17	.82	.65	.55	.35	.29
50	4.42	2.33	1.64	1.29	1.09	.69	.57
75	6.62	3.49	2.45	1.93	1.63	1.03	.85
100	8.83	4.65	3.27	2.58	2.17	1.37	1.13
200	17.66	9.30	6.53	5.15	4.33	2.73	2.25
300	26.48	13.95	9.79	7.72	6.49	4.10	3.37
400	35.31	18.60	13.05	10.29	8.65	5.46	4.49
500	44.14	23.25	16.32	12.87	10.81	6.82	5.61
600	52.96	27.90	19.58	15.44	12.98	8.19	6.73
700	61.79	32.55	22.84	18.01	15.14	9.55	7.85
800	70.62	37.20	26.10	20.58	17.30	10.91	8.97
900	79.44	41.85	29.36	23.16	19.46	12.28	10.09
1000	88.27	46.50	32.63	25.73	21.62	13.64	11.21
2000	176.54	92.99	65.25	51.45	43.24	27.27	22.42
2500	220.67	116.23	81.56	64.32	54.05	34.09	28.03
3000	264.80	139.48	97.87	77.18	64.86	40.91	33.63
4000	353.07	185.97	130.49	102.90	86.48	54.54	44.84
5000	441.33	232.46	163.11	128.63	108.09	68.17	56.05
6000	529.60	278.96	195.73	154.35	129.71	81.81	67.26
7000	617.86	325.45	228.35	180.07	151.33	95.44	78.47
8000	706.13	371.94	260.97	205.80	172.95	109.08	89.68
9000	794.39	418.43	293.59	231.52	194.57	122.71	100.89
10000	882.66	464.92	326.21	257.25	216.18	136.34	112.10
11000	970.92	511.42	358.83	282.97	237.80	149.98	123.31
12000	1059.19	557.91	391.45	308.70	259.42	163.61	134.52
13000	1147.45	604.40	424.07	334.42	281.04	177.25	145.73
14000	1235.72	650.89	456.69	360.14	302.66	190.88	156.94
15000	1323.98	697.38	489.31	385.87	324.27	204.51	168.15
16000	1412.25	743.87	521.93	411.59	345.89	218.15	179.36
17000	1500.51	790.37	554.55	437.32	367.51	231.78	190.57
18000	1588.78	836.86	587.17	463.04	389.13	245.41	201.78
19000	1677.04	883.35	619.79	488.77	410.75	259.05	212.99
20000	1765.31	929.84	652.41	514.49	432.36	272.68	224.19
21000	1853.57	976.33	685.03	540.21	453.98	286.32	235.40
22000	1941.84	1022.83	717.65	565.94	475.60	299.95	246.61
23000	2030.10	1069.32	750.28	591.66	497.22	313.58	257.82
24000	2118.37	1115.81	782.90	617.39	518.84	327.22	269.03
25000	2206.63	1162.30	815.52	643.11	540.45	340.85	280.24
26000	2294.90	1208.79	848.14	668.84	562.07	354.49	291.45
27000	2383.16	1255.29	880.76	694.56	583.69	368.12	302.66
28000	2471.43	1301.78	913.38	720.28	605.31	381.75	313.87
29000	2559.69	1348.27	946.00	746.01	626.93	395.39	325.08
30000	2647.96	1394.76	978.62	771.73	648.54	409.02	336.29
31000	2736.22	1441.25	1011.24	797.46	670.16	422.65	347.50
32000	2824.49	1487.74	1043.86	823.18	691.78	436.29	358.71
33000	2912.75	1534.24	1076.48	848.91	713.40	449.92	369.92
34000	3001.02	1580.73	1109.10	874.63	735.02	463.56	381.13
35000	3089.28	1627.22	1141.72	900.35	756.63	477.19	392.34
36000	3177.55	1673.71	1174.34	926.08	778.25	490.82	403.55
37000	3265.81	1720.20	1206.96	951.80	799.87	504.46	414.76
38000	3354.08	1766.70	1239.58	977.53	821.49	518.09	425.97
39000	3442.34	1813.19	1272.20	1003.25	843.11	531.73	437.17
40000	3530.61	1859.68	1304.82	1028.98	864.72	545.36	448.38
45000	3971.93	2092.14	1467.93	1157.60	972.81	613.53	504.43
50000	4413.26	2324.60	1631.03	1286.22	1080.90	681.70	560.48
55000	4854.58	2557.06	1794.13	1414.84	1188.99	749.87	616.53
60000	5295.91	2789.52	1957.23	1543.46	1297.08	818.04	672.57
65000	5737.24	3021.98	2120.33	1672.08	1405.17	886.21	728.62
70000	6178.56	3254.43	2283.44	1800.70	1513.26	954.38	784.67
75000	6619.89	3486.89	2446.54	1929.33	1621.35	1022.55	840.72
80000	7061.21	3719.35	2609.64	2057.95	1729.44	1090.71	896.76
85000	7502.54	3951.81	2772.74	2186.57	1837.53	1158.88	952.81
90000	7943.86	4184.27	2935.85	2315.19	1945.62	1227.05	1008.86
95000	8385.19	4416.73	3098.95	2443.81	2053.71	1295.22	1064.91
100000	8826.51	4649.19	3262.05	2572.43	2161.80	1363.39	1120.95

16

MONTHLY AMORTIZING PAYMENTS 10.75%

AMOUNT OF LOAN	NUMBER OF YEARS IN TERM						
	20	25	28	29	30	35	40
$ 25	.26	.25	.24	.24	.24	.23	.23
50	.51	.49	.48	.47	.47	.46	.46
75	.77	.73	.71	.71	.71	.69	.69
100	1.02	.97	.95	.94	.94	.92	.91
200	2.04	1.93	1.89	1.88	1.87	1.84	1.82
300	3.05	2.89	2.83	2.82	2.81	2.76	2.73
400	4.07	3.85	3.78	3.76	3.74	3.68	3.64
500	5.08	4.82	4.72	4.69	4.67	4.59	4.55
600	6.10	5.78	5.66	5.63	5.61	5.51	5.46
700	7.11	6.74	6.61	6.57	6.54	6.43	6.36
800	8.13	7.70	7.55	7.51	7.47	7.35	7.27
900	9.14	8.66	8.49	8.45	8.41	8.26	8.18
1000	10.16	9.63	9.43	9.38	9.34	9.18	9.09
2000	20.31	19.25	18.86	18.76	18.67	18.36	18.17
2500	25.39	24.06	23.58	23.45	23.34	22.94	22.71
3000	30.46	28.87	28.29	28.14	28.01	27.53	27.26
4000	40.61	38.49	37.72	37.52	37.34	36.71	36.34
5000	50.77	48.11	47.15	46.90	46.68	45.88	45.42
6000	60.92	57.73	56.58	56.28	56.01	55.06	54.51
7000	71.07	67.35	66.01	65.66	65.35	64.23	63.59
8000	81.22	76.97	75.44	75.04	74.68	73.41	72.68
9000	91.38	86.59	84.87	84.42	84.02	82.58	81.76
10000	101.53	96.21	94.30	93.80	93.35	91.76	90.84
11000	111.68	105.84	103.73	103.18	102.69	100.93	99.93
12000	121.83	115.46	113.16	112.56	112.02	110.11	109.01
13000	131.98	125.08	122.59	121.94	121.36	119.28	118.10
14000	142.14	134.70	132.02	131.32	130.69	128.46	127.18
15000	152.29	144.32	141.45	140.70	140.03	137.63	136.26
16000	162.44	153.94	150.88	150.07	149.36	146.81	145.35
17000	172.59	163.56	160.30	159.45	158.70	155.98	154.43
18000	182.75	173.18	169.73	168.83	168.03	165.16	163.52
19000	192.90	182.80	179.16	178.21	177.37	174.33	172.60
20000	203.05	192.42	188.59	187.59	186.70	183.51	181.68
21000	213.20	202.04	198.02	196.97	196.04	192.68	190.77
22000	223.36	211.67	207.45	206.35	205.37	201.86	199.85
23000	233.51	221.29	216.88	215.73	214.71	211.03	208.94
24000	243.66	230.91	226.31	225.11	224.04	220.21	218.02
25000	253.81	240.53	235.74	234.49	233.38	229.38	227.10
26000	263.96	250.15	245.17	243.87	242.71	238.56	236.19
27000	274.12	259.77	254.60	253.25	252.04	247.73	245.27
28000	284.27	269.39	264.03	262.63	261.38	256.91	254.36
29000	294.42	279.01	273.46	272.01	270.71	266.08	263.44
30000	304.57	288.63	282.89	281.39	280.05	275.26	272.52
31000	314.73	298.25	292.32	290.76	289.38	284.43	281.61
32000	324.88	307.87	301.75	300.14	298.72	293.61	290.69
33000	335.03	317.50	311.18	309.52	308.05	302.78	299.78
34000	345.18	327.12	320.60	318.90	317.39	311.96	308.86
35000	355.34	336.74	330.03	328.28	326.72	321.13	317.94
36000	365.49	346.36	339.46	337.66	336.06	330.31	327.03
37000	375.64	355.98	348.89	347.04	345.39	339.48	336.11
38000	385.79	365.60	358.32	356.42	354.73	348.66	345.20
39000	395.94	375.22	367.75	365.80	364.06	357.83	354.28
40000	406.10	384.84	377.18	375.18	373.40	367.01	363.36
45000	456.86	432.95	424.33	422.08	420.07	412.88	408.78
50000	507.62	481.05	471.47	468.97	466.75	458.76	454.20
55000	558.38	529.16	518.62	515.87	513.42	504.63	499.62
60000	609.14	577.26	565.77	562.77	560.09	550.51	545.04
65000	659.90	625.37	612.92	609.66	606.77	596.38	590.46
70000	710.67	673.47	660.06	656.56	653.44	642.26	635.88
75000	761.43	721.57	707.21	703.46	700.12	688.13	681.30
80000	812.19	769.68	754.36	750.36	746.79	734.01	726.72
85000	862.95	817.78	801.50	797.25	793.46	779.88	772.14
90000	913.71	865.89	848.65	844.15	840.14	825.76	817.56
95000	964.47	913.99	895.80	891.04	886.81	871.63	862.98
100000	1015.23	962.10	942.94	937.94	933.49	917.51	908.40

17

11.00% MONTHLY AMORTIZING PAYMENTS

AMOUNT OF LOAN	NUMBER OF YEARS IN TERM						
	1	2	3	4	5	10	15
$ 25	2.21	1.17	.82	.65	.55	.35	.29
50	4.42	2.34	1.64	1.30	1.09	.69	.57
75	6.63	3.50	2.46	1.94	1.64	1.04	.86
100	8.84	4.67	3.28	2.59	2.18	1.38	1.14
200	17.68	9.33	6.55	5.17	4.35	2.76	2.28
300	26.52	13.99	9.83	7.76	6.53	4.14	3.41
400	35.36	18.65	13.10	10.34	8.70	5.51	4.55
500	44.20	23.31	16.37	12.93	10.88	6.89	5.69
600	53.03	27.97	19.65	15.51	13.05	8.27	6.82
700	61.87	32.63	22.92	18.10	15.22	9.65	7.96
800	70.71	37.29	26.20	20.68	17.40	11.02	9.10
900	79.55	41.95	29.47	23.27	19.57	12.40	10.23
1000	88.39	46.61	32.74	25.85	21.75	13.78	11.37
2000	176.77	93.22	65.48	51.70	43.49	27.56	22.74
2500	220.96	116.52	81.85	64.62	54.36	34.44	28.42
3000	265.15	139.83	98.22	77.54	65.23	41.33	34.10
4000	353.53	186.44	130.96	103.39	86.97	55.11	45.47
5000	441.91	233.04	163.70	129.23	108.72	68.88	56.83
6000	530.29	279.65	196.44	155.08	130.46	82.66	68.20
7000	618.68	326.26	229.18	180.92	152.20	96.43	79.57
8000	707.06	372.87	261.91	206.77	173.94	110.21	90.93
9000	795.44	419.48	294.65	232.61	195.69	123.98	102.30
10000	883.82	466.08	327.39	258.46	217.43	137.76	113.66
11000	972.20	512.69	360.13	284.31	239.17	151.53	125.03
12000	1060.58	559.30	392.87	310.15	260.91	165.31	136.40
13000	1148.97	605.91	425.61	336.00	282.66	179.08	147.76
14000	1237.35	652.51	458.35	361.84	304.40	192.86	159.13
15000	1325.73	699.12	491.09	387.69	326.14	206.63	170.49
16000	1414.11	745.73	523.82	413.53	347.88	220.41	181.86
17000	1502.49	792.34	556.56	439.38	369.63	234.18	193.23
18000	1590.87	838.95	589.30	465.22	391.37	247.96	204.59
19000	1679.26	885.55	622.04	491.07	413.11	261.73	215.96
20000	1767.64	932.16	654.78	516.92	434.85	275.51	227.32
21000	1856.02	978.77	687.52	542.76	456.60	289.28	238.69
22000	1944.40	1025.38	720.26	568.61	478.34	303.06	250.06
23000	2032.78	1071.99	753.00	594.45	500.08	316.83	261.42
24000	2121.16	1118.59	785.73	620.30	521.82	330.61	272.79
25000	2209.55	1165.20	818.47	646.14	543.57	344.38	284.15
26000	2297.93	1211.81	851.21	671.99	565.31	358.16	295.52
27000	2386.31	1258.42	883.95	697.83	587.05	371.93	306.89
28000	2474.69	1305.02	916.69	723.68	608.79	385.71	318.25
29000	2563.07	1351.63	949.43	749.53	630.54	399.48	329.62
30000	2651.45	1398.24	982.17	775.37	652.28	413.26	340.98
31000	2739.84	1444.85	1014.91	801.22	674.02	427.03	352.35
32000	2828.22	1491.46	1047.64	827.06	695.76	440.81	363.72
33000	2916.60	1538.06	1080.38	852.91	717.50	454.58	375.08
34000	3004.98	1584.67	1113.12	878.75	739.25	468.36	386.45
35000	3093.36	1631.28	1145.86	904.60	760.99	482.13	397.81
36000	3181.74	1677.89	1178.60	930.44	782.73	495.91	409.18
37000	3270.13	1724.50	1211.34	956.29	804.47	509.68	420.55
38000	3358.51	1771.10	1244.08	982.13	826.22	523.46	431.91
39000	3446.89	1817.71	1276.81	1007.98	847.96	537.23	443.28
40000	3535.27	1864.32	1309.55	1033.83	869.70	551.01	454.64
45000	3977.18	2097.36	1473.25	1163.05	978.41	619.88	511.47
50000	4419.09	2330.40	1636.94	1292.28	1087.13	688.76	568.30
55000	4861.00	2563.44	1800.63	1421.51	1195.84	757.63	625.13
60000	5302.90	2796.48	1964.33	1550.74	1304.55	826.51	681.96
65000	5744.81	3029.51	2128.02	1679.96	1413.26	895.38	738.79
70000	6186.72	3262.55	2291.72	1809.19	1521.97	964.26	795.62
75000	6628.63	3495.59	2455.41	1938.42	1630.69	1033.13	852.45
80000	7070.54	3728.63	2619.10	2067.65	1739.40	1102.01	909.28
85000	7512.45	3961.67	2782.80	2196.87	1848.11	1170.88	966.11
90000	7954.35	4194.71	2946.49	2326.10	1956.82	1239.76	1022.94
95000	8396.26	4427.75	3110.18	2455.33	2065.54	1308.63	1079.77
100000	8838.17	4660.79	3273.88	2584.56	2174.25	1377.51	1136.60

18

MONTHLY AMORTIZING PAYMENTS 11.00%

AMOUNT OF LOAN	\multicolumn{7}{c}{NUMBER OF YEARS IN TERM}						
	20	25	28	29	30	35	40
$ 25	.26	.25	.25	.24	.24	.24	.24
50	.52	.50	.49	.48	.48	.47	.47
75	.78	.74	.73	.72	.72	.71	.70
100	1.04	.99	.97	.96	.96	.94	.93
200	2.07	1.97	1.93	1.92	1.91	1.88	1.86
300	3.10	2.95	2.89	2.87	2.86	2.82	2.79
400	4.13	3.93	3.85	3.83	3.81	3.75	3.72
500	5.17	4.91	4.81	4.79	4.77	4.69	4.65
600	6.20	5.89	5.77	5.74	5.72	5.63	5.57
700	7.23	6.87	6.74	6.70	6.67	6.56	6.50
800	8.26	7.85	7.70	7.66	7.62	7.50	7.43
900	9.29	8.83	8.66	8.61	8.58	8.44	8.36
1000	10.33	9.81	9.62	9.57	9.53	9.37	9.29
2000	20.65	19.61	19.23	19.14	19.05	18.74	18.57
2500	25.81	24.51	24.04	23.92	23.81	23.43	23.21
3000	30.97	29.41	28.85	28.70	28.57	28.11	27.85
4000	41.29	39.21	38.46	38.27	38.10	37.48	37.14
5000	51.61	49.01	48.08	47.84	47.62	46.85	46.42
6000	61.94	58.81	57.69	57.40	57.14	56.22	55.70
7000	72.26	68.61	67.31	66.97	66.67	65.59	64.99
8000	82.58	78.41	76.92	76.54	76.19	74.96	74.27
9000	92.90	88.22	86.54	86.10	85.71	84.33	83.55
10000	103.22	98.02	96.15	95.67	95.24	93.70	92.83
11000	113.55	107.82	105.77	105.23	104.76	103.07	102.12
12000	123.87	117.62	115.38	114.80	114.28	112.44	111.40
13000	134.19	127.42	125.00	124.37	123.81	121.81	120.68
14000	144.51	137.22	134.61	133.93	133.33	131.18	129.97
15000	154.83	147.02	144.23	143.50	142.85	140.55	139.25
16000	165.16	156.82	153.84	153.07	152.38	149.92	148.53
17000	175.48	166.62	163.46	162.63	161.90	159.29	157.82
18000	185.80	176.43	173.07	172.20	171.42	168.66	167.10
19000	196.12	186.23	182.69	181.76	180.95	178.03	176.38
20000	206.44	196.03	192.30	191.33	190.47	187.40	185.66
21000	216.76	205.83	201.92	200.90	199.99	196.77	194.95
22000	227.09	215.63	211.53	210.46	209.52	206.14	204.23
23000	237.41	225.43	221.15	220.03	219.04	215.51	213.51
24000	247.73	235.23	230.76	229.60	228.56	224.87	222.80
25000	258.05	245.03	240.37	239.16	238.09	234.24	232.08
26000	268.37	254.83	249.99	248.73	247.61	243.61	241.36
27000	278.70	264.64	259.60	258.29	257.13	252.98	250.64
28000	289.02	274.44	269.22	267.86	266.66	262.35	259.93
29000	299.34	284.24	278.83	277.43	276.18	271.72	269.21
30000	309.66	294.04	288.45	286.99	285.70	281.09	278.49
31000	319.98	303.84	298.06	296.56	295.23	290.46	287.78
32000	330.31	313.64	307.68	306.13	304.75	299.83	297.06
33000	340.63	323.44	317.29	315.69	314.27	309.20	306.34
34000	350.95	333.24	326.91	325.26	323.79	318.57	315.63
35000	361.27	343.04	336.52	334.83	333.32	327.94	324.91
36000	371.59	352.85	346.14	344.39	342.84	337.31	334.19
37000	381.91	362.65	355.75	353.96	352.36	346.68	343.47
38000	392.24	372.45	365.37	363.52	361.89	356.05	352.76
39000	402.56	382.25	374.98	373.09	371.41	365.42	362.04
40000	412.88	392.05	384.60	382.66	380.93	374.79	371.32
45000	464.49	441.06	432.67	430.49	428.55	421.64	417.74
50000	516.10	490.06	480.74	478.32	476.17	468.48	464.15
55000	567.71	539.07	528.82	526.15	523.78	515.33	510.57
60000	619.32	588.07	576.89	573.98	571.40	562.18	556.98
65000	670.93	637.08	624.97	621.81	619.02	609.03	603.40
70000	722.54	686.08	673.04	669.65	666.63	655.88	649.81
75000	774.15	735.09	721.11	717.48	714.25	702.72	696.23
80000	825.76	784.10	769.19	765.31	761.86	749.57	742.64
85000	877.37	833.10	817.26	813.14	809.48	796.42	789.06
90000	928.97	882.11	865.34	860.97	857.10	843.27	835.47
95000	980.58	931.11	913.41	908.80	904.71	890.11	881.88
100000	1032.19	980.12	961.48	956.63	952.33	936.96	928.30

11.25% MONTHLY AMORTIZING PAYMENTS

AMOUNT OF LOAN	NUMBER OF YEARS IN TERM						
	1	2	3	4	5	10	15
$ 25	2.22	1.17	.83	.65	.55	.35	.29
50	4.43	2.34	1.65	1.30	1.10	.70	.58
75	6.64	3.51	2.47	1.95	1.65	1.05	.87
100	8.85	4.68	3.29	2.60	2.19	1.40	1.16
200	17.70	9.35	6.58	5.20	4.38	2.79	2.31
300	26.55	14.02	9.86	7.80	6.57	4.18	3.46
400	35.40	18.69	13.15	10.39	8.75	5.57	4.61
500	44.25	23.37	16.43	12.99	10.94	6.96	5.77
600	53.10	28.04	19.72	15.59	13.13	8.36	6.92
700	61.95	32.71	23.01	18.18	15.31	9.75	8.07
800	70.80	37.38	26.29	20.78	17.50	11.14	9.22
900	79.65	42.06	29.58	23.38	19.69	12.53	10.38
1000	88.50	46.73	32.86	25.97	21.87	13.92	11.53
2000	177.00	93.45	65.72	51.94	43.74	27.84	23.05
2500	221.25	116.81	82.15	64.92	54.67	34.80	28.81
3000	265.50	140.18	98.58	77.91	65.61	41.76	34.58
4000	354.00	186.90	131.43	103.87	87.47	55.67	46.10
5000	442.50	233.62	164.29	129.84	109.34	69.59	57.62
6000	530.99	280.35	197.15	155.81	131.21	83.51	69.15
7000	619.49	327.07	230.01	181.77	153.08	97.42	80.67
8000	707.99	373.80	262.86	207.74	174.94	111.34	92.19
9000	796.49	420.52	295.72	233.71	196.81	125.26	103.72
10000	884.99	467.24	328.58	259.68	218.68	139.17	115.24
11000	973.49	513.97	361.43	285.64	240.55	153.09	126.76
12000	1061.98	560.69	394.29	311.61	262.41	167.01	138.29
13000	1150.48	607.42	427.15	337.58	284.28	180.92	149.81
14000	1238.98	654.14	460.01	363.54	306.15	194.84	161.33
15000	1327.48	700.86	492.86	389.51	328.01	208.76	172.86
16000	1415.98	747.59	525.72	415.48	349.88	222.68	184.38
17000	1504.48	794.31	558.58	441.45	371.75	236.59	195.90
18000	1592.97	841.04	591.44	467.41	393.62	250.51	207.43
19000	1681.47	887.76	624.29	493.38	415.48	264.43	218.95
20000	1769.97	934.48	657.15	519.35	437.35	278.34	230.47
21000	1858.47	981.21	690.01	545.31	459.22	292.26	242.00
22000	1946.97	1027.93	722.86	571.28	481.09	306.18	253.52
23000	2035.47	1074.66	755.72	597.25	502.95	320.09	265.04
24000	2123.96	1121.38	788.58	623.22	524.82	334.01	276.57
25000	2212.46	1168.10	821.44	649.18	546.69	347.93	288.09
26000	2300.96	1214.83	854.29	675.15	568.56	361.84	299.61
27000	2389.46	1261.55	887.15	701.12	590.42	375.76	311.14
28000	2477.96	1308.28	920.01	727.08	612.29	389.68	322.66
29000	2566.46	1355.00	952.86	753.05	634.16	403.59	334.18
30000	2654.95	1401.72	985.72	779.02	656.02	417.51	345.71
31000	2743.45	1448.45	1018.58	804.99	677.89	431.43	357.23
32000	2831.95	1495.17	1051.44	830.95	699.76	445.35	368.76
33000	2920.45	1541.90	1084.29	856.92	721.63	459.26	380.28
34000	3008.95	1588.62	1117.15	882.89	743.49	473.18	391.80
35000	3097.45	1635.34	1150.01	908.85	765.36	487.10	403.33
36000	3185.94	1682.07	1182.87	934.82	787.23	501.01	414.85
37000	3274.44	1728.79	1215.72	960.79	809.10	514.93	426.37
38000	3362.94	1775.52	1248.58	986.75	830.96	528.85	437.90
39000	3451.44	1822.24	1281.44	1012.72	852.83	542.76	449.42
40000	3539.94	1868.96	1314.29	1038.69	874.70	556.68	460.94
45000	3982.43	2102.58	1478.58	1168.52	984.03	626.27	518.56
50000	4424.92	2336.20	1642.87	1298.36	1093.37	695.85	576.18
55000	4867.41	2569.82	1807.15	1428.20	1202.71	765.43	633.79
60000	5309.90	2803.44	1971.44	1558.03	1312.04	835.02	691.41
65000	5752.40	3037.06	2135.73	1687.87	1421.38	904.60	749.03
70000	6194.89	3270.68	2300.01	1817.70	1530.72	974.19	806.65
75000	6637.38	3504.30	2464.30	1947.54	1640.05	1043.77	864.26
80000	7079.87	3737.92	2628.58	2077.37	1749.39	1113.36	921.88
85000	7522.36	3971.54	2792.87	2207.21	1858.73	1182.94	979.50
90000	7964.85	4205.16	2957.16	2337.04	1968.06	1252.53	1037.12
95000	8407.34	4438.78	3121.44	2466.88	2077.40	1322.11	1094.73
100000	8849.84	4672.40	3285.73	2596.71	2186.74	1391.69	1152.35

MONTHLY AMORTIZING PAYMENTS 11.25%

AMOUNT OF LOAN	NUMBER OF YEARS IN TERM						
	20	25	28	29	30	35	40
$ 25	.27	.25	.25	.25	.25	.24	.24
50	.53	.50	.50	.49	.49	.48	.48
75	.79	.75	.74	.74	.73	.72	.72
100	1.05	1.00	.99	.98	.98	.96	.95
200	2.10	2.00	1.97	1.96	1.95	1.92	1.90
300	3.15	3.00	2.95	2.93	2.92	2.87	2.85
400	4.20	4.00	3.93	3.91	3.89	3.83	3.80
500	5.25	5.00	4.91	4.88	4.86	4.79	4.75
600	6.30	5.99	5.89	5.86	5.83	5.74	5.69
700	7.35	6.99	6.87	6.83	6.80	6.70	6.64
800	8.40	7.99	7.85	7.81	7.78	7.66	7.59
900	9.45	8.99	8.83	8.78	8.75	8.61	8.54
1000	10.50	9.99	9.81	9.76	9.72	9.57	9.49
2000	20.99	19.97	19.61	19.51	19.43	19.13	18.97
2500	26.24	24.96	24.51	24.39	24.29	23.92	23.71
3000	31.48	29.95	29.41	29.27	29.14	28.70	28.45
4000	41.98	39.93	39.21	39.02	38.86	38.26	37.94
5000	52.47	49.92	49.01	48.78	48.57	47.83	47.42
6000	62.96	59.90	58.81	58.53	58.28	57.39	56.90
7000	73.45	69.88	68.61	68.28	67.99	66.96	66.38
8000	83.95	79.86	78.41	78.04	77.71	76.52	75.87
9000	94.44	89.85	88.22	87.79	87.42	86.09	85.35
10000	104.93	99.83	98.02	97.55	97.13	95.65	94.83
11000	115.42	109.81	107.82	107.30	106.84	105.22	104.31
12000	125.92	119.79	117.62	117.06	116.56	114.78	113.80
13000	136.41	129.78	127.42	126.81	126.27	124.35	123.28
14000	146.90	139.76	137.22	136.56	135.98	133.91	132.76
15000	157.39	149.74	147.02	146.32	145.69	143.48	142.24
16000	167.89	159.72	156.82	156.07	155.41	153.04	151.73
17000	178.38	169.71	166.63	165.83	165.12	162.61	161.21
18000	188.87	179.69	176.43	175.58	174.83	172.17	170.69
19000	199.36	189.67	186.23	185.34	184.54	181.74	180.17
20000	209.86	199.65	196.03	195.09	194.26	191.30	189.66
21000	220.35	209.64	205.83	204.84	203.97	200.87	199.14
22000	230.84	219.62	215.63	214.60	213.68	210.43	208.62
23000	241.33	229.60	225.43	224.35	223.40	220.00	218.10
24000	251.83	239.58	235.23	234.11	233.11	229.56	227.59
25000	262.32	249.56	245.04	243.86	242.82	239.13	237.07
26000	272.81	259.55	254.84	253.62	252.53	248.69	246.55
27000	283.30	269.53	264.64	263.37	262.25	258.26	256.03
28000	293.80	279.51	274.44	273.12	271.96	267.82	265.52
29000	304.29	289.49	284.24	282.88	281.67	277.39	275.00
30000	314.78	299.48	294.04	292.63	291.38	286.95	284.48
31000	325.27	309.46	303.84	302.39	301.10	296.52	293.96
32000	335.77	319.44	313.64	312.14	310.81	306.08	303.45
33000	346.26	329.42	323.44	321.89	320.52	315.65	312.93
34000	356.75	339.41	333.25	331.65	330.23	325.21	322.41
35000	367.24	349.39	343.05	341.40	339.95	334.78	331.90
36000	377.74	359.37	352.85	351.16	349.66	344.34	341.38
37000	388.23	369.35	362.65	360.91	359.37	353.91	350.86
38000	398.72	379.34	372.45	370.67	369.08	363.47	360.34
39000	409.21	389.32	382.25	380.42	378.80	373.04	369.83
40000	419.71	399.30	392.05	390.17	388.51	382.60	379.31
45000	472.17	449.21	441.06	438.95	437.07	430.43	426.72
50000	524.63	499.12	490.07	487.72	485.64	478.25	474.13
55000	577.10	549.04	539.07	536.49	534.20	526.08	521.55
60000	629.56	598.95	588.08	585.26	582.76	573.90	568.96
65000	682.02	648.86	637.08	634.03	631.32	621.73	616.37
70000	734.48	698.77	686.09	682.80	679.89	669.55	663.79
75000	786.95	748.68	735.10	731.57	728.45	717.38	711.20
80000	839.41	798.60	784.10	780.34	777.01	765.20	758.61
85000	891.87	848.51	833.11	829.11	825.58	813.03	806.02
90000	944.34	898.42	882.11	877.89	874.14	860.85	853.44
95000	996.80	948.33	931.12	926.66	922.70	908.67	900.85
100000	1049.26	998.24	980.13	975.43	971.27	956.50	948.26

11.50% MONTHLY AMORTIZING PAYMENTS

AMOUNT OF LOAN	NUMBER OF YEARS IN TERM						
	1	2	3	4	5	10	15
$ 25	2.22	1.18	.83	.66	.55	.36	.30
50	4.44	2.35	1.65	1.31	1.10	.71	.59
75	6.65	3.52	2.48	1.96	1.65	1.06	.88
100	8.87	4.69	3.30	2.61	2.20	1.41	1.17
200	17.73	9.37	6.60	5.22	4.40	2.82	2.34
300	26.59	14.06	9.90	7.83	6.60	4.22	3.51
400	35.45	18.74	13.20	10.44	8.80	5.63	4.68
500	44.31	23.43	16.49	13.05	11.00	7.03	5.85
600	53.17	28.11	19.79	15.66	13.20	8.44	7.01
700	62.04	32.79	23.09	18.27	15.40	9.85	8.18
800	70.90	37.48	26.39	20.88	17.60	11.25	9.35
900	79.76	42.16	29.68	23.49	19.80	12.66	10.52
1000	88.62	46.85	32.98	26.09	22.00	14.06	11.69
2000	177.24	93.69	65.96	52.18	43.99	28.12	23.37
2500	221.54	117.11	82.45	65.23	54.99	35.15	29.21
3000	265.85	140.53	98.93	78.27	65.98	42.18	35.05
4000	354.47	187.37	131.91	104.36	87.98	56.24	46.73
5000	443.08	234.21	164.89	130.45	109.97	70.30	58.41
6000	531.70	281.05	197.86	156.54	131.96	84.36	70.10
7000	620.31	327.89	230.84	182.63	153.95	98.42	81.78
8000	708.93	374.73	263.81	208.72	175.95	112.48	93.46
9000	797.54	421.57	296.79	234.81	197.94	126.54	105.14
10000	886.16	468.41	329.77	260.90	219.93	140.60	116.82
11000	974.77	515.25	362.74	286.98	241.92	154.66	128.51
12000	1063.39	562.09	395.72	313.07	263.92	168.72	140.19
13000	1152.00	608.93	428.69	339.16	285.91	182.78	151.87
14000	1240.62	655.77	461.67	365.25	307.90	196.84	163.55
15000	1329.23	702.61	494.65	391.34	329.89	210.90	175.23
16000	1417.85	749.45	527.62	417.43	351.89	224.96	186.92
17000	1506.46	796.29	560.60	443.52	373.88	239.02	198.60
18000	1595.08	843.13	593.57	469.61	395.87	253.08	210.28
19000	1683.69	889.97	626.55	495.70	417.86	267.14	221.96
20000	1772.31	936.81	659.53	521.79	439.86	281.20	233.64
21000	1860.92	983.65	692.50	547.87	461.85	295.26	245.32
22000	1949.54	1030.49	725.48	573.96	483.84	309.31	257.01
23000	2038.15	1077.33	758.45	600.05	505.83	323.37	268.69
24000	2126.77	1124.17	791.43	626.14	527.83	337.43	280.37
25000	2215.38	1171.01	824.41	652.23	549.82	351.49	292.05
26000	2304.00	1217.85	857.38	678.32	571.81	365.55	303.73
27000	2392.61	1264.69	890.36	704.41	593.81	379.61	315.42
28000	2481.23	1311.53	923.33	730.50	615.80	393.67	327.10
29000	2569.84	1358.37	956.31	756.59	637.79	407.73	338.78
30000	2658.46	1405.21	989.29	782.68	659.78	421.79	350.46
31000	2747.07	1452.05	1022.26	808.76	681.78	435.85	362.14
32000	2835.69	1498.90	1055.24	834.85	703.77	449.91	373.83
33000	2924.30	1545.74	1088.21	860.94	725.76	463.97	385.51
34000	3012.92	1592.58	1121.19	887.03	747.75	478.03	397.19
35000	3101.53	1639.42	1154.17	913.12	769.75	492.09	408.87
36000	3190.15	1686.26	1187.14	939.21	791.74	506.15	420.55
37000	3278.76	1733.10	1220.12	965.30	813.73	520.21	432.24
38000	3367.38	1779.94	1253.09	991.39	835.72	534.27	443.92
39000	3455.99	1826.78	1286.07	1017.48	857.72	548.33	455.60
40000	3544.61	1873.62	1319.05	1043.57	879.71	562.39	467.28
45000	3987.68	2107.82	1483.93	1174.01	989.67	632.68	525.69
50000	4430.76	2342.02	1648.81	1304.46	1099.64	702.98	584.10
55000	4873.83	2576.22	1813.69	1434.90	1209.60	773.28	642.51
60000	5316.91	2810.42	1978.57	1565.35	1319.56	843.58	700.92
65000	5759.98	3044.62	2143.45	1695.79	1429.52	913.88	759.33
70000	6203.06	3278.83	2308.33	1826.24	1539.49	984.17	817.74
75000	6646.13	3513.03	2473.21	1956.68	1649.45	1054.47	876.15
80000	7089.21	3747.23	2638.09	2087.13	1759.41	1124.77	934.56
85000	7532.28	3981.43	2802.97	2217.57	1869.38	1195.07	992.97
90000	7975.36	4215.63	2967.85	2348.02	1979.34	1265.36	1051.38
95000	8418.44	4449.83	3132.73	2478.46	2089.30	1335.66	1109.79
100000	8861.51	4684.04	3297.61	2608.91	2199.27	1405.96	1168.19

22

MONTHLY AMORTIZING PAYMENTS 11.50%

AMOUNT OF LOAN	NUMBER OF YEARS IN TERM						
	20	25	28	29	30	35	40
$ 25	.27	.26	.25	.25	.25	.25	.25
50	.54	.51	.50	.50	.50	.49	.49
75	.80	.77	.75	.75	.75	.74	.73
100	1.07	1.02	1.00	1.00	1.00	.98	.97
200	2.14	2.04	2.00	1.99	1.99	1.96	1.94
300	3.20	3.05	3.00	2.99	2.98	2.93	2.91
400	4.27	4.07	4.00	3.98	3.97	3.91	3.88
500	5.34	5.09	5.00	4.98	4.96	4.89	4.85
600	6.40	6.10	6.00	5.97	5.95	5.86	5.81
700	7.47	7.12	7.00	6.97	6.94	6.84	6.78
800	8.54	8.14	8.00	7.96	7.93	7.81	7.75
900	9.60	9.15	8.99	8.95	8.92	8.79	8.72
1000	10.67	10.17	9.99	9.95	9.91	9.77	9.69
2000	21.33	20.33	19.98	19.89	19.82	19.53	19.37
2500	26.67	25.42	24.98	24.86	24.76	24.41	24.21
3000	32.00	30.50	29.97	29.83	29.71	29.29	29.05
4000	42.66	40.66	39.96	39.78	39.62	39.05	38.74
5000	53.33	50.83	49.95	49.72	49.52	48.81	48.42
6000	63.99	60.99	59.94	59.66	59.42	58.57	58.10
7000	74.66	71.16	69.93	69.61	69.33	68.33	67.78
8000	85.32	81.32	79.91	79.55	79.23	78.09	77.47
9000	95.98	91.49	89.90	89.49	89.13	87.85	87.15
10000	106.65	101.65	99.89	99.44	99.03	97.62	96.83
11000	117.31	111.82	109.88	109.38	108.94	107.38	106.52
12000	127.98	121.98	119.87	119.32	118.84	117.14	116.20
13000	138.64	132.15	129.86	129.27	128.74	126.90	125.88
14000	149.31	142.31	139.85	139.21	138.65	136.66	135.56
15000	159.97	152.48	149.83	149.15	148.55	146.42	145.25
16000	170.63	162.64	159.82	159.09	158.45	156.18	154.93
17000	181.30	172.80	169.81	169.04	168.35	165.94	164.61
18000	191.96	182.97	179.80	178.98	178.26	175.70	174.30
19000	202.63	193.13	189.79	188.92	188.16	185.47	183.98
20000	213.29	203.30	199.78	198.87	198.06	195.23	193.66
21000	223.96	213.46	209.77	208.81	207.97	204.99	203.34
22000	234.62	223.63	219.75	218.75	217.87	214.75	213.03
23000	245.28	233.79	229.74	228.70	227.77	224.51	222.71
24000	255.95	243.96	239.73	238.64	237.67	234.27	232.39
25000	266.61	254.12	249.72	248.58	247.58	244.03	242.08
26000	277.28	264.29	259.71	258.53	257.48	253.79	251.76
27000	287.94	274.45	269.70	268.47	267.38	263.55	261.44
28000	298.61	284.62	279.69	278.41	277.29	273.32	271.12
29000	309.27	294.78	289.67	288.36	287.19	283.08	280.81
30000	319.93	304.95	299.66	298.30	297.09	292.84	290.49
31000	330.60	315.11	309.65	308.24	307.00	302.60	300.17
32000	341.26	325.28	319.64	318.18	316.90	312.36	309.86
33000	351.93	335.44	329.63	328.13	326.80	322.12	319.54
34000	362.59	345.60	339.62	338.07	336.70	331.88	329.22
35000	373.26	355.77	349.61	348.01	346.61	341.64	338.90
36000	383.92	365.93	359.59	357.96	356.51	351.40	348.59
37000	394.58	376.10	369.58	367.90	366.41	361.16	358.27
38000	405.25	386.26	379.57	377.84	376.32	370.93	367.95
39000	415.91	396.43	389.56	387.79	386.22	380.69	377.63
40000	426.58	406.59	399.55	397.73	396.12	390.45	387.32
45000	479.90	457.42	449.49	447.45	445.64	439.25	435.73
50000	533.22	508.24	499.43	497.16	495.15	488.06	484.15
55000	586.54	559.06	549.38	546.88	544.67	536.86	532.56
60000	639.86	609.89	599.32	596.59	594.18	585.67	580.97
65000	693.18	660.71	649.26	646.31	643.69	634.47	629.39
70000	746.51	711.53	699.21	696.02	693.21	683.28	677.80
75000	799.83	762.36	749.15	745.74	742.72	732.09	726.22
80000	853.15	813.18	799.09	795.45	792.24	780.89	774.63
85000	906.47	864.00	849.04	845.17	841.75	829.70	823.04
90000	959.79	914.83	898.98	894.89	891.27	878.50	871.46
95000	1013.11	965.65	948.92	944.60	940.78	927.31	919.87
100000	1066.43	1016.47	998.86	994.32	990.30	976.11	968.29

11.75% MONTHLY AMORTIZING PAYMENTS

AMOUNT OF LOAN	NUMBER OF YEARS IN TERM						
	1	2	3	4	5	10	15
$ 25	2.22	1.18	.83	.66	.56	.36	.30
50	4.44	2.35	1.66	1.32	1.11	.72	.60
75	6.66	3.53	2.49	1.97	1.66	1.07	.89
100	8.88	4.70	3.31	2.63	2.22	1.43	1.19
200	17.75	9.40	6.62	5.25	4.43	2.85	2.37
300	26.62	14.09	9.93	7.87	6.64	4.27	3.56
400	35.50	18.79	13.24	10.49	8.85	5.69	4.74
500	44.37	23.48	16.55	13.11	11.06	7.11	5.93
600	53.24	28.18	19.86	15.73	13.28	8.53	7.11
700	62.12	32.87	23.17	18.35	15.49	9.95	8.29
800	70.99	37.57	26.48	20.97	17.70	11.37	9.48
900	79.86	42.27	29.79	23.60	19.91	12.79	10.66
1000	88.74	46.96	33.10	26.22	22.12	14.21	11.85
2000	177.47	93.92	66.20	52.43	44.24	28.41	23.69
2500	221.83	117.40	82.74	65.53	55.30	35.51	29.61
3000	266.20	140.88	99.29	78.64	66.36	42.61	35.53
4000	354.93	187.83	132.39	104.85	88.48	56.82	47.37
5000	443.66	234.79	165.48	131.06	110.60	71.02	59.21
6000	532.40	281.75	198.58	157.27	132.71	85.22	71.05
7000	621.13	328.70	231.67	183.48	154.83	99.43	82.89
8000	709.86	375.66	264.77	209.70	176.95	113.63	94.74
9000	798.59	422.62	297.86	235.91	199.07	127.83	106.58
10000	887.32	469.57	330.96	262.12	221.19	142.03	118.42
11000	976.06	516.53	364.05	288.33	243.31	156.24	130.26
12000	1064.79	563.49	397.15	314.54	265.42	170.44	142.10
13000	1153.52	610.44	430.24	340.75	287.54	184.64	153.94
14000	1242.25	657.40	463.34	366.96	309.66	198.85	165.78
15000	1330.98	704.36	496.43	393.17	331.78	213.05	177.62
16000	1419.72	751.31	529.53	419.39	353.90	227.25	189.47
17000	1508.45	798.27	562.62	445.60	376.02	241.46	201.31
18000	1597.18	845.23	595.72	471.81	398.13	255.66	213.15
19000	1685.91	892.18	628.81	498.02	420.25	269.86	224.99
20000	1774.64	939.14	661.91	524.23	442.37	284.06	236.83
21000	1863.37	986.10	695.00	550.44	464.49	298.27	248.67
22000	1952.11	1033.05	728.10	576.65	486.61	312.47	260.51
23000	2040.84	1080.01	761.19	602.86	508.73	326.67	272.36
24000	2129.57	1126.97	794.29	629.08	530.84	340.88	284.20
25000	2218.30	1173.93	827.38	655.29	552.96	355.08	296.04
26000	2307.03	1220.88	860.48	681.50	575.08	369.28	307.88
27000	2395.77	1267.84	893.57	707.71	597.20	383.48	319.72
28000	2484.50	1314.80	926.67	733.92	619.32	397.69	331.56
29000	2573.23	1361.75	959.76	760.13	641.44	411.89	343.40
30000	2661.96	1408.71	992.86	786.34	663.55	426.09	355.24
31000	2750.69	1455.67	1025.95	812.55	685.67	440.30	367.09
32000	2839.43	1502.62	1059.05	838.77	707.79	454.50	378.93
33000	2928.16	1549.58	1092.14	864.98	729.91	468.70	390.77
34000	3016.89	1596.54	1125.24	891.19	752.03	482.91	402.61
35000	3105.62	1643.50	1158.33	917.40	774.15	497.11	414.45
36000	3194.35	1690.45	1191.43	943.61	796.26	511.31	426.29
37000	3283.08	1737.41	1224.52	969.82	818.38	525.51	438.13
38000	3371.82	1784.36	1257.62	996.03	840.50	539.72	449.97
39000	3460.55	1831.32	1290.71	1022.24	862.62	553.92	461.82
40000	3549.28	1878.28	1323.81	1048.46	884.74	568.12	473.66
45000	3992.94	2113.06	1489.28	1179.51	995.33	639.14	532.86
50000	4436.60	2347.85	1654.76	1310.57	1105.92	710.15	592.07
55000	4880.26	2582.63	1820.23	1441.62	1216.51	781.17	651.28
60000	5323.92	2817.41	1985.71	1572.68	1327.10	852.18	710.48
65000	5767.58	3052.20	2151.18	1703.74	1437.70	923.20	769.69
70000	6211.24	3286.98	2316.66	1834.79	1548.29	994.21	828.90
75000	6654.90	3521.77	2482.13	1965.85	1658.88	1065.23	888.10
80000	7098.56	3756.55	2647.61	2096.91	1769.47	1136.24	947.31
85000	7542.21	3991.33	2813.08	2227.96	1880.06	1207.26	1006.52
90000	7985.87	4226.12	2978.56	2359.02	1990.65	1278.27	1065.72
95000	8429.53	4460.90	3144.03	2490.07	2101.25	1349.28	1124.93
100000	8873.19	4695.69	3309.51	2621.13	2211.84	1420.30	1184.14

24

MONTHLY AMORTIZING PAYMENTS 11.75%

AMOUNT OF LOAN	NUMBER OF YEARS IN TERM						
	20	25	28	29	30	35	40
$ 25	.28	.26	.26	.26	.26	.25	.25
50	.55	.52	.51	.51	.51	.50	.50
75	.82	.78	.77	.76	.76	.75	.75
100	1.09	1.04	1.02	1.02	1.01	1.00	.99
200	2.17	2.07	2.04	2.03	2.02	2.00	1.98
300	3.26	3.11	3.06	3.04	3.03	2.99	2.97
400	4.34	4.14	4.08	4.06	4.04	3.99	3.96
500	5.42	5.18	5.09	5.07	5.05	4.98	4.95
600	6.51	6.21	6.11	6.08	6.06	5.98	5.94
700	7.59	7.25	7.13	7.10	7.07	6.98	6.92
800	8.67	8.28	8.15	8.11	8.08	7.97	7.91
900	9.76	9.32	9.16	9.12	9.09	8.97	8.90
1000	10.84	10.35	10.18	10.14	10.10	9.96	9.89
2000	21.68	20.70	20.36	20.27	20.19	19.92	19.77
2500	27.10	25.87	25.45	25.34	25.24	24.90	24.71
3000	32.52	31.05	30.54	30.40	30.29	29.88	29.66
4000	43.35	41.40	40.71	40.54	40.38	39.84	39.54
5000	54.19	51.74	50.89	50.67	50.48	49.79	49.42
6000	65.03	62.09	61.07	60.80	60.57	59.75	59.30
7000	75.86	72.44	71.24	70.94	70.66	69.71	69.19
8000	86.70	82.79	81.42	81.07	80.76	79.67	79.07
9000	97.54	93.14	91.60	91.20	90.85	89.63	88.96
10000	108.38	103.48	101.77	101.33	100.95	99.58	98.84
11000	119.21	113.83	111.95	111.47	111.04	109.54	108.73
12000	130.05	124.18	122.13	121.60	121.13	119.50	118.61
13000	140.89	134.53	132.30	131.73	131.23	129.46	128.49
14000	151.72	144.88	142.48	141.87	141.32	139.42	138.38
15000	162.56	155.22	152.66	152.00	151.42	149.37	148.26
16000	173.40	165.57	162.84	162.13	161.51	159.33	158.14
17000	184.24	175.92	173.01	172.26	171.60	169.29	168.03
18000	195.07	186.27	183.19	182.40	181.70	179.25	177.91
19000	205.91	196.62	193.37	192.53	191.79	189.21	187.79
20000	216.75	206.96	203.54	202.66	201.89	199.16	197.68
21000	227.58	217.31	213.72	212.80	211.98	209.12	207.56
22000	238.42	227.66	223.90	222.93	222.08	219.08	217.45
23000	249.26	238.01	234.07	233.06	232.17	229.04	227.33
24000	260.09	248.36	244.25	243.20	242.26	239.00	237.21
25000	270.93	258.70	254.43	253.33	252.36	248.95	247.10
26000	281.77	269.05	264.60	263.46	262.45	258.91	256.98
27000	292.61	279.40	274.78	273.59	272.55	268.87	266.86
28000	303.44	289.75	284.96	283.73	282.64	278.83	276.75
29000	314.28	300.10	295.14	293.86	292.73	288.79	286.63
30000	325.12	310.44	305.31	303.99	302.83	298.74	296.51
31000	335.95	320.79	315.49	314.13	312.92	308.70	306.40
32000	346.79	331.14	325.67	324.26	323.02	318.66	316.28
33000	357.63	341.49	335.84	334.39	333.11	328.62	326.17
34000	368.47	351.84	346.02	344.52	343.20	338.57	336.05
35000	379.30	362.18	356.20	354.66	353.30	348.53	345.93
36000	390.14	372.53	366.37	364.79	363.39	358.49	355.82
37000	400.98	382.88	376.55	374.92	373.49	368.45	365.70
38000	411.81	393.23	386.73	385.06	383.58	378.41	375.58
39000	422.65	403.58	396.90	395.19	393.67	388.36	385.47
40000	433.49	413.92	407.08	405.32	403.77	398.32	395.35
45000	487.67	465.66	457.97	455.99	454.24	448.11	444.77
50000	541.86	517.40	508.85	506.65	504.71	497.90	494.19
55000	596.04	569.14	559.74	557.32	555.18	547.69	543.61
60000	650.23	620.88	610.62	607.98	605.65	597.48	593.02
65000	704.41	672.62	661.50	658.64	656.12	647.27	642.44
70000	758.60	724.36	712.39	709.31	706.59	697.06	691.86
75000	812.79	776.10	763.27	759.97	757.06	746.85	741.28
80000	866.97	827.84	814.16	810.64	807.53	796.64	790.70
85000	921.16	879.58	865.04	861.30	858.00	846.43	840.11
90000	975.34	931.32	915.93	911.97	908.47	896.22	889.53
95000	1029.53	983.06	966.81	962.63	958.94	946.01	938.95
100000	1083.71	1034.80	1017.70	1013.30	1009.41	995.80	988.37

25

12.00% MONTHLY AMORTIZING PAYMENTS

AMOUNT OF LOAN	NUMBER OF YEARS IN TERM						
	1	2	3	4	5	10	15
$ 25	2.23	1.18	.84	.66	.56	.36	.31
50	4.45	2.36	1.67	1.32	1.12	.72	.61
75	6.67	3.54	2.50	1.98	1.67	1.08	.91
100	8.89	4.71	3.33	2.64	2.23	1.44	1.21
200	17.77	9.42	6.65	5.27	4.45	2.87	2.41
300	26.66	14.13	9.97	7.91	6.68	4.31	3.61
400	35.54	18.83	13.29	10.54	8.90	5.74	4.81
500	44.43	23.54	16.61	13.17	11.13	7.18	6.01
600	53.31	28.25	19.93	15.81	13.35	8.61	7.21
700	62.20	32.96	23.26	18.44	15.58	10.05	8.41
800	71.08	37.66	26.58	21.07	17.80	11.48	9.61
900	79.97	42.37	29.90	23.71	20.03	12.92	10.81
1000	88.85	47.08	33.22	26.34	22.25	14.35	12.01
2000	177.70	94.15	66.43	52.67	44.49	28.70	24.01
2500	222.13	117.69	83.04	65.84	55.62	35.87	30.01
3000	266.55	141.23	99.65	79.01	66.74	43.05	36.01
4000	355.40	188.30	132.86	105.34	88.99	57.39	48.01
5000	444.25	235.37	166.08	131.67	111.23	71.74	60.01
6000	533.10	282.45	199.29	158.01	133.47	86.09	72.02
7000	621.95	329.52	232.51	184.34	155.72	100.43	84.02
8000	710.80	376.59	265.72	210.68	177.96	114.78	96.02
9000	799.64	423.67	298.93	237.01	200.21	129.13	108.02
10000	888.49	470.74	332.15	263.34	222.45	143.48	120.02
11000	977.34	517.81	365.36	289.68	244.69	157.82	132.02
12000	1066.19	564.89	398.58	316.01	266.94	172.17	144.03
13000	1155.04	611.96	431.79	342.34	289.18	186.52	156.03
14000	1243.89	659.03	465.01	368.68	311.43	200.86	168.03
15000	1332.74	706.11	498.22	395.01	333.67	215.21	180.03
16000	1421.59	753.18	531.43	421.35	355.92	229.56	192.03
17000	1510.43	800.25	564.65	447.68	378.16	243.91	204.03
18000	1599.28	847.33	597.86	474.01	400.41	258.25	216.04
19000	1688.13	894.40	631.08	500.35	422.65	272.60	228.04
20000	1776.98	941.47	664.29	526.68	444.89	286.95	240.04
21000	1865.83	988.55	697.51	553.02	467.14	301.29	252.04
22000	1954.68	1035.62	730.72	579.35	489.38	315.64	264.04
23000	2043.53	1082.69	763.93	605.68	511.63	329.99	276.04
24000	2132.38	1129.77	797.15	632.02	533.87	344.34	288.05
25000	2221.22	1176.84	830.36	658.35	556.12	358.68	300.05
26000	2310.07	1223.92	863.58	684.68	578.36	373.03	312.05
27000	2398.92	1270.99	896.79	711.02	600.61	387.38	324.05
28000	2487.77	1318.06	930.01	737.35	622.85	401.72	336.05
29000	2576.62	1365.14	963.22	763.69	645.09	416.07	348.05
30000	2665.47	1412.21	996.43	790.02	667.34	430.42	360.06
31000	2754.32	1459.28	1029.65	816.35	689.58	444.76	372.06
32000	2843.17	1506.36	1062.86	842.69	711.83	459.11	384.06
33000	2932.02	1553.43	1096.08	869.02	734.07	473.46	396.06
34000	3020.86	1600.50	1129.29	895.36	756.32	487.81	408.06
35000	3109.71	1647.58	1162.51	921.69	778.56	502.15	420.06
36000	3198.56	1694.65	1195.72	948.02	800.81	516.50	432.07
37000	3287.41	1741.72	1228.93	974.36	823.05	530.85	444.07
38000	3376.26	1788.80	1262.15	1000.69	845.29	545.19	456.07
39000	3465.11	1835.87	1295.36	1027.02	867.54	559.54	468.07
40000	3553.96	1882.94	1328.58	1053.36	889.78	573.89	480.07
45000	3998.20	2118.31	1494.65	1185.03	1001.01	645.62	540.08
50000	4442.44	2353.68	1660.72	1316.70	1112.23	717.36	600.09
55000	4886.69	2589.05	1826.79	1448.37	1223.45	789.10	660.10
60000	5330.93	2824.41	1992.86	1580.04	1334.67	860.83	720.11
65000	5775.18	3059.78	2158.94	1711.70	1445.89	932.57	780.11
70000	6219.42	3295.15	2325.01	1843.37	1557.12	1004.30	840.12
75000	6663.66	3530.52	2491.08	1975.04	1668.34	1076.04	900.13
80000	7107.91	3765.88	2657.15	2106.71	1779.56	1147.77	960.14
85000	7552.15	4001.25	2823.22	2238.38	1890.78	1219.51	1020.15
90000	7996.40	4236.62	2989.29	2370.05	2002.01	1291.24	1080.16
95000	8440.64	4471.98	3155.36	2501.72	2113.23	1362.98	1140.16
100000	8884.88	4707.35	3321.44	2633.39	2224.45	1434.71	1200.17

26

AMOUNT OF LOAN	NUMBER OF YEARS IN TERM						
	20	**25**	**28**	**29**	**30**	**35**	**40**
$ 25	.28	.27	.26	.26	.26	.26	.26
50	.56	.53	.52	.52	.52	.51	.51
75	.83	.79	.78	.78	.78	.77	.76
100	1.11	1.06	1.04	1.04	1.03	1.02	1.01
200	2.21	2.11	2.08	2.07	2.06	2.04	2.02
300	3.31	3.16	3.11	3.10	3.09	3.05	3.03
400	4.41	4.22	4.15	4.13	4.12	4.07	4.04
500	5.51	5.27	5.19	5.17	5.15	5.08	5.05
600	6.61	6.32	6.22	6.20	6.18	6.10	6.06
700	7.71	7.38	7.26	7.23	7.21	7.11	7.06
800	8.81	8.43	8.30	8.26	8.23	8.13	8.07
900	9.91	9.48	9.33	9.30	9.26	9.14	9.08
1000	11.02	10.54	10.37	10.33	10.29	10.16	10.09
2000	22.03	21.07	20.74	20.65	20.58	20.32	20.17
2500	27.53	26.34	25.92	25.81	25.72	25.39	25.22
3000	33.04	31.60	31.10	30.98	30.86	30.47	30.26
4000	44.05	42.13	41.47	41.30	41.15	40.63	40.34
5000	55.06	52.67	51.84	51.62	51.44	50.78	50.43
6000	66.07	63.20	62.20	61.95	61.72	60.94	60.51
7000	77.08	73.73	72.57	72.27	72.01	71.09	70.60
8000	88.09	84.26	82.93	82.59	82.29	81.25	80.68
9000	99.10	94.80	93.30	92.92	92.58	91.40	90.77
10000	110.11	105.33	103.67	103.24	102.87	101.56	100.85
11000	121.12	115.86	114.03	113.56	113.15	111.72	110.94
12000	132.14	126.39	124.40	123.89	123.44	121.87	121.02
13000	143.15	136.92	134.76	134.21	133.72	132.03	131.11
14000	154.16	147.46	145.13	144.54	144.01	142.18	141.19
15000	165.17	157.99	155.50	154.86	154.30	152.34	151.28
16000	176.18	168.52	165.86	165.18	164.58	162.49	161.36
17000	187.19	179.05	176.23	175.51	174.87	172.65	171.45
18000	198.20	189.59	186.60	185.83	185.16	182.80	181.53
19000	209.21	200.12	196.96	196.15	195.44	192.96	191.62
20000	220.22	210.65	207.33	206.48	205.73	203.11	201.70
21000	231.23	221.18	217.69	216.80	216.01	213.27	211.79
22000	242.24	231.71	228.06	227.12	226.30	223.43	221.87
23000	253.25	242.25	238.43	237.45	236.59	233.58	231.96
24000	264.27	252.78	248.79	247.77	246.87	243.74	242.04
25000	275.28	263.31	259.16	258.09	257.16	253.89	252.13
26000	286.29	273.84	269.52	268.42	267.44	264.05	262.21
27000	297.30	284.38	279.89	278.74	277.73	274.20	272.30
28000	308.31	294.91	290.26	289.07	288.02	284.36	282.38
29000	319.32	305.44	300.62	299.39	298.30	294.51	292.47
30000	330.33	315.97	310.99	309.71	308.59	304.67	302.55
31000	341.34	326.50	321.36	320.04	318.87	314.83	312.64
32000	352.35	337.04	331.72	330.36	329.16	324.98	322.72
33000	363.36	347.57	342.09	340.68	339.45	335.14	332.81
34000	374.37	358.10	352.45	351.01	349.73	345.29	342.89
35000	385.39	368.63	362.82	361.33	360.02	355.45	352.98
36000	396.40	379.17	373.19	371.65	370.31	365.60	363.06
37000	407.41	389.70	383.55	381.98	380.59	375.76	373.15
38000	418.42	400.23	393.92	392.30	390.88	385.91	383.23
39000	429.43	410.76	404.28	402.62	401.16	396.07	393.32
40000	440.44	421.29	414.65	412.95	411.45	406.22	403.40
45000	495.49	473.96	466.48	464.57	462.88	457.00	453.83
50000	550.55	526.62	518.31	516.18	514.31	507.78	504.25
55000	605.60	579.28	570.14	567.80	565.74	558.56	554.68
60000	660.66	631.94	621.97	619.42	617.17	609.33	605.10
65000	715.71	684.60	673.80	671.04	668.60	660.11	655.53
70000	770.77	737.26	725.63	722.66	720.03	710.89	705.95
75000	825.82	789.92	777.46	774.27	771.46	761.67	756.38
80000	880.87	842.58	829.30	825.89	822.90	812.44	806.80
85000	935.93	895.25	881.13	877.51	874.33	863.22	857.23
90000	990.98	947.91	932.96	929.13	925.76	914.00	907.65
95000	1046.04	1000.57	984.79	980.75	977.19	964.78	958.08
100000	1101.09	1053.23	1036.62	1032.36	1028.62	1015.55	1008.50

12.25% MONTHLY AMORTIZING PAYMENTS

AMOUNT OF LOAN	NUMBER OF YEARS IN TERM						
	1	2	3	4	5	10	15
$ 25	2.23	1.18	.84	.67	.56	.37	.31
50	4.45	2.36	1.67	1.33	1.12	.73	.61
75	6.68	3.54	2.51	1.99	1.68	1.09	.92
100	8.90	4.72	3.34	2.65	2.24	1.45	1.22
200	17.80	9.44	6.67	5.30	4.48	2.90	2.44
300	26.69	14.16	10.01	7.94	6.72	4.35	3.65
400	35.59	18.88	13.34	10.59	8.95	5.80	4.87
500	44.49	23.60	16.67	13.23	11.19	7.25	6.09
600	53.38	28.32	20.01	15.88	13.43	8.70	7.30
700	62.28	33.04	23.34	18.52	15.66	10.15	8.52
800	71.18	37.76	26.67	21.17	17.90	11.60	9.74
900	80.07	42.48	30.01	23.82	20.14	13.05	10.95
1000	88.97	47.20	33.34	26.46	22.38	14.50	12.17
2000	177.94	94.39	66.67	52.92	44.75	28.99	24.33
2500	222.42	117.98	83.34	66.15	55.93	36.23	30.41
3000	266.90	141.58	100.01	79.38	67.12	43.48	36.49
4000	355.87	188.77	133.34	105.83	89.49	57.97	48.66
5000	444.83	235.96	166.67	132.29	111.86	72.46	60.82
6000	533.80	283.15	200.01	158.75	134.23	86.96	72.98
7000	622.77	330.34	233.34	185.20	156.60	101.45	85.15
8000	711.73	377.53	266.68	211.66	178.97	115.94	97.31
9000	800.70	424.72	300.01	238.12	201.34	130.43	109.47
10000	889.66	471.91	333.34	264.57	223.71	144.92	121.63
11000	978.63	519.10	366.68	291.03	246.09	159.42	133.80
12000	1067.59	566.29	400.01	317.49	268.46	173.91	145.96
13000	1156.56	613.48	433.34	343.94	290.83	188.40	158.12
14000	1245.53	660.67	466.68	370.40	313.20	202.89	170.29
15000	1334.49	707.86	500.01	396.86	335.57	217.38	182.45
16000	1423.46	755.05	533.35	423.31	357.94	231.88	194.61
17000	1512.42	802.24	566.68	449.77	380.31	246.37	206.78
18000	1601.39	849.43	600.01	476.23	402.68	260.86	218.94
19000	1690.35	896.62	633.35	502.68	425.05	275.35	231.10
20000	1779.32	943.81	666.68	529.14	447.42	289.84	243.26
21000	1868.29	991.00	700.01	555.60	469.80	304.34	255.43
22000	1957.25	1038.19	733.35	582.05	492.17	318.83	267.59
23000	2046.22	1085.38	766.68	608.51	514.54	333.32	279.75
24000	2135.18	1132.57	800.02	634.97	536.91	347.81	291.92
25000	2224.15	1179.76	833.35	661.42	559.28	362.30	304.08
26000	2313.12	1226.95	866.68	687.88	581.65	376.80	316.24
27000	2402.08	1274.14	900.02	714.34	604.02	391.29	328.41
28000	2491.05	1321.33	933.35	740.79	626.39	405.78	340.57
29000	2580.01	1368.52	966.69	767.25	648.76	420.27	352.73
30000	2668.98	1415.70	1000.02	793.71	671.13	434.76	364.89
31000	2757.94	1462.90	1033.35	820.16	693.51	449.26	377.06
32000	2846.91	1510.09	1066.69	846.62	715.88	463.75	389.22
33000	2935.88	1557.29	1100.02	873.08	738.25	478.24	401.38
34000	3024.84	1604.48	1133.36	899.53	760.62	492.73	413.55
35000	3113.81	1651.67	1166.69	925.99	782.99	507.22	425.71
36000	3202.77	1698.86	1200.02	952.45	805.36	521.72	437.87
37000	3291.74	1746.05	1233.36	978.90	827.73	536.21	450.04
38000	3380.70	1793.24	1266.69	1005.36	850.10	550.70	462.20
39000	3469.67	1840.43	1300.02	1031.82	872.47	565.19	474.36
40000	3558.64	1887.62	1333.36	1058.28	894.84	579.68	486.52
45000	4003.47	2123.57	1500.03	1190.56	1006.70	652.14	547.34
50000	4448.29	2359.52	1666.70	1322.84	1118.55	724.60	608.15
55000	4893.12	2595.47	1833.37	1455.13	1230.41	797.06	668.97
60000	5337.95	2831.42	2000.04	1587.41	1342.26	869.52	729.78
65000	5782.78	3067.37	2166.70	1719.69	1454.12	941.98	790.60
70000	6227.61	3303.33	2333.37	1851.97	1565.97	1014.44	851.41
75000	6672.44	3539.28	2500.04	1984.26	1677.83	1086.90	912.23
80000	7117.27	3775.23	2666.71	2116.55	1789.68	1159.36	973.04
85000	7562.10	4011.18	2833.38	2248.83	1901.54	1231.82	1033.86
90000	8006.93	4247.13	3000.05	2381.11	2013.39	1304.28	1094.67
95000	8451.75	4483.08	3166.72	2513.40	2125.25	1376.74	1155.49
100000	8896.58	4719.04	3333.39	2645.68	2237.10	1449.20	1216.30

28

MONTHLY AMORTIZING PAYMENTS 12.25%

AMOUNT OF LOAN	NUMBER OF YEARS IN TERM						
	20	25	28	29	30	35	40
$ 25	.28	.27	.27	.27	.27	.26	.26
50	.56	.54	.53	.53	.53	.52	.52
75	.84	.81	.80	.79	.79	.78	.78
100	1.12	1.08	1.06	1.06	1.05	1.04	1.03
200	2.24	2.15	2.12	2.11	2.10	2.08	2.06
300	3.36	3.22	3.17	3.16	3.15	3.11	3.09
400	4.48	4.29	4.23	4.21	4.20	4.15	4.12
500	5.60	5.36	5.28	5.26	5.24	5.18	5.15
600	6.72	6.44	6.34	6.31	6.29	6.22	6.18
700	7.83	7.51	7.39	7.37	7.34	7.25	7.21
800	8.95	8.58	8.45	8.42	8.39	8.29	8.23
900	10.07	9.65	9.51	9.47	9.44	9.32	9.26
1000	11.19	10.72	10.56	10.52	10.48	10.36	10.29
2000	22.38	21.44	21.12	21.04	20.96	20.71	20.58
2500	27.97	26.80	26.40	26.29	26.20	25.89	25.72
3000	33.56	32.16	31.67	31.55	31.44	31.07	30.87
4000	44.75	42.87	42.23	42.07	41.92	41.42	41.15
5000	55.93	53.59	52.79	52.58	52.40	51.77	51.44
6000	67.12	64.31	63.34	63.10	62.88	62.13	61.73
7000	78.30	75.03	73.90	73.61	73.36	72.48	72.01
8000	89.49	85.74	84.45	84.13	83.84	82.83	82.30
9000	100.68	96.46	95.01	94.64	94.32	93.19	92.59
10000	111.86	107.18	105.57	105.16	104.79	103.54	102.87
11000	123.05	117.90	116.12	115.67	115.27	113.90	113.16
12000	134.23	128.61	126.68	126.19	125.75	124.25	123.45
13000	145.42	139.33	137.24	136.70	136.23	134.60	133.73
14000	156.60	150.05	147.79	147.22	146.71	144.96	144.02
15000	167.79	160.77	158.35	157.73	157.19	155.31	154.31
16000	178.98	171.48	168.90	168.25	167.67	165.66	164.59
17000	190.16	182.20	179.46	178.76	178.15	176.02	174.88
18000	201.35	192.92	190.02	189.28	188.63	186.37	185.17
19000	212.53	203.64	200.57	199.79	199.11	196.73	195.46
20000	223.72	214.35	211.13	210.31	209.58	207.08	205.74
21000	234.90	225.07	221.69	220.82	220.06	217.43	216.03
22000	246.09	235.79	232.24	231.34	230.54	227.79	226.32
23000	257.27	246.51	242.80	241.85	241.02	238.14	236.60
24000	268.46	257.22	253.35	252.37	251.50	248.49	246.89
25000	279.65	267.94	263.91	262.88	261.98	258.85	257.18
26000	290.83	278.66	274.47	273.40	272.46	269.20	267.46
27000	302.02	289.38	285.02	283.91	282.94	279.56	277.75
28000	313.20	300.09	295.58	294.43	293.42	289.91	288.04
29000	324.39	310.81	306.14	304.94	303.89	300.26	298.32
30000	335.57	321.53	316.69	315.46	314.37	310.62	308.61
31000	346.76	332.25	327.25	325.97	324.85	320.97	318.90
32000	357.95	342.96	337.80	336.49	335.33	331.32	329.18
33000	369.13	353.68	348.36	347.00	345.81	341.68	339.47
34000	380.32	364.40	358.92	357.52	356.29	352.03	349.76
35000	391.50	375.12	369.47	368.03	366.77	362.38	360.05
36000	402.69	385.83	380.03	378.55	377.25	372.74	370.33
37000	413.87	396.55	390.58	389.06	387.73	383.09	380.62
38000	425.06	407.27	401.14	399.58	398.21	393.45	390.91
39000	436.25	417.99	411.70	410.09	408.68	403.80	401.19
40000	447.43	428.70	422.25	420.61	419.16	414.15	411.48
45000	503.36	482.29	475.03	473.18	471.56	465.92	462.91
50000	559.29	535.88	527.82	525.76	523.95	517.69	514.35
55000	615.22	589.46	580.60	578.34	576.35	569.46	565.78
60000	671.14	643.05	633.38	630.91	628.74	621.23	617.22
65000	727.07	696.64	686.16	683.49	681.14	673.00	668.65
70000	783.00	750.23	738.94	736.06	733.53	724.76	720.09
75000	838.93	803.81	791.72	788.64	785.93	776.53	771.52
80000	894.86	857.40	844.50	841.21	838.32	828.30	822.95
85000	950.78	910.99	897.28	893.79	890.72	880.07	874.39
90000	1006.71	964.57	950.06	946.36	943.11	931.84	925.82
95000	1062.64	1018.16	1002.85	998.94	995.51	983.61	977.26
100000	1118.57	1071.75	1055.63	1051.51	1047.90	1035.38	1028.69

12.50% MONTHLY AMORTIZING PAYMENTS

AMOUNT OF LOAN	NUMBER OF YEARS IN TERM						
	1	2	3	4	5	10	15
$ 25	2.23	1.19	.84	.67	.57	.37	.31
50	4.46	2.37	1.68	1.33	1.13	.74	.62
75	6.69	3.55	2.51	2.00	1.69	1.10	.93
100	8.91	4.74	3.35	2.66	2.25	1.47	1.24
200	17.82	9.47	6.70	5.32	4.50	2.93	2.47
300	26.73	14.20	10.04	7.98	6.75	4.40	3.70
400	35.64	18.93	13.39	10.64	9.00	5.86	4.94
500	44.55	23.66	16.73	13.29	11.25	7.32	6.17
600	53.45	28.39	20.08	15.95	13.50	8.79	7.40
700	62.36	33.12	23.42	18.61	15.75	10.25	8.63
800	71.27	37.85	26.77	21.27	18.00	11.72	9.87
900	80.18	42.58	30.11	23.93	20.25	13.18	11.10
1000	89.09	47.31	33.46	26.58	22.50	14.64	12.33
2000	178.17	94.62	66.91	53.16	45.00	29.28	24.66
2500	222.71	118.27	83.64	66.45	56.25	36.60	30.82
3000	267.25	141.93	100.37	79.74	67.50	43.92	36.98
4000	356.34	189.23	133.82	106.32	90.00	58.56	49.31
5000	445.42	236.54	167.27	132.90	112.49	73.19	61.63
6000	534.50	283.85	200.73	159.48	134.99	87.83	73.96
7000	623.59	331.16	234.18	186.06	157.49	102.47	86.28
8000	712.67	378.46	267.63	212.64	179.99	117.11	98.61
9000	801.75	425.77	301.09	239.22	202.49	131.74	110.93
10000	890.83	473.08	334.54	265.80	224.98	146.38	123.26
11000	979.92	520.39	367.99	292.38	247.48	161.02	135.58
12000	1069.00	567.69	401.45	318.96	269.98	175.66	147.91
13000	1158.08	615.00	434.90	345.54	292.48	190.29	160.23
14000	1247.17	662.31	468.36	372.12	314.98	204.93	172.56
15000	1336.25	709.61	501.81	398.70	337.47	219.57	184.88
16000	1425.33	756.92	535.26	425.28	359.97	234.21	197.21
17000	1514.41	804.23	568.72	451.86	382.47	248.84	209.53
18000	1603.50	851.54	602.17	478.44	404.97	263.48	221.86
19000	1692.58	898.84	635.62	505.02	427.47	278.12	234.18
20000	1781.66	946.15	669.08	531.60	449.96	292.76	246.51
21000	1870.75	993.46	702.53	558.18	472.46	307.39	258.83
22000	1959.83	1040.77	735.98	584.76	494.96	322.03	271.16
23000	2048.91	1088.07	769.44	611.34	517.46	336.67	283.49
24000	2137.99	1135.38	802.89	637.92	539.96	351.31	295.81
25000	2227.08	1182.69	836.35	664.50	562.45	365.95	308.14
26000	2316.16	1230.00	869.80	691.08	584.95	380.58	320.46
27000	2405.24	1277.30	903.25	717.66	607.45	395.22	332.79
28000	2494.33	1324.61	936.71	744.24	629.95	409.86	345.11
29000	2583.41	1371.92	970.16	770.82	652.45	424.50	357.44
30000	2672.49	1419.22	1003.61	797.40	674.94	439.13	369.76
31000	2761.57	1466.53	1037.07	823.98	697.44	453.77	382.09
32000	2850.66	1513.84	1070.52	850.56	719.94	468.41	394.41
33000	2939.74	1561.15	1103.97	877.14	742.44	483.05	406.74
34000	3028.82	1608.45	1137.43	903.72	764.93	497.68	419.06
35000	3117.91	1655.76	1170.88	930.30	787.43	512.32	431.39
36000	3206.99	1703.07	1204.34	956.88	809.93	526.96	443.71
37000	3296.07	1750.38	1237.79	983.46	832.43	541.60	456.04
38000	3385.15	1797.68	1271.24	1010.04	854.93	556.23	468.36
39000	3474.24	1844.99	1304.70	1036.62	877.42	570.87	480.69
40000	3563.32	1892.30	1338.15	1063.20	899.92	585.51	493.01
45000	4008.73	2128.83	1505.42	1196.10	1012.41	658.70	554.64
50000	4454.15	2365.37	1672.69	1329.00	1124.90	731.89	616.27
55000	4899.56	2601.91	1839.95	1461.90	1237.39	805.07	677.89
60000	5344.98	2838.44	2007.22	1594.80	1349.88	878.26	739.52
65000	5790.39	3074.98	2174.49	1727.70	1462.37	951.45	801.14
70000	6235.81	3311.52	2341.76	1860.60	1574.86	1024.64	862.77
75000	6681.22	3548.05	2509.03	1993.50	1687.35	1097.83	924.40
80000	7126.63	3784.59	2676.30	2126.40	1799.84	1171.01	986.02
85000	7572.05	4021.13	2843.56	2259.30	1912.33	1244.20	1047.65
90000	8017.46	4257.66	3010.83	2392.20	2024.82	1317.39	1109.27
95000	8462.88	4494.20	3178.10	2525.10	2137.31	1390.58	1170.90
100000	8908.29	4730.74	3345.37	2658.00	2249.80	1463.77	1232.53

AMOUNT OF LOAN	NUMBER OF YEARS IN TERM						
	20	25	28	29	30	35	40
$ 25	.29	.28	.27	.27	.27	.27	.27
50	.57	.55	.54	.54	.54	.53	.53
75	.86	.82	.81	.81	.81	.80	.79
100	1.14	1.10	1.08	1.08	1.07	1.06	1.05
200	2.28	2.19	2.15	2.15	2.14	2.12	2.10
300	3.41	3.28	3.23	3.22	3.21	3.17	3.15
400	4.55	4.37	4.30	4.29	4.27	4.23	4.20
500	5.69	5.46	5.38	5.36	5.34	5.28	5.25
600	6.82	6.55	6.45	6.43	6.41	6.34	6.30
700	7.96	7.64	7.53	7.50	7.48	7.39	7.35
800	9.09	8.73	8.60	8.57	8.54	8.45	8.40
900	10.23	9.82	9.68	9.64	9.61	9.50	9.45
1000	11.37	10.91	10.75	10.71	10.68	10.56	10.49
2000	22.73	21.81	21.50	21.42	21.35	21.11	20.98
2500	28.41	27.26	26.87	26.77	26.69	26.39	26.23
3000	34.09	32.72	32.25	32.13	32.02	31.66	31.47
4000	45.45	43.62	42.99	42.83	42.70	42.22	41.96
5000	56.81	54.52	53.74	53.54	53.37	52.77	52.45
6000	68.17	65.43	64.49	64.25	64.04	63.32	62.94
7000	79.53	76.33	75.23	74.96	74.71	73.87	73.43
8000	90.90	87.23	85.98	85.66	85.39	84.43	83.92
9000	102.26	98.14	96.73	96.37	96.06	94.98	94.41
10000	113.62	109.04	107.48	107.08	106.73	105.53	104.90
11000	124.98	119.94	118.22	117.79	117.40	116.08	115.39
12000	136.34	130.85	128.97	128.49	128.08	126.64	125.88
13000	147.70	141.75	139.72	139.20	138.75	137.19	136.36
14000	159.06	152.65	150.46	149.91	149.42	147.74	146.85
15000	170.43	163.56	161.21	160.62	160.09	158.29	157.34
16000	181.79	174.46	171.96	171.32	170.77	168.85	167.83
17000	193.15	185.37	182.71	182.03	181.44	179.40	178.32
18000	204.51	196.27	193.45	192.74	192.11	189.95	188.81
19000	215.87	207.17	204.20	203.45	202.78	200.50	199.30
20000	227.23	218.08	214.95	214.15	213.46	211.06	209.79
21000	238.59	228.98	225.69	224.86	224.13	221.61	220.28
22000	249.96	239.88	236.44	235.57	234.80	232.16	230.77
23000	261.32	250.79	247.19	246.28	245.47	242.71	241.26
24000	272.68	261.69	257.94	256.98	256.15	253.27	251.75
25000	284.04	272.59	268.68	267.69	266.82	263.82	262.23
26000	295.40	283.50	279.43	278.40	277.49	274.37	272.72
27000	306.76	294.40	290.18	289.11	288.16	284.92	283.21
28000	318.12	305.30	300.92	299.81	298.84	295.48	293.70
29000	329.49	316.21	311.67	310.52	309.51	306.03	304.19
30000	340.85	327.11	322.42	321.23	320.18	316.58	314.68
31000	352.21	338.01	333.17	331.93	330.85	327.13	325.17
32000	363.57	348.92	343.91	342.64	341.53	337.69	335.66
33000	374.93	359.82	354.66	353.35	352.20	348.24	346.15
34000	386.29	370.73	365.41	364.06	362.87	358.79	356.64
35000	397.65	381.63	376.15	374.76	373.55	369.34	367.13
36000	409.02	392.53	386.90	385.47	384.22	379.90	377.62
37000	420.38	403.44	397.65	396.18	394.89	390.45	388.11
38000	431.74	414.34	408.40	406.89	405.56	401.00	398.59
39000	443.10	425.24	419.14	417.59	416.24	411.55	409.08
40000	454.46	436.15	429.89	428.30	426.91	422.11	419.57
45000	511.27	490.66	483.63	481.84	480.27	474.87	472.02
50000	568.08	545.18	537.36	535.38	533.63	527.63	524.46
55000	624.88	599.70	591.10	588.91	587.00	580.39	576.91
60000	681.69	654.22	644.83	642.45	640.36	633.16	629.36
65000	738.50	708.74	698.57	695.99	693.72	685.92	681.80
70000	795.30	763.25	752.30	749.52	747.09	738.68	734.25
75000	852.11	817.77	806.04	803.06	800.45	791.45	786.69
80000	908.92	872.29	859.78	856.60	853.81	844.21	839.14
85000	965.72	926.81	913.51	910.13	907.17	896.97	891.59
90000	1022.53	981.32	967.25	963.67	960.54	949.73	944.03
95000	1079.34	1035.84	1020.98	1017.21	1013.90	1002.50	996.48
100000	1136.15	1090.36	1074.72	1070.75	1067.26	1055.26	1048.92

12.75% MONTHLY AMORTIZING PAYMENTS

AMOUNT OF LOAN	NUMBER OF YEARS IN TERM						
	1	2	3	4	5	10	15
$ 25	2.23	1.19	.84	.67	.57	.37	.32
50	4.47	2.38	1.68	1.34	1.14	.74	.63
75	6.70	3.56	2.52	2.01	1.70	1.11	.94
100	8.93	4.75	3.36	2.68	2.27	1.48	1.25
200	17.85	9.49	6.72	5.35	4.53	2.96	2.50
300	26.77	14.23	10.08	8.02	6.79	4.44	3.75
400	35.69	18.97	13.43	10.69	9.06	5.92	5.00
500	44.61	23.72	16.79	13.36	11.32	7.40	6.25
600	53.53	28.46	20.15	16.03	13.58	8.88	7.50
700	62.45	33.20	23.51	18.70	15.84	10.35	8.75
800	71.37	37.94	26.86	21.37	18.11	11.83	10.00
900	80.29	42.69	30.22	24.04	20.37	13.31	11.24
1000	89.21	47.43	33.58	26.71	22.63	14.79	12.49
2000	178.41	94.85	67.15	53.41	45.26	29.57	24.98
2500	223.01	118.57	83.94	66.76	56.57	36.96	31.23
3000	267.61	142.28	100.73	80.12	67.88	44.36	37.47
4000	356.81	189.70	134.30	106.82	90.51	59.14	49.96
5000	446.01	237.13	167.87	133.52	113.13	73.92	62.45
6000	535.21	284.55	201.45	160.23	135.76	88.71	74.94
7000	624.41	331.98	235.02	186.93	158.38	103.49	87.42
8000	713.61	379.40	268.59	213.63	181.01	118.28	99.91
9000	802.81	426.83	302.17	240.34	203.63	133.06	112.40
10000	892.01	474.25	335.74	267.04	226.26	147.84	124.89
11000	981.21	521.67	369.32	293.74	248.88	162.63	137.38
12000	1070.41	569.10	402.89	320.45	271.51	177.41	149.87
13000	1159.61	616.52	436.46	347.15	294.13	192.20	162.35
14000	1248.81	663.95	470.04	373.86	316.76	206.98	174.84
15000	1338.01	711.37	503.61	400.56	339.38	221.76	187.33
16000	1427.21	758.80	537.18	427.26	362.01	236.55	199.82
17000	1516.41	806.22	570.76	453.97	384.64	251.33	212.31
18000	1605.61	853.65	604.33	480.67	407.26	266.12	224.80
19000	1694.81	901.07	637.90	507.37	429.89	280.90	237.28
20000	1784.01	948.49	671.48	534.08	452.51	295.68	249.77
21000	1873.21	995.92	705.05	560.78	475.14	310.47	262.26
22000	1962.41	1043.34	738.63	587.48	497.76	325.25	274.75
23000	2051.61	1090.77	772.20	614.19	520.39	340.04	287.24
24000	2140.81	1138.19	805.77	640.89	543.01	354.82	299.73
25000	2230.01	1185.62	839.35	667.59	565.64	369.60	312.21
26000	2319.21	1233.04	872.92	694.30	588.26	384.39	324.70
27000	2408.41	1280.47	906.49	721.00	610.89	399.17	337.19
28000	2497.61	1327.89	940.07	747.71	633.51	413.96	349.68
29000	2586.81	1375.31	973.64	774.41	656.14	428.74	362.17
30000	2676.01	1422.74	1007.21	801.11	678.76	443.52	374.66
31000	2765.21	1470.16	1040.79	827.82	701.39	458.31	387.14
32000	2854.41	1517.59	1074.36	854.52	724.01	473.09	399.63
33000	2943.61	1565.01	1107.94	881.22	746.64	487.88	412.12
34000	3032.81	1612.44	1141.51	907.93	769.27	502.66	424.61
35000	3122.01	1659.86	1175.08	934.63	791.89	517.44	437.10
36000	3211.21	1707.29	1208.66	961.33	814.52	532.23	449.59
37000	3300.41	1754.71	1242.23	988.04	837.14	547.01	462.07
38000	3389.61	1802.14	1275.80	1014.74	859.77	561.80	474.56
39000	3478.81	1849.56	1309.38	1041.44	882.39	576.58	487.05
40000	3568.01	1896.98	1342.95	1068.15	905.02	591.36	499.54
45000	4014.01	2134.11	1510.82	1201.67	1018.14	665.28	561.98
50000	4460.01	2371.23	1678.69	1335.18	1131.27	739.20	624.42
55000	4906.01	2608.35	1846.56	1468.70	1244.40	813.12	686.87
60000	5352.01	2845.47	2014.42	1602.22	1357.52	887.04	749.31
65000	5798.01	3082.60	2182.29	1735.74	1470.65	960.96	811.75
70000	6244.01	3319.72	2350.16	1869.26	1583.78	1034.88	874.19
75000	6690.01	3556.84	2518.03	2002.77	1696.90	1108.80	936.63
80000	7136.01	3793.96	2685.90	2136.29	1810.03	1182.72	999.07
85000	7582.01	4031.09	2853.77	2269.81	1923.16	1256.64	1061.52
90000	8028.01	4268.21	3021.63	2403.33	2036.28	1330.56	1123.96
95000	8474.01	4505.33	3189.50	2536.85	2149.41	1404.48	1186.40
100000	8920.01	4742.45	3357.37	2670.36	2262.54	1478.40	1248.84

AMOUNT OF LOAN	NUMBER OF YEARS IN TERM						
	20	25	28	29	30	35	40
$ 25	.29	.28	.28	.28	.28	.27	.27
50	.58	.56	.55	.55	.55	.54	.54
75	.87	.84	.83	.82	.82	.81	.81
100	1.16	1.11	1.10	1.10	1.09	1.08	1.07
200	2.31	2.22	2.19	2.19	2.18	2.16	2.14
300	3.47	3.33	3.29	3.28	3.27	3.23	3.21
400	4.62	4.44	4.38	4.37	4.35	4.31	4.28
500	5.77	5.55	5.47	5.46	5.44	5.38	5.35
600	6.93	6.66	6.57	6.55	6.53	6.46	6.42
700	8.08	7.77	7.66	7.64	7.61	7.53	7.49
800	9.24	8.88	8.76	8.73	8.70	8.61	8.56
900	10.39	9.99	9.85	9.82	9.79	9.68	9.63
1000	11.54	11.10	10.94	10.91	10.87	10.76	10.70
2000	23.08	22.19	21.88	21.81	21.74	21.51	21.39
2500	28.85	27.73	27.35	27.26	27.17	26.88	26.73
3000	34.62	33.28	32.82	32.71	32.61	32.26	32.08
4000	46.16	44.37	43.76	43.61	43.47	43.01	42.77
5000	57.70	55.46	54.70	54.51	54.34	53.76	53.46
6000	69.23	66.55	65.64	65.41	65.21	64.52	64.16
7000	80.77	77.64	76.58	76.31	76.07	75.27	74.85
8000	92.31	88.73	87.52	87.21	86.94	86.02	85.54
9000	103.85	99.82	98.45	98.11	97.81	96.77	96.23
10000	115.39	110.91	109.39	109.01	108.67	107.52	106.92
11000	126.92	122.00	120.33	119.91	119.54	118.28	117.62
12000	138.46	133.09	131.27	130.81	130.41	129.03	128.31
13000	150.00	144.18	142.21	141.71	141.28	139.78	139.00
14000	161.54	155.27	153.15	152.61	152.14	150.53	149.69
15000	173.08	166.36	164.09	163.51	163.01	161.28	160.38
16000	184.61	177.45	175.03	174.41	173.88	172.04	171.08
17000	196.15	188.54	185.97	185.31	184.74	182.79	181.77
18000	207.69	199.63	196.90	196.21	195.61	193.54	192.46
19000	219.23	210.72	207.84	207.11	206.48	204.29	203.15
20000	230.77	221.82	218.78	218.01	217.34	215.04	213.84
21000	242.31	232.91	229.72	228.92	228.21	225.80	224.54
22000	253.84	244.00	240.66	239.82	239.08	236.55	235.23
23000	265.38	255.09	251.60	250.72	249.94	247.30	245.92
24000	276.92	266.18	262.54	261.62	260.81	258.05	256.61
25000	288.46	277.27	273.48	272.52	271.68	268.80	267.30
26000	300.00	288.36	284.42	283.42	282.55	279.56	278.00
27000	311.53	299.45	295.35	294.32	293.41	290.31	288.69
28000	323.07	310.54	306.29	305.22	304.28	301.06	299.38
29000	334.61	321.63	317.23	316.12	315.15	311.81	310.07
30000	346.15	332.72	328.17	327.02	326.01	322.56	320.76
31000	357.69	343.81	339.11	337.92	336.88	333.32	331.46
32000	369.22	354.90	350.05	348.82	347.75	344.07	342.15
33000	380.76	365.99	360.99	359.72	358.61	354.82	352.84
34000	392.30	377.08	371.93	370.62	369.48	365.57	363.53
35000	403.84	388.17	382.86	381.52	380.35	376.32	374.22
36000	415.38	399.26	393.80	392.42	391.21	387.08	384.92
37000	426.92	410.35	404.74	403.32	402.08	397.83	395.61
38000	438.45	421.44	415.68	414.22	412.95	408.58	406.30
39000	449.99	432.54	426.62	425.12	423.82	419.33	416.99
40000	461.53	443.63	437.56	436.02	434.68	430.08	427.68
45000	519.22	499.08	492.25	490.53	489.02	483.84	481.14
50000	576.91	554.53	546.95	545.03	543.35	537.60	534.60
55000	634.60	609.98	601.64	599.53	597.69	591.36	588.06
60000	692.29	665.44	656.34	654.03	652.02	645.12	641.52
65000	749.98	720.89	711.03	708.54	706.36	698.88	694.98
70000	807.67	776.34	765.72	763.04	760.69	752.64	748.44
75000	865.36	831.79	820.42	817.54	815.02	806.40	801.90
80000	923.05	887.25	875.11	872.04	869.36	860.16	855.36
85000	980.74	942.70	929.81	926.55	923.69	913.92	908.82
90000	1038.44	998.15	984.50	981.05	978.03	967.68	962.28
95000	1096.13	1053.60	1039.20	1035.55	1032.36	1021.44	1015.74
100000	1153.82	1109.06	1093.89	1090.05	1086.70	1075.20	1069.20

13.00% MONTHLY AMORTIZING PAYMENTS

AMOUNT OF LOAN	NUMBER OF YEARS IN TERM						
	1	2	3	4	5	10	15
$ 25	2.24	1.19	.85	.68	.57	.38	.32
50	4.47	2.38	1.69	1.35	1.14	.75	.64
75	6.70	3.57	2.53	2.02	1.71	1.12	.95
100	8.94	4.76	3.37	2.69	2.28	1.50	1.27
200	17.87	9.51	6.74	5.37	4.56	2.99	2.54
300	26.80	14.27	10.11	8.05	6.83	4.48	3.80
400	35.73	19.02	13.48	10.74	9.11	5.98	5.07
500	44.66	23.78	16.85	13.42	11.38	7.47	6.33
600	53.60	28.53	20.22	16.10	13.66	8.96	7.60
700	62.53	33.28	23.59	18.78	15.93	10.46	8.86
800	71.46	38.04	26.96	21.47	18.21	11.95	10.13
900	80.39	42.79	30.33	24.15	20.48	13.44	11.39
1000	89.32	47.55	33.70	26.83	22.76	14.94	12.66
2000	178.64	95.09	67.39	53.66	45.51	29.87	25.31
2500	223.30	118.86	84.24	67.07	56.89	37.33	31.64
3000	267.96	142.63	101.09	80.49	68.26	44.80	37.96
4000	357.27	190.17	134.78	107.31	91.02	59.73	50.61
5000	446.59	237.71	168.47	134.14	113.77	74.66	63.27
6000	535.91	285.26	202.17	160.97	136.52	89.59	75.92
7000	625.23	332.80	235.86	187.80	159.28	104.52	88.57
8000	714.54	380.34	269.56	214.62	182.03	119.45	101.22
9000	803.86	427.88	303.25	241.45	204.78	134.38	113.88
10000	893.18	475.42	336.94	268.28	227.54	149.32	126.53
11000	982.50	522.97	370.64	295.11	250.29	164.25	139.18
12000	1071.81	570.51	404.33	321.93	273.04	179.18	151.83
13000	1161.13	618.05	438.03	348.76	295.79	194.11	164.49
14000	1250.45	665.59	471.72	375.59	318.55	209.04	177.14
15000	1339.76	713.13	505.41	402.42	341.30	223.97	189.79
16000	1429.08	760.67	539.11	429.24	364.05	238.90	202.44
17000	1518.40	808.22	572.80	456.07	386.81	253.83	215.10
18000	1607.72	855.76	606.50	482.90	409.56	268.76	227.75
19000	1697.03	903.30	640.19	509.73	432.31	283.70	240.40
20000	1786.35	950.84	673.88	536.55	455.07	298.63	253.05
21000	1875.67	998.38	707.58	563.38	477.82	313.56	265.71
22000	1964.99	1045.93	741.27	590.21	500.57	328.49	278.36
23000	2054.30	1093.47	774.97	617.04	523.33	343.42	291.01
24000	2143.62	1141.01	808.66	643.86	546.08	358.35	303.66
25000	2232.94	1188.55	842.35	670.69	568.83	373.28	316.32
26000	2322.25	1236.09	876.05	697.52	591.58	388.21	328.97
27000	2411.57	1283.63	909.74	724.35	614.34	403.14	341.62
28000	2500.89	1331.18	943.44	751.17	637.09	418.08	354.27
29000	2590.21	1378.72	977.13	778.00	659.84	433.01	366.93
30000	2679.52	1426.26	1010.82	804.83	682.60	447.94	379.58
31000	2768.84	1473.80	1044.52	831.66	705.35	462.87	392.23
32000	2858.16	1521.34	1078.21	858.48	728.10	477.80	404.88
33000	2947.48	1568.89	1111.91	885.31	750.86	492.73	417.53
34000	3036.79	1616.43	1145.60	912.14	773.61	507.66	430.19
35000	3126.11	1663.97	1179.29	938.97	796.36	522.59	442.84
36000	3215.43	1711.51	1212.99	965.79	819.12	537.52	455.49
37000	3304.74	1759.05	1246.68	992.62	841.87	552.45	468.14
38000	3394.06	1806.59	1280.38	1019.45	864.62	567.39	480.80
39000	3483.38	1854.14	1314.07	1046.28	887.37	582.32	493.45
40000	3572.70	1901.68	1347.76	1073.10	910.13	597.25	506.10
45000	4019.28	2139.39	1516.23	1207.24	1023.89	671.90	569.36
50000	4465.87	2377.10	1684.70	1341.38	1137.66	746.56	632.63
55000	4912.46	2614.81	1853.17	1475.52	1251.42	821.21	695.89
60000	5359.04	2852.51	2021.64	1609.65	1365.19	895.87	759.15
65000	5805.63	3090.22	2190.11	1743.79	1478.95	970.52	822.41
70000	6252.21	3327.93	2358.58	1877.93	1592.72	1045.18	885.67
75000	6698.80	3565.64	2527.05	2012.07	1706.49	1119.84	948.94
80000	7145.39	3803.35	2695.52	2146.20	1820.25	1194.49	1012.20
85000	7591.97	4041.06	2863.99	2280.34	1934.02	1269.15	1075.46
90000	8038.56	4278.77	3032.46	2414.48	2047.78	1343.80	1138.72
95000	8485.15	4516.48	3200.93	2548.62	2161.55	1418.46	1201.99
100000	8931.73	4754.19	3369.40	2682.75	2275.31	1493.11	1265.25

AMOUNT OF LOAN	NUMBER OF YEARS IN TERM						
	20	25	28	29	30	35	40
$ 25	.30	.29	.28	.28	.28	.28	.28
50	.59	.57	.56	.56	.56	.55	.55
75	.88	.85	.84	.84	.83	.83	.82
100	1.18	1.13	1.12	1.11	1.11	1.10	1.09
200	2.35	2.26	2.23	2.22	2.22	2.20	2.18
300	3.52	3.39	3.34	3.33	3.32	3.29	3.27
400	4.69	4.52	4.46	4.44	4.43	4.39	4.36
500	5.86	5.64	5.57	5.55	5.54	5.48	5.45
600	7.03	6.77	6.68	6.66	6.64	6.58	6.54
700	8.21	7.90	7.80	7.77	7.75	7.67	7.63
800	9.38	9.03	8.91	8.88	8.85	8.77	8.72
900	10.55	10.16	10.02	9.99	9.96	9.86	9.81
1000	11.72	11.28	11.14	11.10	11.07	10.96	10.90
2000	23.44	22.56	22.27	22.19	22.13	21.91	21.80
2500	29.29	28.20	27.83	27.74	27.66	27.38	27.24
3000	35.15	33.84	33.40	33.29	33.19	32.86	32.69
4000	46.87	45.12	44.53	44.38	44.25	43.81	43.59
5000	58.58	56.40	55.66	55.48	55.31	54.76	54.48
6000	70.30	67.68	66.79	66.57	66.38	65.72	65.38
7000	82.02	78.95	77.92	77.67	77.44	76.67	76.27
8000	93.73	90.23	89.06	88.76	88.50	87.62	87.17
9000	105.45	101.51	100.19	99.85	99.56	98.57	98.06
10000	117.16	112.79	111.32	110.95	110.62	109.52	108.96
11000	128.88	124.07	122.45	122.04	121.69	120.48	119.85
12000	140.59	135.35	133.58	133.14	132.75	131.43	130.75
13000	152.31	146.62	144.71	144.23	143.81	142.38	141.64
14000	164.03	157.90	155.84	155.33	154.87	153.33	152.54
15000	175.74	169.18	166.98	166.42	165.93	164.28	163.43
16000	187.46	180.46	178.11	177.51	177.00	175.24	174.33
17000	199.17	191.74	189.24	188.61	188.06	186.19	185.22
18000	210.89	203.02	200.37	199.70	199.12	197.14	196.12
19000	222.60	214.29	211.50	210.80	210.18	208.09	207.01
20000	234.32	225.57	222.63	221.89	221.24	219.04	217.91
21000	246.04	236.85	233.76	232.99	232.31	230.00	228.80
22000	257.75	248.13	244.89	244.08	243.37	240.95	239.70
23000	269.47	259.41	256.03	255.17	254.43	251.90	250.59
24000	281.18	270.69	267.16	266.27	265.49	262.85	261.49
25000	292.90	281.96	278.29	277.36	276.55	273.80	272.38
26000	304.61	293.24	289.42	288.46	287.62	284.76	283.28
27000	316.33	304.52	300.55	299.55	298.68	295.71	294.17
28000	328.05	315.80	311.68	310.65	309.74	306.66	305.07
29000	339.76	327.08	322.81	321.74	320.80	317.61	315.96
30000	351.48	338.36	333.95	332.83	331.86	328.56	326.86
31000	363.19	349.63	345.08	343.93	342.93	339.51	337.75
32000	374.91	360.91	356.21	355.02	353.99	350.47	348.65
33000	386.62	372.19	367.34	366.12	365.05	361.42	359.54
34000	398.34	383.47	378.47	377.21	376.11	372.37	370.44
35000	410.06	394.75	389.60	388.31	387.17	383.32	381.33
36000	421.77	406.03	400.73	399.40	398.24	394.27	392.23
37000	433.49	417.30	411.86	410.49	409.30	405.23	403.13
38000	445.20	428.58	423.00	421.59	420.36	416.18	414.02
39000	456.92	439.86	434.13	432.68	431.42	427.13	424.92
40000	468.64	451.14	445.26	443.78	442.48	438.08	435.81
45000	527.21	507.53	500.92	499.25	497.79	492.84	490.29
50000	585.79	563.92	556.57	554.72	553.10	547.60	544.76
55000	644.37	620.31	612.23	610.19	608.41	602.36	599.24
60000	702.95	676.71	667.89	665.66	663.72	657.12	653.71
65000	761.53	733.10	723.54	721.14	719.03	711.88	708.19
70000	820.11	789.49	779.20	776.61	774.34	766.64	762.66
75000	878.69	845.88	834.86	832.08	829.65	821.40	817.14
80000	937.27	902.27	890.51	887.55	884.96	876.16	871.62
85000	995.84	958.67	946.17	943.02	940.27	930.92	926.09
90000	1054.42	1015.06	1001.83	998.49	995.58	985.68	980.57
95000	1113.00	1071.45	1057.48	1053.97	1050.89	1040.44	1035.04
100000	1171.58	1127.84	1113.14	1109.44	1106.20	1095.20	1089.52

13.25% MONTHLY AMORTIZING PAYMENTS

AMOUNT OF LOAN	NUMBER OF YEARS IN TERM						
	1	2	3	4	5	10	15
$ 25	2.24	1.20	.85	.68	.58	.38	.33
50	4.48	2.39	1.70	1.35	1.15	.76	.65
75	6.71	3.58	2.54	2.03	1.72	1.14	.97
100	8.95	4.77	3.39	2.70	2.29	1.51	1.29
200	17.89	9.54	6.77	5.40	4.58	3.02	2.57
300	26.84	14.30	10.15	8.09	6.87	4.53	3.85
400	35.78	19.07	13.53	10.79	9.16	6.04	5.13
500	44.72	23.83	16.91	13.48	11.45	7.54	6.41
600	53.67	28.60	20.29	16.18	13.73	9.05	7.70
700	62.61	33.37	23.68	18.87	16.02	10.56	8.98
800	71.55	38.13	27.06	21.57	18.31	12.07	10.26
900	80.50	42.90	30.44	24.26	20.60	13.58	11.54
1000	89.44	47.66	33.82	26.96	22.89	15.08	12.82
2000	178.87	95.32	67.63	53.91	45.77	30.16	25.64
2500	223.59	119.15	84.54	67.38	57.21	37.70	32.05
3000	268.31	142.98	101.45	80.86	68.65	45.24	38.46
4000	357.74	190.64	135.26	107.81	91.53	60.32	51.27
5000	447.18	238.30	169.08	134.76	114.41	75.40	64.09
6000	536.61	285.96	202.89	161.72	137.29	90.48	76.91
7000	626.05	333.62	236.71	188.67	160.17	105.56	89.73
8000	715.48	381.28	270.52	215.62	183.06	120.64	102.54
9000	804.92	428.94	304.34	242.57	205.94	135.72	115.36
10000	894.35	476.60	338.15	269.52	228.82	150.79	128.18
11000	983.79	524.26	371.96	296.47	251.70	165.87	141.00
12000	1073.22	571.92	405.78	323.43	274.58	180.95	153.81
13000	1162.65	619.58	439.59	350.38	297.46	196.03	166.63
14000	1252.09	667.24	473.41	377.33	320.34	211.11	179.45
15000	1341.52	714.90	507.22	404.28	343.22	226.19	192.27
16000	1430.96	762.55	541.04	431.23	366.11	241.27	205.08
17000	1520.39	810.21	574.85	458.18	388.99	256.35	217.90
18000	1609.83	857.87	608.67	485.14	411.87	271.43	230.72
19000	1699.26	905.53	642.48	512.09	434.75	286.50	243.53
20000	1788.70	953.19	676.29	539.04	457.63	301.58	256.35
21000	1878.13	1000.85	710.11	565.99	480.51	316.66	269.17
22000	1967.57	1048.51	743.92	592.94	503.39	331.74	281.99
23000	2057.00	1096.17	777.74	619.90	526.27	346.82	294.80
24000	2146.44	1143.83	811.55	646.85	549.16	361.90	307.62
25000	2235.87	1191.49	845.37	673.80	572.04	376.98	320.44
26000	2325.30	1239.15	879.18	700.75	594.92	392.06	333.26
27000	2414.74	1286.81	913.00	727.70	617.80	407.14	346.07
28000	2504.17	1334.47	946.81	754.65	640.68	422.21	358.89
29000	2593.61	1382.13	980.63	781.61	663.56	437.29	371.71
30000	2683.04	1429.79	1014.44	808.56	686.44	452.37	384.53
31000	2772.48	1477.44	1048.25	835.51	709.32	467.45	397.34
32000	2861.91	1525.10	1082.07	862.46	732.21	482.53	410.16
33000	2951.35	1572.76	1115.88	889.41	755.09	497.61	422.98
34000	3040.78	1620.42	1149.70	916.36	777.97	512.69	435.80
35000	3130.22	1668.08	1183.51	943.32	800.85	527.77	448.61
36000	3219.65	1715.74	1217.33	970.27	823.73	542.85	461.43
37000	3309.09	1763.40	1251.14	997.22	846.61	557.92	474.25
38000	3398.52	1811.06	1284.96	1024.17	869.49	573.00	487.06
39000	3487.95	1858.72	1318.77	1051.12	892.37	588.08	499.88
40000	3577.39	1906.38	1352.58	1078.07	915.26	603.16	512.70
45000	4024.56	2144.68	1521.66	1212.83	1029.66	678.56	576.79
50000	4471.74	2382.97	1690.73	1347.59	1144.07	753.95	640.87
55000	4918.91	2621.27	1859.80	1482.35	1258.47	829.34	704.96
60000	5366.08	2859.57	2028.87	1617.11	1372.88	904.74	769.05
65000	5813.25	3097.86	2197.95	1751.87	1487.29	980.13	833.13
70000	6260.43	3336.16	2367.02	1886.63	1601.69	1055.53	897.22
75000	6707.60	3574.46	2536.09	2021.39	1716.10	1130.92	961.31
80000	7154.77	3812.75	2705.16	2156.14	1830.51	1206.32	1025.39
85000	7601.95	4051.05	2874.24	2290.90	1944.91	1281.71	1089.48
90000	8049.12	4289.35	3043.31	2425.66	2059.32	1357.11	1153.57
95000	8496.29	4527.64	3212.38	2560.42	2173.72	1432.50	1217.65
100000	8943.47	4765.94	3381.45	2695.18	2288.13	1507.89	1281.74

36

AMOUNT OF LOAN	NUMBER OF YEARS IN TERM						
	20	25	28	29	30	35	40
$ 25	.30	.29	.29	.29	.29	.28	.28
50	.60	.58	.57	.57	.57	.56	.56
75	.90	.87	.85	.85	.85	.84	.84
100	1.19	1.15	1.14	1.13	1.13	1.12	1.11
200	2.38	2.30	2.27	2.26	2.26	2.24	2.22
300	3.57	3.45	3.40	3.39	3.38	3.35	3.33
400	4.76	4.59	4.53	4.52	4.51	4.47	4.44
500	5.95	5.74	5.67	5.65	5.63	5.58	5.55
600	7.14	6.89	6.80	6.78	6.76	6.70	6.66
700	8.33	8.03	7.93	7.91	7.89	7.81	7.77
800	9.52	9.18	9.06	9.04	9.01	8.93	8.88
900	10.71	10.33	10.20	10.16	10.14	10.04	9.99
1000	11.90	11.47	11.33	11.29	11.26	11.16	11.10
2000	23.79	22.94	22.65	22.58	22.52	22.31	22.20
2500	29.74	28.67	28.32	28.23	28.15	27.89	27.75
3000	35.69	34.41	33.98	33.87	33.78	33.46	33.30
4000	47.58	45.87	45.30	45.16	45.04	44.61	44.40
5000	59.48	57.34	56.63	56.45	56.29	55.77	55.50
6000	71.37	68.81	67.95	67.74	67.55	66.92	66.60
7000	83.27	80.27	79.28	79.03	78.81	78.07	77.70
8000	95.16	91.74	90.60	90.32	90.07	89.22	88.79
9000	107.05	103.21	101.93	101.60	101.32	100.38	99.89
10000	118.95	114.68	113.25	112.89	112.58	111.53	110.99
11000	130.84	126.14	124.58	124.18	123.84	122.68	122.09
12000	142.74	137.61	135.90	135.47	135.10	133.83	133.19
13000	154.63	149.08	147.22	146.76	146.36	144.99	144.29
14000	166.53	160.54	158.55	158.05	157.61	156.14	155.39
15000	178.42	172.01	169.87	169.34	168.87	167.29	166.49
16000	190.31	183.48	181.20	180.63	180.13	178.44	177.58
17000	202.21	194.94	192.52	191.92	191.39	189.60	188.68
18000	214.10	206.41	203.85	203.20	202.64	200.75	199.78
19000	226.00	217.88	215.17	214.49	213.90	211.90	210.88
20000	237.89	229.35	226.50	225.78	225.16	223.05	221.98
21000	249.79	240.81	237.82	237.07	236.42	234.21	233.08
22000	261.68	252.28	249.15	248.36	247.68	245.36	244.18
23000	273.57	263.75	260.47	259.65	258.93	256.51	255.28
24000	285.47	275.21	271.79	270.94	270.19	267.66	266.37
25000	297.36	286.68	283.12	282.23	281.45	278.82	277.47
26000	309.26	298.15	294.44	293.52	292.71	289.97	288.57
27000	321.15	309.61	305.77	304.80	303.96	301.12	299.67
28000	333.05	321.08	317.09	316.09	315.22	312.27	310.77
29000	344.94	332.55	328.42	327.38	326.48	323.43	321.87
30000	356.83	344.02	339.74	338.67	337.74	334.58	332.97
31000	368.73	355.48	351.07	349.96	348.99	345.73	344.06
32000	380.62	366.95	362.39	361.25	360.25	356.88	355.16
33000	392.52	378.42	373.72	372.54	371.51	368.03	366.26
34000	404.41	389.88	385.04	383.83	382.77	379.19	377.36
35000	416.31	401.35	396.36	395.11	394.03	390.34	388.46
36000	428.20	412.82	407.69	406.40	405.28	401.49	399.56
37000	440.09	424.28	419.01	417.69	416.54	412.64	410.66
38000	451.99	435.75	430.34	428.98	427.80	423.80	421.76
39000	463.88	447.22	441.66	440.27	439.06	434.95	432.85
40000	475.78	458.69	452.99	451.56	450.31	446.10	443.95
45000	535.25	516.02	509.61	508.00	506.60	501.86	499.45
50000	594.72	573.36	566.23	564.45	562.89	557.63	554.94
55000	654.19	630.69	622.86	620.89	619.18	613.39	610.43
60000	713.66	688.03	679.48	677.34	675.47	669.15	665.93
65000	773.13	745.36	736.10	733.78	731.76	724.91	721.42
70000	832.61	802.70	792.72	790.22	788.05	780.67	776.91
75000	892.08	860.03	849.35	846.67	844.34	836.44	832.41
80000	951.55	917.37	905.97	903.11	900.62	892.20	887.90
85000	1011.02	974.70	962.59	959.56	956.91	947.96	943.39
90000	1070.49	1032.04	1019.22	1016.00	1013.20	1003.72	998.89
95000	1129.96	1089.37	1075.84	1072.45	1069.49	1059.49	1054.38
100000	1189.44	1146.71	1132.46	1128.89	1125.78	1115.25	1109.87

13.50% MONTHLY AMORTIZING PAYMENTS

AMOUNT OF LOAN	NUMBER OF YEARS IN TERM						
	1	2	3	4	5	10	15
$ 25	2.24	1.20	.85	.68	.58	.39	.33
50	4.48	2.39	1.70	1.36	1.16	.77	.65
75	6.72	3.59	2.55	2.04	1.73	1.15	.98
100	8.96	4.78	3.40	2.71	2.31	1.53	1.30
200	17.92	9.56	6.79	5.42	4.61	3.05	2.60
300	26.87	14.34	10.19	8.13	6.91	4.57	3.90
400	35.83	19.12	13.58	10.84	9.21	6.10	5.20
500	44.78	23.89	16.97	13.54	11.51	7.62	6.50
600	53.74	28.67	20.37	16.25	13.81	9.14	7.79
700	62.69	33.45	23.76	18.96	16.11	10.66	9.09
800	71.65	38.23	27.15	21.67	18.41	12.19	10.39
900	80.60	43.00	30.55	24.37	20.71	13.71	11.69
1000	89.56	47.78	33.94	27.08	23.01	15.23	12.99
2000	179.11	95.56	67.88	54.16	46.02	30.46	25.97
2500	223.89	119.45	84.84	67.70	57.53	38.07	32.46
3000	268.66	143.34	101.81	81.23	69.03	45.69	38.95
4000	358.21	191.11	135.75	108.31	92.04	60.91	51.94
5000	447.77	238.89	169.68	135.39	115.05	76.14	64.92
6000	537.32	286.67	203.62	162.46	138.06	91.37	77.90
7000	626.87	334.44	237.55	189.54	161.07	106.60	90.89
8000	716.42	382.22	271.49	216.62	184.08	121.82	103.87
9000	805.97	430.00	305.42	243.69	207.09	137.05	116.85
10000	895.53	477.78	339.36	270.77	230.10	152.28	129.84
11000	985.08	525.55	373.29	297.84	253.11	167.51	142.82
12000	1074.63	573.33	407.23	324.92	276.12	182.73	155.80
13000	1164.18	621.11	441.16	352.00	299.13	197.96	168.79
14000	1253.73	668.88	475.10	379.07	322.14	213.19	181.77
15000	1343.29	716.66	509.03	406.15	345.15	228.42	194.75
16000	1432.84	764.44	542.97	433.23	368.16	243.64	207.74
17000	1522.39	812.21	576.90	460.30	391.17	258.87	220.72
18000	1611.94	859.99	610.84	487.38	414.18	274.10	233.70
19000	1701.49	907.77	644.78	514.46	437.19	289.33	246.69
20000	1791.05	955.55	678.71	541.53	460.20	304.55	259.67
21000	1880.60	1003.32	712.65	568.61	483.21	319.78	272.65
22000	1970.15	1051.10	746.58	595.68	506.22	335.01	285.64
23000	2059.70	1098.88	780.52	622.76	529.23	350.24	298.62
24000	2149.25	1146.65	814.45	649.84	552.24	365.46	311.60
25000	2238.81	1194.43	848.39	676.91	575.25	380.69	324.58
26000	2328.36	1242.21	882.32	703.99	598.26	395.92	337.57
27000	2417.91	1289.98	916.26	731.07	621.27	411.15	350.55
28000	2507.46	1337.76	950.19	758.14	644.28	426.37	363.53
29000	2597.01	1385.54	984.13	785.22	667.29	441.60	376.52
30000	2686.57	1433.32	1018.06	812.29	690.30	456.83	389.50
31000	2776.12	1481.09	1052.00	839.37	713.31	472.06	402.48
32000	2865.67	1528.87	1085.93	866.45	736.32	487.28	415.47
33000	2955.22	1576.65	1119.87	893.52	759.33	502.51	428.45
34000	3044.77	1624.42	1153.80	920.60	782.34	517.74	441.43
35000	3134.33	1672.20	1187.74	947.68	805.35	532.97	454.42
36000	3223.88	1719.98	1221.68	974.75	828.36	548.19	467.40
37000	3313.43	1767.75	1255.61	1001.83	851.37	563.42	480.38
38000	3402.98	1815.53	1289.55	1028.91	874.38	578.65	493.37
39000	3492.53	1863.31	1323.48	1055.98	897.39	593.87	506.35
40000	3582.09	1911.09	1357.42	1083.06	920.40	609.10	519.33
45000	4029.85	2149.97	1527.09	1218.44	1035.45	685.24	584.25
50000	4477.61	2388.86	1696.77	1353.82	1150.50	761.38	649.16
55000	4925.37	2627.74	1866.45	1489.20	1265.55	837.51	714.08
60000	5373.13	2866.63	2036.12	1624.58	1380.60	913.65	779.00
65000	5820.89	3105.51	2205.80	1759.97	1495.64	989.79	843.91
70000	6268.65	3344.40	2375.48	1895.35	1610.69	1065.93	908.83
75000	6716.41	3583.28	2545.15	2030.73	1725.74	1142.06	973.74
80000	7164.17	3822.17	2714.83	2166.11	1840.79	1218.20	1038.66
85000	7611.93	4061.05	2884.50	2301.49	1955.84	1294.34	1103.58
90000	8059.69	4299.94	3054.18	2436.87	2070.89	1370.47	1168.49
95000	8507.45	4538.82	3223.86	2572.26	2185.94	1446.61	1233.41
100000	8955.21	4777.71	3393.53	2707.64	2300.99	1522.75	1298.32

38

MONTHLY AMORTIZING PAYMENTS 13.50%

AMOUNT OF LOAN	20	25	28	29	30	35	40
$ 25	.31	.30	.29	.29	.29	.29	.29
50	.61	.59	.58	.58	.58	.57	.57
75	.91	.88	.87	.87	.86	.86	.85
100	1.21	1.17	1.16	1.15	1.15	1.14	1.14
200	2.42	2.34	2.31	2.30	2.30	2.28	2.27
300	3.63	3.50	3.46	3.45	3.44	3.41	3.40
400	4.83	4.67	4.61	4.60	4.59	4.55	4.53
500	6.04	5.83	5.76	5.75	5.73	5.68	5.66
600	7.25	7.00	6.92	6.90	6.88	6.82	6.79
700	8.46	8.16	8.07	8.04	8.02	7.95	7.92
800	9.66	9.33	9.22	9.19	9.17	9.09	9.05
900	10.87	10.50	10.37	10.34	10.31	10.22	10.18
1000	12.08	11.66	11.52	11.49	11.46	11.36	11.31
2000	24.15	23.32	23.04	22.97	22.91	22.71	22.61
2500	30.19	29.15	28.80	28.72	28.64	28.39	28.26
3000	36.23	34.97	34.56	34.46	34.37	34.07	33.91
4000	48.30	46.63	46.08	45.94	45.82	45.42	45.22
5000	60.37	58.29	57.60	57.43	57.28	56.77	56.52
6000	72.45	69.94	69.12	68.91	68.73	68.13	67.82
7000	84.52	81.60	80.63	80.39	80.18	79.48	79.12
8000	96.59	93.26	92.15	91.88	91.64	90.83	90.43
9000	108.67	104.91	103.67	103.36	103.09	102.19	101.73
10000	120.74	116.57	115.19	114.85	114.55	113.54	113.03
11000	132.82	128.23	126.71	126.33	126.00	124.89	124.33
12000	144.89	139.88	138.23	137.81	137.45	136.25	135.64
13000	156.96	151.54	149.75	149.30	148.91	147.60	146.94
14000	169.04	163.20	161.26	160.78	160.36	158.95	158.24
15000	181.11	174.85	172.78	172.27	171.82	170.31	169.54
16000	193.18	186.51	184.30	183.75	183.27	181.66	180.85
17000	205.26	198.16	195.82	195.23	194.73	193.01	192.15
18000	217.33	209.82	207.34	206.72	206.18	204.37	203.45
19000	229.41	221.48	218.86	218.20	217.63	215.72	214.75
20000	241.48	233.13	230.37	229.69	229.09	227.07	226.06
21000	253.55	244.79	241.89	241.17	240.54	238.43	237.36
22000	265.63	256.45	253.41	252.65	252.00	249.78	248.66
23000	277.70	268.10	264.93	264.14	263.45	261.13	259.97
24000	289.77	279.76	276.45	275.62	274.90	272.49	271.27
25000	301.85	291.42	287.97	287.11	286.36	283.84	282.57
26000	313.92	303.07	299.49	298.59	297.81	295.19	293.87
27000	326.00	314.73	311.00	310.07	309.27	306.55	305.18
28000	338.07	326.39	322.52	321.56	320.72	317.90	316.48
29000	350.14	338.04	334.04	333.04	332.17	329.25	327.78
30000	362.22	349.70	345.56	344.53	343.63	340.61	339.08
31000	374.29	361.35	357.08	356.01	355.08	351.96	350.39
32000	386.36	373.01	368.60	367.49	366.54	363.31	361.69
33000	398.44	384.67	380.12	378.98	377.99	374.67	372.99
34000	410.51	396.32	391.63	390.46	389.45	386.02	384.29
35000	422.59	407.98	403.15	401.95	400.90	397.37	395.60
36000	434.66	419.64	414.67	413.43	412.35	408.73	406.90
37000	446.73	431.29	426.19	424.92	423.81	420.08	418.20
38000	458.81	442.95	437.71	436.40	435.26	431.43	429.50
39000	470.88	454.61	449.23	447.88	446.72	442.79	440.81
40000	482.95	466.26	460.74	459.37	458.17	454.14	452.11
45000	543.32	524.55	518.34	516.79	515.44	510.91	508.62
50000	603.69	582.83	575.93	574.21	572.71	567.68	565.14
55000	664.06	641.11	633.52	631.63	629.98	624.44	621.65
60000	724.43	699.39	691.11	689.05	687.25	681.21	678.16
65000	784.80	757.67	748.71	746.47	744.52	737.98	734.67
70000	845.17	815.96	806.30	803.89	801.79	794.74	791.19
75000	905.54	874.24	863.89	861.31	859.06	851.51	847.70
80000	965.90	932.52	921.48	918.73	916.33	908.28	904.21
85000	1026.27	990.80	979.08	976.15	973.61	965.04	960.73
90000	1086.64	1049.09	1036.67	1033.57	1030.88	1021.81	1017.24
95000	1147.01	1107.37	1094.26	1090.99	1088.15	1078.58	1073.75
100000	1207.38	1165.65	1151.85	1148.41	1145.42	1135.35	1130.27

13.75% MONTHLY AMORTIZING PAYMENTS

AMOUNT OF LOAN	NUMBER OF YEARS IN TERM						
	1	2	3	4	5	10	15
$ 25	2.25	1.20	.86	.69	.58	.39	.33
50	4.49	2.40	1.71	1.37	1.16	.77	.66
75	6.73	3.60	2.56	2.05	1.74	1.16	.99
100	8.97	4.79	3.41	2.73	2.32	1.54	1.32
200	17.94	9.58	6.82	5.45	4.63	3.08	2.63
300	26.91	14.37	10.22	8.17	6.95	4.62	3.95
400	35.87	19.16	13.63	10.89	9.26	6.16	5.26
500	44.84	23.95	17.03	13.61	11.57	7.69	6.58
600	53.81	28.74	20.44	16.33	13.89	9.23	7.89
700	62.77	33.53	23.84	19.05	16.20	10.77	9.21
800	71.74	38.32	27.25	21.77	18.52	12.31	10.52
900	80.71	43.11	30.66	24.49	20.83	13.84	11.84
1000	89.67	47.90	34.06	27.21	23.14	15.38	13.15
2000	179.34	95.79	68.12	54.41	46.28	30.76	26.30
2500	224.18	119.74	85.15	68.01	57.85	38.45	32.88
3000	269.01	143.69	102.17	81.61	69.42	46.14	39.45
4000	358.68	191.58	136.23	108.81	92.56	61.51	52.60
5000	448.35	239.48	170.29	136.01	115.70	76.89	65.75
6000	538.02	287.37	204.34	163.21	138.84	92.27	78.90
7000	627.69	335.27	238.40	190.41	161.98	107.64	92.05
8000	717.36	383.16	272.46	217.61	185.12	123.02	105.20
9000	807.03	431.06	306.51	244.82	208.25	138.40	118.35
10000	896.70	478.95	340.57	272.02	231.39	153.77	131.50
11000	986.37	526.85	374.62	299.22	254.53	169.15	144.65
12000	1076.04	574.74	408.68	326.42	277.67	184.53	157.80
13000	1165.71	622.64	442.74	353.62	300.81	199.90	170.95
14000	1255.38	670.53	476.79	380.82	323.95	215.28	184.10
15000	1345.05	718.43	510.85	408.02	347.09	230.66	197.25
16000	1434.72	766.32	544.91	435.22	370.23	246.03	210.40
17000	1524.39	814.22	578.96	462.43	393.37	261.41	223.55
18000	1614.06	862.11	613.02	489.63	416.50	276.79	236.70
19000	1703.73	910.01	647.08	516.83	439.64	292.16	249.85
20000	1793.40	957.90	681.13	544.03	462.78	307.54	263.00
21000	1883.07	1005.80	715.19	571.23	485.92	322.92	276.15
22000	1972.73	1053.69	749.24	598.43	509.06	338.29	289.30
23000	2062.40	1101.59	783.30	625.63	532.20	353.67	302.45
24000	2152.07	1149.48	817.36	652.83	555.34	369.05	315.60
25000	2241.74	1197.38	851.41	680.04	578.48	384.42	328.75
26000	2331.41	1245.27	885.47	707.24	601.61	399.80	341.90
27000	2421.08	1293.17	919.53	734.44	624.75	415.18	355.05
28000	2510.75	1341.06	953.58	761.64	647.89	430.55	368.20
29000	2600.42	1388.96	987.64	788.84	671.03	445.93	381.35
30000	2690.09	1436.85	1021.69	816.04	694.17	461.31	394.50
31000	2779.76	1484.75	1055.75	843.24	717.31	476.68	407.65
32000	2869.43	1532.64	1089.81	870.44	740.45	492.06	420.80
33000	2959.10	1580.54	1123.86	897.65	763.59	507.44	433.95
34000	3048.77	1628.43	1157.92	924.85	786.73	522.81	447.10
35000	3138.44	1676.33	1191.98	952.05	809.86	538.19	460.25
36000	3228.11	1724.22	1226.03	979.25	833.00	553.57	473.40
37000	3317.78	1772.11	1260.09	1006.45	856.14	568.94	486.55
38000	3407.45	1820.01	1294.15	1033.65	879.28	584.32	499.70
39000	3497.12	1867.90	1328.20	1060.85	902.42	599.70	512.85
40000	3586.79	1915.80	1362.26	1088.05	925.56	615.07	526.00
45000	4035.13	2155.27	1532.54	1224.06	1041.25	691.96	591.75
50000	4483.48	2394.75	1702.82	1360.07	1156.95	768.84	657.50
55000	4931.83	2634.22	1873.10	1496.07	1272.64	845.72	723.25
60000	5380.18	2873.70	2043.38	1632.08	1388.34	922.61	789.00
65000	5828.52	3113.17	2213.67	1768.09	1504.03	999.49	854.75
70000	6276.87	3352.65	2383.95	1904.09	1619.72	1076.37	920.50
75000	6725.22	3592.12	2554.23	2040.10	1735.42	1153.26	986.25
80000	7173.57	3831.59	2724.51	2176.10	1851.11	1230.14	1051.99
85000	7621.92	4071.07	2894.79	2312.11	1966.81	1307.02	1117.74
90000	8070.26	4310.54	3065.07	2448.12	2082.50	1383.91	1183.49
95000	8518.61	4550.02	3235.36	2584.12	2198.20	1460.79	1249.24
100000	8966.96	4789.49	3405.64	2720.13	2313.89	1537.67	1314.99

40

MONTHLY AMORTIZING PAYMENTS 13.75%

AMOUNT OF LOAN	NUMBER OF YEARS IN TERM						
	20	25	28	29	30	35	40
$ 25	.31	.30	.30	.30	.30	.29	.29
50	.62	.60	.59	.59	.59	.58	.58
75	.92	.89	.88	.88	.88	.87	.87
100	1.23	1.19	1.18	1.17	1.17	1.16	1.16
200	2.46	2.37	2.35	2.34	2.34	2.32	2.31
300	3.68	3.56	3.52	3.51	3.50	3.47	3.46
400	4.91	4.74	4.69	4.68	4.67	4.63	4.61
500	6.13	5.93	5.86	5.84	5.83	5.78	5.76
600	7.36	7.11	7.03	7.01	7.00	6.94	6.91
700	8.58	8.30	8.20	8.18	8.16	8.09	8.06
800	9.81	9.48	9.38	9.35	9.33	9.25	9.21
900	11.03	10.67	10.55	10.52	10.49	10.40	10.36
1000	12.26	11.85	11.72	11.68	11.66	11.56	11.51
2000	24.51	23.70	23.43	23.36	23.31	23.11	23.02
2500	30.64	29.62	29.29	29.20	29.13	28.89	28.77
3000	36.77	35.54	35.14	35.04	34.96	34.67	34.53
4000	49.02	47.39	46.86	46.72	46.61	46.22	46.03
5000	61.28	59.24	58.57	58.40	58.26	57.78	57.54
6000	73.53	71.08	70.28	70.08	69.91	69.33	69.05
7000	85.78	82.93	82.00	81.76	81.56	80.89	80.55
8000	98.04	94.78	93.71	93.44	93.21	92.44	92.06
9000	110.29	106.62	105.42	105.12	104.87	104.00	103.57
10000	122.55	118.47	117.14	116.80	116.52	115.55	115.07
11000	134.80	130.32	128.85	128.48	128.17	127.11	126.58
12000	147.05	142.16	140.56	140.16	139.82	138.66	138.09
13000	159.31	154.01	152.28	151.84	151.47	150.22	149.59
14000	171.56	165.86	163.99	163.52	163.12	161.77	161.10
15000	183.82	177.70	175.70	175.20	174.77	173.33	172.61
16000	196.07	189.55	187.41	186.88	186.42	184.88	184.11
17000	208.32	201.40	199.13	198.56	198.07	196.44	195.62
18000	220.58	213.24	210.84	210.24	209.73	207.99	207.13
19000	232.83	225.09	222.55	221.92	221.38	219.55	218.64
20000	245.09	236.94	234.27	233.60	233.03	231.10	230.14
21000	257.34	248.78	245.98	245.28	244.68	242.66	241.65
22000	269.59	260.63	257.69	256.96	256.33	254.21	253.16
23000	281.85	272.48	269.41	268.64	267.98	265.77	264.66
24000	294.10	284.32	281.12	280.32	279.63	277.32	276.17
25000	306.36	296.17	292.83	292.00	291.28	288.88	287.68
26000	318.61	308.02	304.55	303.68	302.93	300.43	299.18
27000	330.86	319.86	316.26	315.36	314.59	311.99	310.69
28000	343.12	331.71	327.97	327.04	326.24	323.54	322.20
29000	355.37	343.56	339.68	338.72	337.89	335.10	333.70
30000	367.63	355.40	351.40	350.40	349.54	346.65	345.21
31000	379.88	367.25	363.11	362.08	361.19	358.21	356.72
32000	392.13	379.10	374.82	373.76	372.84	369.76	368.22
33000	404.39	390.94	386.54	385.44	384.49	381.32	379.73
34000	416.64	402.79	398.25	397.12	396.14	392.87	391.24
35000	428.90	414.64	409.96	408.80	407.79	404.42	402.74
36000	441.15	426.48	421.68	420.48	419.45	415.98	414.25
37000	453.40	438.33	433.39	432.16	431.10	427.53	425.76
38000	465.66	450.18	445.10	443.84	442.75	439.09	437.27
39000	477.91	462.02	456.82	455.52	454.40	450.64	448.77
40000	490.17	473.87	468.53	467.20	466.05	462.20	460.28
45000	551.44	533.10	527.00	525.60	524.31	519.97	517.81
50000	612.71	592.34	585.66	584.00	582.56	577.75	575.35
55000	673.98	651.57	644.23	642.40	640.82	635.52	632.88
60000	735.25	710.80	702.79	700.80	699.07	693.30	690.42
65000	796.52	770.04	761.36	759.20	757.33	751.07	747.95
70000	857.79	829.27	819.92	817.60	815.58	808.84	805.48
75000	919.06	888.50	878.49	876.00	873.84	866.62	863.02
80000	980.33	947.74	937.05	934.40	932.10	924.39	920.55
85000	1041.60	1006.97	995.62	992.80	990.35	982.17	978.09
90000	1102.87	1066.20	1054.18	1051.20	1048.61	1039.94	1035.62
95000	1164.14	1125.44	1112.75	1109.60	1106.86	1097.72	1093.16
100000	1225.41	1184.67	1171.32	1168.00	1165.12	1155.49	1150.69

41

14.00% MONTHLY AMORTIZING PAYMENTS

AMOUNT OF LOAN	NUMBER OF YEARS IN TERM						
	1	2	3	4	5	10	15
$ 25	2.25	1.21	.86	.69	.59	.39	.34
50	4.49	2.41	1.71	1.37	1.17	.78	.67
75	6.74	3.61	2.57	2.05	1.75	1.17	1.00
100	8.98	4.81	3.42	2.74	2.33	1.56	1.34
200	17.96	9.61	6.84	5.47	4.66	3.11	2.67
300	26.94	14.41	10.26	8.20	6.99	4.66	4.00
400	35.92	19.21	13.68	10.94	9.31	6.22	5.33
500	44.90	24.01	17.09	13.67	11.64	7.77	6.66
600	53.88	28.81	20.51	16.40	13.97	9.32	8.00
700	62.86	33.61	23.93	19.13	16.29	10.87	9.33
800	71.83	38.42	27.35	21.87	18.62	12.43	10.66
900	80.81	43.22	30.76	24.60	20.95	13.98	11.99
1000	89.79	48.02	34.18	27.33	23.27	15.53	13.32
2000	179.58	96.03	68.36	54.66	46.54	31.06	26.64
2500	224.47	120.04	85.45	68.32	58.18	38.82	33.30
3000	269.37	144.04	102.54	81.98	69.81	46.58	39.96
4000	359.15	192.06	136.72	109.31	93.08	62.11	53.27
5000	448.94	240.07	170.89	136.64	116.35	77.64	66.59
6000	538.73	288.08	205.07	163.96	139.61	93.16	79.91
7000	628.51	336.10	239.25	191.29	162.88	108.69	93.23
8000	718.30	384.11	273.43	218.62	186.15	124.22	106.54
9000	808.09	432.12	307.60	245.94	209.42	139.74	119.86
10000	897.88	480.13	341.78	273.27	232.69	155.27	133.18
11000	987.66	528.15	375.96	300.60	255.96	170.80	146.50
12000	1077.45	576.16	410.14	327.92	279.22	186.32	159.81
13000	1167.24	624.17	444.31	355.25	302.49	201.85	173.13
14000	1257.02	672.19	478.49	382.58	325.76	217.38	186.45
15000	1346.81	720.20	512.67	409.90	349.03	232.90	199.77
16000	1436.60	768.21	546.85	437.23	372.30	248.43	213.08
17000	1526.39	816.22	581.02	464.56	395.57	263.96	226.40
18000	1616.17	864.24	615.20	491.88	418.83	279.48	239.72
19000	1705.96	912.25	649.38	519.21	442.10	295.01	253.04
20000	1795.75	960.26	683.56	546.53	465.37	310.54	266.35
21000	1885.53	1008.28	717.74	573.86	488.64	326.06	279.67
22000	1975.32	1056.29	751.91	601.19	511.91	341.59	292.99
23000	2065.11	1104.30	786.09	628.51	535.17	357.12	306.31
24000	2154.90	1152.31	820.27	655.84	558.44	372.64	319.62
25000	2244.68	1200.33	854.45	683.17	581.71	388.17	332.94
26000	2334.47	1248.34	888.62	710.49	604.98	403.70	346.26
27000	2424.26	1296.35	922.80	737.82	628.25	419.22	359.58
28000	2514.04	1344.37	956.98	765.15	651.52	434.75	372.89
29000	2603.83	1392.38	991.16	792.47	674.78	450.28	386.21
30000	2693.62	1440.39	1025.33	819.80	698.05	465.80	399.53
31000	2783.41	1488.40	1059.51	847.13	721.32	481.33	412.84
32000	2873.19	1536.42	1093.69	874.45	744.59	496.86	426.16
33000	2962.98	1584.43	1127.87	901.78	767.86	512.38	439.48
34000	3052.77	1632.44	1162.04	929.11	791.13	527.91	452.80
35000	3142.55	1680.46	1196.22	956.43	814.39	543.44	466.11
36000	3232.34	1728.47	1230.40	983.76	837.66	558.96	479.43
37000	3322.13	1776.48	1264.58	1011.08	860.93	574.49	492.75
38000	3411.92	1824.49	1298.75	1038.41	884.20	590.02	506.07
39000	3501.70	1872.51	1332.93	1065.74	907.47	605.54	519.38
40000	3591.49	1920.52	1367.11	1093.06	930.74	621.07	532.70
45000	4040.43	2160.58	1538.75	1229.70	1047.08	698.70	599.29
50000	4489.36	2400.65	1708.89	1366.33	1163.42	776.34	665.88
55000	4938.30	2640.71	1879.77	1502.96	1279.76	853.97	732.46
60000	5387.23	2880.78	2050.66	1639.59	1396.10	931.60	799.05
65000	5836.17	3120.84	2221.55	1776.23	1512.44	1009.24	865.64
70000	6285.10	3360.91	2392.44	1912.86	1628.78	1086.87	932.22
75000	6734.04	3600.97	2563.33	2049.49	1745.12	1164.50	998.81
80000	7182.97	3841.04	2734.22	2186.12	1861.47	1242.14	1065.40
85000	7631.91	4081.10	2905.10	2322.76	1977.81	1319.77	1131.99
90000	8080.85	4321.16	3075.99	2459.39	2094.15	1397.40	1198.57
95000	8529.78	4561.23	3246.88	2596.02	2210.49	1475.04	1265.16
100000	8978.72	4801.29	3417.77	2732.65	2326.83	1552.67	1331.75

AMOUNT OF LOAN	NUMBER OF YEARS IN TERM						
	20	25	28	29	30	35	40
$ 25	.32	.31	.30	.30	.30	.30	.30
50	.63	.61	.60	.60	.60	.59	.59
75	.94	.91	.90	.90	.89	.89	.88
100	1.25	1.21	1.20	1.19	1.19	1.18	1.18
200	2.49	2.41	2.39	2.38	2.37	2.36	2.35
300	3.74	3.62	3.58	3.57	3.56	3.53	3.52
400	4.98	4.82	4.77	4.76	4.74	4.71	4.69
500	6.22	6.02	5.96	5.94	5.93	5.88	5.86
600	7.47	7.23	7.15	7.13	7.11	7.06	7.03
700	8.71	8.43	8.34	8.32	8.30	8.23	8.20
800	9.95	9.64	9.53	9.51	9.48	9.41	9.37
900	11.20	10.84	10.72	10.69	10.67	10.59	10.55
1000	12.44	12.04	11.91	11.88	11.85	11.76	11.72
2000	24.88	24.08	23.82	23.76	23.70	23.52	23.43
2500	31.09	30.10	29.78	29.70	29.63	29.40	29.28
3000	37.31	36.12	35.73	35.63	35.55	35.28	35.14
4000	49.75	48.16	47.64	47.51	47.40	47.03	46.85
5000	62.18	60.19	59.55	59.39	59.25	58.79	58.56
6000	74.62	72.23	71.46	71.26	71.10	70.55	70.27
7000	87.05	84.27	83.36	83.14	82.95	82.30	81.98
8000	99.49	96.31	95.27	95.02	94.79	94.06	93.70
9000	111.92	108.34	107.18	106.89	106.64	105.82	105.41
10000	124.36	120.38	119.09	118.77	118.49	117.57	117.12
11000	136.79	132.42	131.00	130.65	130.34	129.33	128.83
12000	149.23	144.46	142.91	142.52	142.19	141.09	140.54
13000	161.66	156.49	154.81	154.40	154.04	152.84	152.25
14000	174.10	168.53	166.72	166.27	165.89	164.60	163.96
15000	186.53	180.57	178.63	178.15	177.74	176.36	175.68
16000	198.97	192.61	190.54	190.03	189.58	188.11	187.39
17000	211.40	204.64	202.45	201.90	201.43	199.87	199.10
18000	223.84	216.68	214.36	213.78	213.28	211.63	210.81
19000	236.27	228.72	226.26	225.66	225.13	223.38	222.52
20000	248.71	240.76	238.17	237.53	236.98	235.14	234.23
21000	261.14	252.79	250.08	249.41	248.83	246.90	245.94
22000	273.58	264.83	261.99	261.29	260.68	258.65	257.66
23000	286.01	276.87	273.90	273.16	272.53	270.41	269.37
24000	298.45	288.91	285.81	285.04	284.37	282.17	281.08
25000	310.89	300.95	297.71	296.91	296.22	293.92	292.79
26000	323.32	312.98	309.62	308.79	308.07	305.68	304.50
27000	335.76	325.02	321.53	320.67	319.92	317.44	316.21
28000	348.19	337.06	333.44	332.54	331.77	329.19	327.92
29000	360.63	349.10	345.35	344.42	343.62	340.95	339.64
30000	373.06	361.13	357.26	356.30	355.47	352.71	351.35
31000	385.50	373.17	369.16	368.17	367.32	364.46	363.06
32000	397.93	385.21	381.07	380.05	379.16	376.22	374.77
33000	410.37	397.25	392.98	391.93	391.01	387.98	386.48
34000	422.80	409.28	404.89	403.80	402.86	399.73	398.19
35000	435.24	421.32	416.80	415.68	414.71	411.49	409.90
36000	447.67	433.36	428.71	427.56	426.56	423.25	421.62
37000	460.11	445.40	440.61	439.43	438.41	435.00	433.33
38000	472.54	457.43	452.52	451.31	450.26	446.76	445.04
39000	484.98	469.47	464.43	463.18	462.10	458.52	456.75
40000	497.41	481.51	476.34	475.06	473.95	470.27	468.46
45000	559.59	541.70	535.88	534.44	533.20	529.06	527.02
50000	621.77	601.89	595.42	593.82	592.44	587.84	585.58
55000	683.94	662.07	654.97	653.21	651.68	646.63	644.13
60000	746.12	722.26	714.51	712.59	710.93	705.41	702.69
65000	808.29	782.45	774.05	771.97	770.17	764.19	761.25
70000	870.47	842.64	833.59	831.35	829.42	822.98	819.80
75000	932.65	902.83	893.13	890.73	888.66	881.76	878.36
80000	994.82	963.01	952.67	950.12	947.90	940.54	936.92
85000	1057.00	1023.20	1012.22	1009.50	1007.15	999.33	995.47
90000	1119.17	1083.39	1071.76	1068.88	1066.39	1058.11	1054.03
95000	1181.35	1143.58	1131.30	1128.26	1125.63	1116.89	1112.59
100000	1243.53	1203.77	1190.84	1187.64	1184.88	1175.68	1171.15

14.25% MONTHLY AMORTIZING PAYMENTS

AMOUNT OF LOAN	NUMBER OF YEARS IN TERM						
	1	2	3	4	5	10	15
$ 25	2.25	1.21	.86	.69	.59	.40	.34
50	4.50	2.41	1.72	1.38	1.17	.79	.68
75	6.75	3.61	2.58	2.06	1.76	1.18	1.02
100	9.00	4.82	3.43	2.75	2.34	1.57	1.35
200	17.99	9.63	6.86	5.50	4.68	3.14	2.70
300	26.98	14.44	10.29	8.24	7.02	4.71	4.05
400	35.97	19.26	13.72	10.99	9.36	6.28	5.40
500	44.96	24.07	17.15	13.73	11.70	7.84	6.75
600	53.95	28.88	20.58	16.48	14.04	9.41	8.10
700	62.94	33.70	24.01	19.22	16.38	10.98	9.45
800	71.93	38.51	27.44	21.97	18.72	12.55	10.79
900	80.92	43.32	30.87	24.71	21.06	14.11	12.14
1000	89.91	48.14	34.30	27.46	23.40	15.68	13.49
2000	179.81	96.27	68.60	54.91	46.80	31.36	26.98
2500	224.77	120.33	85.75	68.64	58.50	39.20	33.72
3000	269.72	144.40	102.90	82.36	70.20	47.04	40.46
4000	359.62	192.53	137.20	109.81	93.60	62.71	53.95
5000	449.53	240.66	171.50	137.27	117.00	78.39	67.43
6000	539.43	288.79	205.80	164.72	140.39	94.07	80.92
7000	629.34	336.92	240.10	192.17	163.79	109.75	94.41
8000	719.24	385.05	274.40	219.62	187.19	125.42	107.89
9000	809.15	433.18	308.70	247.07	210.59	141.10	121.38
10000	899.05	481.32	343.00	274.53	233.99	156.78	134.86
11000	988.96	529.45	377.30	301.98	257.38	172.46	148.35
12000	1078.86	577.58	411.60	329.43	280.78	188.13	161.83
13000	1168.77	625.71	445.89	356.88	304.18	203.81	175.32
14000	1258.67	673.84	480.19	384.33	327.58	219.49	188.81
15000	1348.58	721.97	514.49	411.79	350.98	235.16	202.29
16000	1438.48	770.10	548.79	439.24	374.37	250.84	215.78
17000	1528.39	818.23	583.09	466.69	397.77	266.52	229.26
18000	1618.29	866.36	617.39	494.14	421.17	282.20	242.75
19000	1708.20	914.50	651.69	521.59	444.57	297.87	256.24
20000	1798.10	962.63	685.99	549.05	467.97	313.55	269.72
21000	1888.01	1010.76	720.29	576.50	491.36	329.23	283.21
22000	1977.91	1058.89	754.59	603.95	514.76	344.91	296.69
23000	2067.82	1107.02	788.89	631.40	538.16	360.58	310.18
24000	2157.72	1155.15	823.19	658.85	561.56	376.26	323.66
25000	2247.62	1203.28	857.48	686.31	584.96	391.94	337.15
26000	2337.53	1251.41	891.78	713.76	608.35	407.62	350.64
27000	2427.43	1299.54	926.08	741.21	631.75	423.29	364.12
28000	2517.34	1347.67	960.38	768.66	655.15	438.97	377.61
29000	2607.24	1395.81	994.68	796.11	678.55	454.65	391.09
30000	2697.15	1443.94	1028.98	823.57	701.95	470.32	404.58
31000	2787.05	1492.07	1063.28	851.02	725.34	486.00	418.06
32000	2876.96	1540.20	1097.58	878.47	748.74	501.68	431.55
33000	2966.86	1588.33	1131.88	905.92	772.14	517.36	445.04
34000	3056.77	1636.46	1166.18	933.37	795.54	533.03	458.52
35000	3146.67	1684.59	1200.48	960.83	818.94	548.71	472.01
36000	3236.58	1732.72	1234.78	988.28	842.34	564.39	485.49
37000	3326.48	1780.85	1269.07	1015.73	865.73	580.07	498.98
38000	3416.39	1828.99	1303.37	1043.18	889.13	595.74	512.47
39000	3506.29	1877.12	1337.67	1070.63	912.53	611.42	525.95
40000	3596.20	1925.25	1371.97	1098.09	935.93	627.10	539.44
45000	4045.72	2165.90	1543.47	1235.35	1052.92	705.48	606.87
50000	4495.24	2406.56	1714.96	1372.61	1169.91	783.87	674.29
55000	4944.77	2647.21	1886.46	1509.87	1286.90	862.26	741.72
60000	5394.29	2887.87	2057.96	1647.13	1403.89	940.64	809.15
65000	5843.82	3128.52	2229.45	1784.39	1520.88	1019.03	876.58
70000	6293.34	3369.18	2400.95	1921.65	1637.87	1097.42	944.01
75000	6742.86	3609.84	2572.44	2058.91	1754.86	1175.80	1011.44
80000	7192.39	3850.49	2743.94	2196.17	1871.85	1254.19	1078.87
85000	7641.91	4091.15	2915.44	2333.43	1988.84	1332.58	1146.30
90000	8091.44	4331.80	3086.93	2470.69	2105.83	1410.96	1213.73
95000	8540.96	4572.46	3258.43	2607.95	2222.82	1489.35	1281.16
100000	8990.48	4813.11	3429.92	2745.21	2339.81	1567.74	1348.58

44

MONTHLY AMORTIZING PAYMENTS 14.25%

AMOUNT OF LOAN	NUMBER OF YEARS IN TERM						
	20	25	28	29	30	35	40
$ 25	.32	.31	.31	.31	.31	.30	.30
50	.64	.62	.61	.61	.61	.60	.60
75	.95	.92	.91	.91	.91	.90	.90
100	1.27	1.23	1.22	1.21	1.21	1.20	1.20
200	2.53	2.45	2.43	2.42	2.41	2.40	2.39
300	3.79	3.67	3.64	3.63	3.62	3.59	3.58
400	5.05	4.90	4.85	4.83	4.82	4.79	4.77
500	6.31	6.12	6.06	6.04	6.03	5.98	5.96
600	7.58	7.34	7.27	7.25	7.23	7.18	7.15
700	8.84	8.57	8.48	8.46	8.44	8.38	8.35
800	10.10	9.79	9.69	9.66	9.64	9.57	9.54
900	11.36	11.01	10.90	10.87	10.85	10.77	10.73
1000	12.62	12.23	12.11	12.08	12.05	11.96	11.92
2000	25.24	24.46	24.21	24.15	24.10	23.92	23.84
2500	31.55	30.58	30.27	30.19	30.12	29.90	29.80
3000	37.86	36.69	36.32	36.23	36.14	35.88	35.75
4000	50.47	48.92	48.42	48.30	48.19	47.84	47.67
5000	63.09	61.15	60.53	60.37	60.24	59.80	59.59
6000	75.71	73.38	72.63	72.45	72.29	71.76	71.50
7000	88.33	85.61	84.73	84.52	84.33	83.72	83.42
8000	100.94	97.84	96.84	96.59	96.38	95.68	95.33
9000	113.56	110.07	108.94	108.67	108.43	107.64	107.25
10000	126.18	122.30	121.05	120.74	120.47	119.60	119.17
11000	138.79	134.53	133.15	132.81	132.52	131.55	131.08
12000	151.41	146.76	145.26	144.89	144.57	143.51	143.00
13000	164.03	158.99	157.36	156.96	156.61	155.47	154.92
14000	176.65	171.21	169.46	169.03	168.66	167.43	166.83
15000	189.26	183.44	181.57	181.11	180.71	179.39	178.75
16000	201.88	195.67	193.67	193.18	192.75	191.35	190.66
17000	214.50	207.90	205.78	205.25	204.80	203.31	202.58
18000	227.11	220.13	217.88	217.33	216.85	215.27	214.50
19000	239.73	232.36	229.99	229.40	228.90	227.23	226.41
20000	252.35	244.59	242.09	241.47	240.94	239.19	238.33
21000	264.97	256.82	254.19	253.55	252.99	251.14	250.25
22000	277.58	269.05	266.30	265.62	265.04	263.10	262.16
23000	290.20	281.28	278.40	277.69	277.08	275.06	274.08
24000	302.82	293.51	290.51	289.77	289.13	287.02	285.99
25000	315.43	305.74	302.61	301.84	301.18	298.98	297.91
26000	328.05	317.97	314.72	313.92	313.22	310.94	309.83
27000	340.67	330.20	326.82	325.99	325.27	322.90	321.74
28000	353.29	342.42	338.92	338.06	337.32	334.86	333.66
29000	365.90	354.65	351.03	350.14	349.36	346.82	345.58
30000	378.52	366.88	363.13	362.21	361.41	358.78	357.49
31000	391.14	379.11	375.24	374.28	373.46	370.73	369.41
32000	403.76	391.34	387.34	386.36	385.50	382.69	381.32
33000	416.37	403.57	399.45	398.43	397.55	394.65	393.24
34000	428.99	415.80	411.55	410.50	409.60	406.61	405.16
35000	441.61	428.03	423.65	422.58	421.65	418.57	417.07
36000	454.22	440.26	435.76	434.65	433.69	430.53	428.99
37000	466.84	452.49	447.86	446.72	445.74	442.49	440.91
38000	479.46	464.72	459.97	458.80	457.79	454.45	452.82
39000	492.08	476.95	472.07	470.87	469.83	466.41	464.74
40000	504.69	489.18	484.18	482.94	481.88	478.37	476.65
45000	567.78	550.32	544.70	543.31	542.11	538.16	536.24
50000	630.86	611.47	605.22	603.68	602.35	597.96	595.82
55000	693.95	672.62	665.74	664.05	662.58	657.75	655.40
60000	757.04	733.76	726.26	724.41	722.82	717.55	714.98
65000	820.12	794.91	786.78	784.78	783.05	777.34	774.56
70000	883.21	856.05	847.30	845.15	843.29	837.14	834.14
75000	946.29	917.20	907.82	905.51	903.52	896.93	893.72
80000	1009.38	978.35	968.35	965.88	963.75	956.73	953.30
85000	1072.47	1039.49	1028.87	1026.25	1023.99	1016.52	1012.88
90000	1135.55	1100.64	1089.39	1086.62	1084.22	1076.32	1072.47
95000	1198.64	1161.79	1149.91	1146.98	1144.46	1136.11	1132.05
100000	1261.72	1222.93	1210.43	1207.35	1204.69	1195.91	1191.63

45

14.50% MONTHLY AMORTIZING PAYMENTS

AMOUNT OF LOAN	NUMBER OF YEARS IN TERM						
	1	2	3	4	5	10	15
$ 25	2.26	1.21	.87	.69	.59	.40	.35
50	4.51	2.42	1.73	1.38	1.18	.80	.69
75	6.76	3.62	2.59	2.07	1.77	1.19	1.03
100	9.01	4.83	3.45	2.76	2.36	1.59	1.37
200	18.01	9.65	6.89	5.52	4.71	3.17	2.74
300	27.01	14.48	10.33	8.28	7.06	4.75	4.10
400	36.01	19.30	13.77	11.04	9.42	6.34	5.47
500	45.02	24.13	17.22	13.79	11.77	7.92	6.83
600	54.02	28.95	20.66	16.55	14.12	9.50	8.20
700	63.02	33.78	24.10	19.31	16.47	11.09	9.56
800	72.02	38.60	27.54	22.07	18.83	12.67	10.93
900	81.03	43.43	30.98	24.83	21.18	14.25	12.29
1000	90.03	48.25	34.43	27.58	23.53	15.83	13.66
2000	180.05	96.50	68.85	55.16	47.06	31.66	27.32
2500	225.06	120.63	86.06	68.95	58.83	39.58	34.14
3000	270.07	144.75	103.27	82.74	70.59	47.49	40.97
4000	360.10	193.00	137.69	110.32	94.12	63.32	54.63
5000	450.12	241.25	172.11	137.89	117.65	79.15	68.28
6000	540.14	289.50	206.53	165.47	141.17	94.98	81.94
7000	630.16	337.75	240.95	193.05	164.70	110.81	95.59
8000	720.19	386.00	275.37	220.63	188.23	126.63	109.25
9000	810.21	434.25	309.79	248.21	211.76	142.46	122.90
10000	900.23	482.50	344.21	275.78	235.29	158.29	136.56
11000	990.25	530.75	378.64	303.36	258.82	174.12	150.21
12000	1080.28	579.00	413.06	330.94	282.34	189.95	163.87
13000	1170.30	627.25	447.48	358.52	305.87	205.78	177.52
14000	1260.32	675.50	481.90	386.10	329.40	221.61	191.18
15000	1350.34	723.75	516.32	413.67	352.93	237.44	204.83
16000	1440.37	772.00	550.74	441.25	376.46	253.26	218.49
17000	1530.39	820.25	585.16	468.83	399.99	269.09	232.14
18000	1620.41	868.49	619.58	496.41	423.51	284.92	245.80
19000	1710.43	916.74	654.00	523.99	447.04	300.75	259.45
20000	1800.46	964.99	688.42	551.56	470.57	316.58	273.11
21000	1890.48	1013.24	722.85	579.14	494.10	332.41	286.76
22000	1980.50	1061.49	757.27	606.72	517.63	348.24	300.42
23000	2070.52	1109.74	791.69	634.30	541.16	364.06	314.07
24000	2160.55	1157.99	826.11	661.88	564.68	379.89	327.73
25000	2250.57	1206.24	860.53	689.45	588.21	395.72	341.38
26000	2340.59	1254.49	894.95	717.03	611.74	411.55	355.04
27000	2430.61	1302.74	929.37	744.61	635.27	427.38	368.69
28000	2520.64	1350.99	963.79	772.19	658.80	443.21	382.35
29000	2610.66	1399.24	998.21	799.77	682.33	459.04	396.00
30000	2700.68	1447.49	1032.63	827.34	705.85	474.87	409.66
31000	2790.70	1495.74	1067.06	854.92	729.38	490.69	423.31
32000	2880.73	1543.99	1101.48	882.50	752.91	506.52	436.97
33000	2970.75	1592.24	1135.90	910.08	776.44	522.35	450.62
34000	3060.77	1640.49	1170.32	937.66	799.97	538.18	464.28
35000	3150.79	1688.73	1204.74	965.23	823.49	554.01	477.93
36000	3240.82	1736.98	1239.16	992.81	847.02	569.84	491.59
37000	3330.84	1785.23	1273.58	1020.39	870.55	585.67	505.24
38000	3420.86	1833.48	1308.00	1047.97	894.08	601.49	518.90
39000	3510.88	1881.73	1342.42	1075.55	917.61	617.32	532.55
40000	3600.91	1929.98	1376.84	1103.12	941.14	633.15	546.21
45000	4051.02	2171.23	1548.95	1241.01	1058.78	712.30	614.48
50000	4501.13	2412.48	1721.05	1378.90	1176.42	791.44	682.76
55000	4951.25	2653.72	1893.16	1516.79	1294.06	870.58	751.03
60000	5401.36	2894.97	2065.26	1654.68	1411.70	949.73	819.31
65000	5851.47	3136.22	2237.37	1792.57	1529.34	1028.87	887.58
70000	6301.58	3377.46	2409.47	1930.46	1646.98	1108.01	955.86
75000	6751.70	3618.71	2581.58	2068.35	1764.63	1187.16	1024.13
80000	7201.81	3859.96	2753.68	2206.24	1882.27	1266.30	1092.41
85000	7651.92	4101.21	2925.79	2344.13	1999.91	1345.44	1160.68
90000	8102.03	4342.45	3097.89	2482.02	2117.55	1424.59	1228.96
95000	8552.15	4583.70	3270.00	2619.91	2235.19	1503.73	1297.23
100000	9002.26	4824.95	3442.10	2757.80	2352.83	1582.87	1365.51

46

MONTHLY AMORTIZING PAYMENTS 14.50%

AMOUNT OF LOAN	NUMBER OF YEARS IN TERM						
	20	25	28	29	30	35	40
$ 25	.32	.32	.31	.31	.31	.31	.31
50	.64	.63	.62	.62	.62	.61	.61
75	.96	.94	.93	.93	.92	.92	.91
100	1.28	1.25	1.24	1.23	1.23	1.22	1.22
200	2.56	2.49	2.47	2.46	2.45	2.44	2.43
300	3.84	3.73	3.70	3.69	3.68	3.65	3.64
400	5.12	4.97	4.93	4.91	4.90	4.87	4.85
500	6.40	6.22	6.16	6.14	6.13	6.09	6.07
600	7.68	7.46	7.39	7.37	7.35	7.30	7.28
700	8.96	8.70	8.62	8.59	8.58	8.52	8.49
800	10.24	9.94	9.85	9.82	9.80	9.73	9.70
900	11.52	11.18	11.08	11.05	11.03	10.95	10.91
1000	12.80	12.43	12.31	12.28	12.25	12.17	12.13
2000	25.60	24.85	24.61	24.55	24.50	24.33	24.25
2500	32.00	31.06	30.76	30.68	30.62	30.41	30.31
3000	38.40	37.27	36.91	36.82	36.74	36.49	36.37
4000	51.20	49.69	49.21	49.09	48.99	48.65	48.49
5000	64.00	62.11	61.51	61.36	61.23	60.81	60.61
6000	76.80	74.53	73.81	73.63	73.48	72.98	72.73
7000	89.60	86.96	86.11	85.90	85.72	85.14	84.85
8000	102.40	99.38	98.41	98.17	97.97	97.30	96.98
9000	115.20	111.80	110.71	110.44	110.22	109.46	109.10
10000	128.00	124.22	123.01	122.72	122.46	121.62	121.22
11000	140.80	136.64	135.31	134.99	134.71	133.78	133.34
12000	153.60	149.06	147.61	147.26	146.95	145.95	145.46
13000	166.60	161.49	159.91	159.53	159.20	158.11	157.58
14000	179.20	173.91	172.22	171.80	171.44	170.27	169.70
15000	192.00	186.33	184.52	184.07	183.69	182.43	181.82
16000	204.80	198.75	196.82	196.34	195.93	194.59	193.95
17000	217.60	211.17	209.12	208.61	208.18	206.75	206.07
18000	230.40	223.59	221.42	220.88	220.43	218.92	218.19
19000	243.20	236.02	233.72	233.16	232.67	231.08	230.31
20000	256.00	248.44	246.02	245.43	244.92	243.24	242.43
21000	268.80	260.86	258.32	257.70	257.16	255.40	254.55
22000	281.60	273.28	270.62	269.97	269.41	267.56	266.67
23000	294.40	285.70	282.92	282.24	281.65	279.72	278.80
24000	307.20	298.12	295.22	294.51	293.90	291.89	290.92
25000	320.00	310.55	307.52	306.78	306.14	304.05	303.04
26000	332.80	322.97	319.82	319.05	318.39	316.21	315.16
27000	345.60	335.39	332.12	331.32	330.64	328.37	327.28
28000	358.40	347.81	344.43	343.60	342.88	340.53	339.40
29000	371.20	360.23	356.73	355.87	355.13	352.69	351.52
30000	384.00	372.65	369.03	368.14	367.37	364.86	363.64
31000	396.80	385.08	381.33	380.41	379.62	377.02	375.77
32000	409.60	397.50	393.63	392.68	391.86	389.18	387.89
33000	422.40	409.92	405.93	404.95	404.11	401.34	400.01
34000	435.20	422.34	418.23	417.22	416.35	413.50	412.13
35000	448.00	434.76	430.53	429.49	428.60	425.66	424.25
36000	460.80	447.18	442.83	441.76	440.85	437.83	436.37
37000	473.60	459.61	455.13	454.04	453.09	449.99	448.49
38000	486.40	472.03	467.43	466.31	465.34	462.15	460.62
39000	499.20	484.45	479.73	478.58	477.58	474.31	472.74
40000	512.00	496.87	492.03	490.85	489.83	486.47	484.86
45000	576.00	558.98	553.54	552.20	551.06	547.28	545.46
50000	640.00	621.09	615.04	613.56	612.28	608.09	606.07
55000	704.00	683.19	676.55	674.92	673.51	668.90	666.68
60000	768.00	745.30	738.05	736.27	734.74	729.71	727.28
65000	832.00	807.41	799.55	797.63	795.97	790.52	787.89
70000	896.00	869.52	861.06	858.98	857.19	851.32	848.50
75000	960.00	931.63	922.56	920.34	918.42	912.13	909.10
80000	1024.00	993.74	984.06	981.69	979.65	972.94	969.71
85000	1088.00	1055.84	1045.57	1043.05	1040.88	1033.75	1030.32
90000	1152.00	1117.95	1107.07	1104.40	1102.11	1094.56	1090.92
95000	1216.00	1180.06	1168.57	1165.76	1163.33	1155.37	1151.53
100000	1280.00	1242.17	1230.08	1227.12	1224.56	1216.18	1212.14

47

14.75% MONTHLY AMORTIZING PAYMENTS

AMOUNT OF LOAN	NUMBER OF YEARS IN TERM						
	1	2	3	4	5	10	15
$ 25	2.26	1.21	.87	.70	.60	.40	.35
50	4.51	2.42	1.73	1.39	1.19	.80	.70
75	6.77	3.63	2.60	2.08	1.78	1.20	1.04
100	9.02	4.84	3.46	2.78	2.37	1.60	1.39
200	18.03	9.68	6.91	5.55	4.74	3.20	2.77
300	27.05	14.52	10.37	8.32	7.10	4.80	4.15
400	36.06	19.35	13.82	11.09	9.47	6.40	5.54
500	45.08	24.19	17.28	13.86	11.83	8.00	6.92
600	54.09	29.03	20.73	16.63	14.20	9.59	8.30
700	63.10	33.86	24.19	19.40	16.57	11.19	9.68
800	72.12	38.70	27.64	22.17	18.93	12.79	11.07
900	81.13	43.54	31.09	24.94	21.30	14.39	12.45
1000	90.15	48.37	34.55	27.71	23.66	15.99	13.83
2000	180.29	96.74	69.09	55.41	47.32	31.97	27.66
2500	225.36	120.92	86.36	69.27	59.15	39.96	34.57
3000	270.43	145.11	103.63	83.12	70.98	47.95	41.48
4000	360.57	193.48	138.18	110.82	94.64	63.93	55.31
5000	450.71	241.84	172.72	138.53	118.30	79.91	69.13
6000	540.85	290.21	207.26	166.23	141.96	95.89	82.96
7000	630.99	338.58	241.81	193.93	165.62	111.87	96.78
8000	721.13	386.95	276.35	221.64	189.28	127.85	110.61
9000	811.27	435.32	310.89	249.34	212.94	143.83	124.43
10000	901.41	483.68	345.44	277.05	236.59	159.81	138.26
11000	991.55	532.05	379.98	304.75	260.25	175.79	152.08
12000	1081.69	580.42	414.52	332.46	283.91	191.77	165.91
13000	1171.83	628.79	449.06	360.16	307.57	207.75	179.73
14000	1261.97	677.16	483.61	387.86	331.23	223.74	193.56
15000	1352.11	725.52	518.15	415.57	354.89	239.72	207.38
16000	1442.25	773.89	552.69	443.27	378.55	255.70	221.21
17000	1532.39	822.26	587.24	470.98	402.21	271.68	235.03
18000	1622.53	870.63	621.78	498.68	425.87	287.66	248.86
19000	1712.67	919.00	656.32	526.38	449.52	303.64	262.68
20000	1802.81	967.36	690.87	554.09	473.18	319.62	276.51
21000	1892.95	1015.73	725.41	581.79	496.84	335.60	290.33
22000	1983.09	1064.10	759.95	609.50	520.50	351.58	304.16
23000	2073.23	1112.47	794.49	637.20	544.16	367.56	317.98
24000	2163.37	1160.84	829.04	664.91	567.82	383.54	331.81
25000	2253.51	1209.20	863.58	692.61	591.48	399.52	345.63
26000	2343.66	1257.57	898.12	720.31	615.14	415.50	359.46
27000	2433.80	1305.94	932.67	748.02	638.80	431.49	373.28
28000	2523.94	1354.31	967.21	775.72	662.45	447.47	387.11
29000	2614.08	1402.68	1001.75	803.43	686.11	463.45	400.93
30000	2704.22	1451.04	1036.30	831.13	709.77	479.43	414.76
31000	2794.36	1499.41	1070.84	858.83	733.43	495.41	428.58
32000	2884.50	1547.78	1105.38	886.54	757.09	511.39	442.41
33000	2974.64	1596.15	1139.92	914.24	780.75	527.37	456.23
34000	3064.78	1644.52	1174.47	941.95	804.41	543.35	470.06
35000	3154.92	1692.88	1209.01	969.65	828.07	559.33	483.88
36000	3245.06	1741.25	1243.55	997.36	851.73	575.31	497.71
37000	3335.20	1789.62	1278.10	1025.06	875.38	591.29	511.53
38000	3425.34	1837.99	1312.64	1052.76	899.04	607.27	525.36
39000	3515.48	1886.36	1347.18	1080.47	922.70	623.25	539.18
40000	3605.62	1934.72	1381.73	1108.17	946.36	639.23	553.01
45000	4056.32	2176.56	1554.44	1246.69	1064.66	719.14	622.13
50000	4507.02	2418.40	1727.16	1385.21	1182.95	799.04	691.26
55000	4957.73	2660.24	1899.87	1523.74	1301.24	878.95	760.38
60000	5408.43	2902.08	2072.59	1662.26	1419.54	958.85	829.51
65000	5859.13	3143.92	2245.30	1800.78	1537.83	1038.75	898.63
70000	6309.83	3385.76	2418.02	1939.30	1656.13	1118.66	967.76
75000	6760.53	3627.60	2590.73	2077.82	1774.42	1198.56	1036.88
80000	7211.24	3869.44	2763.45	2216.34	1892.72	1278.46	1106.01
85000	7661.94	4111.28	2936.16	2354.86	2011.01	1358.37	1175.13
90000	8112.64	4353.12	3108.88	2493.38	2129.31	1438.27	1244.26
95000	8563.34	4594.96	3281.59	2631.90	2247.60	1518.18	1313.38
100000	9014.04	4836.80	3454.31	2770.42	2365.90	1598.08	1382.51

MONTHLY AMORTIZING PAYMENTS 14.75%

AMOUNT OF LOAN	NUMBER OF YEARS IN TERM						
	20	25	28	29	30	35	40
$ 25	.33	.32	.32	.32	.32	.31	.31
50	.65	.64	.63	.63	.63	.62	.62
75	.98	.95	.94	.94	.94	.93	.93
100	1.30	1.27	1.25	1.25	1.25	1.24	1.24
200	2.60	2.53	2.50	2.50	2.49	2.48	2.47
300	3.90	3.79	3.75	3.75	3.74	3.71	3.70
400	5.20	5.05	5.00	4.99	4.98	4.95	4.94
500	6.50	6.31	6.25	6.24	6.23	6.19	6.17
600	7.80	7.57	7.50	7.49	7.47	7.42	7.40
700	9.09	8.84	8.75	8.73	8.72	8.66	8.63
800	10.39	10.10	10.00	9.98	9.96	9.90	9.87
900	11.69	11.36	11.25	11.23	11.21	11.13	11.10
1000	12.99	12.62	12.50	12.47	12.45	12.37	12.33
2000	25.97	25.23	25.00	24.94	24.89	24.73	24.66
2500	32.46	31.54	31.25	31.18	31.12	30.92	30.82
3000	38.96	37.85	37.50	37.41	37.34	37.10	36.99
4000	51.94	50.46	50.00	49.88	49.78	49.46	49.31
5000	64.92	63.08	62.49	62.35	62.23	61.83	61.64
6000	77.91	75.69	74.99	74.82	74.67	74.19	73.97
7000	90.89	88.31	87.49	87.29	87.12	86.56	86.29
8000	103.87	100.92	99.99	99.76	99.56	98.92	98.62
9000	116.86	113.54	112.49	112.23	112.01	111.29	110.95
10000	129.84	126.15	124.98	124.70	124.45	123.65	123.27
11000	142.82	138.77	137.48	137.17	136.90	136.02	135.60
12000	155.81	151.38	149.98	149.64	149.34	148.38	147.93
13000	168.79	164.00	162.48	162.11	161.79	160.75	160.25
14000	181.77	176.61	174.97	174.57	174.23	173.11	172.58
15000	194.76	189.22	187.47	187.04	186.68	185.48	184.91
16000	207.74	201.84	199.97	199.51	199.12	197.84	197.23
17000	220.73	214.45	212.47	211.98	211.57	210.21	209.56
18000	233.71	227.07	224.97	224.45	224.01	222.57	221.89
19000	246.69	239.68	237.46	236.92	236.46	234.94	234.21
20000	259.68	252.30	249.96	249.39	248.90	247.30	246.54
21000	272.66	264.91	262.46	261.86	261.34	259.66	258.87
22000	285.64	277.53	274.96	274.33	273.79	272.03	271.19
23000	298.63	290.14	287.45	286.80	286.23	284.39	283.52
24000	311.61	302.76	299.95	299.27	298.68	296.76	295.85
25000	324.59	315.37	312.45	311.74	311.12	309.12	308.17
26000	337.58	327.99	324.95	324.21	323.57	321.49	320.50
27000	350.56	340.60	337.45	336.68	336.01	333.85	332.83
28000	363.54	353.22	349.94	349.14	348.46	346.22	345.15
29000	376.53	365.83	362.44	361.61	360.90	358.58	357.48
30000	389.51	378.44	374.94	374.08	373.35	370.95	369.81
31000	402.50	391.06	387.44	386.55	385.79	383.31	382.13
32000	415.48	403.67	399.93	399.02	398.24	395.68	394.46
33000	428.46	416.29	412.43	411.49	410.68	408.04	406.79
34000	441.45	428.90	424.93	423.96	423.13	420.41	419.11
35000	454.43	441.52	437.43	436.43	435.57	432.77	431.44
36000	467.41	454.13	449.93	448.90	448.02	445.14	443.77
37000	480.40	466.75	462.42	461.37	460.46	457.50	456.09
38000	493.38	479.36	474.92	473.84	472.91	469.87	468.42
39000	506.36	491.98	487.42	486.31	485.35	482.23	480.75
40000	519.35	504.59	499.92	498.78	497.80	494.59	493.07
45000	584.26	567.66	562.41	561.12	560.02	556.42	554.71
50000	649.18	630.74	624.89	623.47	622.24	618.24	616.34
55000	714.10	693.81	687.38	685.82	684.47	680.07	677.97
60000	779.02	756.88	749.87	748.16	746.69	741.89	739.61
65000	843.94	819.96	812.36	810.51	808.91	803.71	801.24
70000	908.85	883.03	874.85	872.85	871.14	865.54	862.87
75000	973.77	946.10	937.34	935.20	933.36	927.36	924.51
80000	1038.69	1009.18	999.83	997.55	995.59	989.18	986.14
85000	1103.61	1072.25	1062.32	1059.89	1057.81	1051.01	1047.77
90000	1168.52	1135.32	1124.81	1122.24	1120.03	1112.83	1109.41
95000	1233.44	1198.40	1187.30	1184.59	1182.26	1174.66	1171.04
100000	1298.36	1261.47	1249.78	1246.93	1244.48	1236.48	1232.67

49

15.00% MONTHLY AMORTIZING PAYMENTS

AMOUNT OF LOAN	NUMBER OF YEARS IN TERM						
	1	2	3	4	5	10	15
$ 25	2.26	1.22	.87	.70	.60	.41	.35
50	4.52	2.43	1.74	1.40	1.19	.81	.70
75	6.77	3.64	2.60	2.09	1.79	1.22	1.05
100	9.03	4.85	3.47	2.79	2.38	1.62	1.40
200	18.06	9.70	6.94	5.57	4.76	3.23	2.80
300	27.08	14.55	10.40	8.35	7.14	4.85	4.20
400	36.11	19.40	13.87	11.14	9.52	6.46	5.60
500	45.13	24.25	17.34	13.92	11.90	8.07	7.00
600	54.16	29.10	20.80	16.70	14.28	9.69	8.40
700	63.19	33.95	24.27	19.49	16.66	11.30	9.80
800	72.21	38.79	27.74	22.27	19.04	12.91	11.20
900	81.24	43.64	31.20	25.05	21.42	14.53	12.60
1000	90.26	48.49	34.67	27.84	23.79	16.14	14.00
2000	180.52	96.98	69.34	55.67	47.58	32.27	28.00
2500	225.65	121.22	86.67	69.58	59.48	40.34	34.99
3000	270.78	145.46	104.00	83.50	71.37	48.41	41.99
4000	361.04	193.95	138.67	111.33	95.16	64.54	55.99
5000	451.30	242.44	173.33	139.16	118.95	80.67	69.98
6000	541.55	290.92	208.00	166.99	142.74	96.81	83.98
7000	631.81	339.41	242.66	194.82	166.53	112.94	97.98
8000	722.07	387.90	277.33	222.65	190.32	129.07	111.97
9000	812.33	436.38	311.99	250.48	214.11	145.21	125.97
10000	902.59	484.87	346.66	278.31	237.90	161.34	139.96
11000	992.85	533.36	381.32	306.14	261.69	177.47	153.96
12000	1083.10	581.84	415.99	333.97	285.48	193.61	167.96
13000	1173.36	630.33	450.65	361.80	309.27	209.74	181.95
14000	1263.62	678.82	485.32	389.64	333.06	225.87	195.95
15000	1353.88	727.30	519.98	417.47	356.85	242.01	209.94
16000	1444.14	775.79	554.65	445.30	380.64	258.14	223.94
17000	1534.40	824.28	589.32	473.13	404.43	274.27	237.93
18000	1624.65	872.76	623.98	500.96	428.22	290.41	251.93
19000	1714.91	921.25	658.65	528.79	452.01	306.54	265.93
20000	1805.17	969.74	693.31	556.62	475.80	322.67	279.92
21000	1895.43	1018.22	727.98	584.45	499.59	338.81	293.92
22000	1985.69	1066.71	762.64	612.28	523.38	354.94	307.91
23000	2075.95	1115.20	797.31	640.11	547.17	371.08	321.91
24000	2166.20	1163.68	831.97	667.94	570.96	387.21	335.91
25000	2256.46	1212.17	866.64	695.77	594.75	403.34	349.90
26000	2346.72	1260.66	901.30	723.60	618.54	419.48	363.90
27000	2436.98	1309.14	935.97	751.44	642.33	435.61	377.89
28000	2527.24	1357.63	970.63	779.27	666.12	451.74	391.89
29000	2617.50	1406.12	1005.30	807.10	689.91	467.88	405.89
30000	2707.75	1454.60	1039.96	834.93	713.70	484.01	419.88
31000	2798.01	1503.09	1074.63	862.76	737.49	500.14	433.88
32000	2888.27	1551.58	1109.30	890.59	761.28	516.28	447.87
33000	2978.53	1600.06	1143.96	918.42	785.07	532.41	461.87
34000	3068.79	1648.55	1178.63	946.25	808.86	548.54	475.86
35000	3159.05	1697.04	1213.29	974.08	832.65	564.68	489.86
36000	3249.30	1745.52	1247.96	1001.91	856.44	580.81	503.86
37000	3339.56	1794.01	1282.62	1029.74	880.23	596.94	517.85
38000	3429.82	1842.50	1317.29	1057.57	904.02	613.08	531.85
39000	3520.08	1890.98	1351.95	1085.40	927.81	629.21	545.84
40000	3610.34	1939.47	1386.62	1113.23	951.60	645.34	559.84
45000	4061.63	2181.90	1559.94	1252.39	1070.55	726.01	629.82
50000	4512.92	2424.34	1733.27	1391.54	1189.50	806.68	699.80
55000	4964.21	2666.77	1906.60	1530.70	1308.45	887.35	769.78
60000	5415.50	2909.20	2079.92	1669.85	1427.40	968.01	839.76
65000	5866.80	3151.64	2253.25	1809.00	1546.35	1048.68	909.74
70000	6318.09	3394.07	2426.58	1948.16	1665.30	1129.35	979.72
75000	6769.38	3636.50	2599.90	2087.31	1784.25	1210.02	1049.70
80000	7220.67	3878.94	2773.23	2226.46	1903.20	1290.68	1119.67
85000	7671.96	4121.37	2946.56	2365.62	2022.15	1371.35	1189.65
90000	8123.25	4363.80	3119.88	2504.77	2141.10	1452.02	1259.63
95000	8574.54	4606.24	3293.21	2643.93	2260.05	1532.69	1329.61
100000	9025.84	4848.67	3466.54	2783.08	2379.00	1613.35	1399.59

MONTHLY AMORTIZING PAYMENTS 15.00%

AMOUNT OF LOAN	NUMBER OF YEARS IN TERM						
	20	25	28	29	30	35	40
$ 25	.33	.33	.32	.32	.32	.32	.32
50	.66	.65	.64	.64	.64	.63	.63
75	.99	.97	.96	.96	.95	.95	.94
100	1.32	1.29	1.27	1.27	1.27	1.26	1.26
200	2.64	2.57	2.54	2.54	2.53	2.52	2.51
300	3.96	3.85	3.81	3.81	3.80	3.78	3.76
400	5.27	5.13	5.08	5.07	5.06	5.03	5.02
500	6.59	6.41	6.35	6.34	6.33	6.29	6.27
600	7.91	7.69	7.62	7.61	7.59	7.55	7.52
700	9.22	8.97	8.89	8.87	8.86	8.80	8.78
800	10.54	10.25	10.16	10.14	10.12	10.06	10.03
900	11.86	11.53	11.43	11.41	11.38	11.32	11.28
1000	13.17	12.81	12.70	12.67	12.65	12.57	12.54
2000	26.34	25.62	25.40	25.34	25.29	25.14	25.07
2500	32.92	32.03	31.74	31.67	31.62	31.43	31.34
3000	39.51	38.43	38.09	38.01	37.94	37.71	37.60
4000	52.68	51.24	50.79	50.68	50.58	50.28	50.13
5000	65.84	64.05	63.48	63.34	63.23	62.85	62.67
6000	79.01	76.85	76.18	76.01	75.87	75.41	75.20
7000	92.18	89.66	88.87	88.68	88.52	87.98	87.73
8000	105.35	102.47	101.57	101.35	101.16	100.55	100.26
9000	118.52	115.28	114.26	114.02	113.80	113.12	112.80
10000	131.68	128.09	126.96	126.68	126.45	125.69	125.33
11000	144.85	140.90	139.65	139.35	139.09	138.25	137.86
12000	158.02	153.70	152.35	152.02	151.74	150.82	150.39
13000	171.19	166.51	165.05	164.69	164.38	163.39	162.92
14000	184.36	179.32	177.74	177.36	177.03	175.96	175.46
15000	197.52	192.13	190.44	190.02	189.67	188.53	187.99
16000	210.69	204.94	203.13	202.69	202.32	201.10	200.52
17000	223.86	217.75	215.83	215.36	214.96	213.66	213.05
18000	237.03	230.55	228.52	228.03	227.60	226.23	225.59
19000	250.20	243.36	241.22	240.70	240.25	238.80	238.12
20000	263.36	256.17	253.91	253.36	252.89	251.37	250.65
21000	276.53	268.98	266.61	266.03	265.54	263.94	263.18
22000	289.70	281.79	279.30	278.70	278.18	276.50	275.71
23000	302.87	294.60	292.00	291.37	290.83	289.07	288.25
24000	316.03	307.40	304.69	304.04	303.47	301.64	300.78
25000	329.20	320.21	317.39	316.70	316.12	314.21	313.31
26000	342.37	333.02	330.09	329.37	328.76	326.78	325.84
27000	355.54	345.83	342.78	342.04	341.40	339.34	338.38
28000	368.71	358.64	355.48	354.71	354.05	351.91	350.91
29000	381.87	371.45	368.17	367.38	366.69	364.48	363.44
30000	395.04	384.25	380.87	380.04	379.34	377.05	375.97
31000	408.21	397.06	393.56	392.71	391.98	389.62	388.50
32000	421.38	409.87	406.26	405.38	404.63	402.19	401.04
33000	434.55	422.68	418.95	418.05	417.27	414.75	413.57
34000	447.71	435.49	431.65	430.72	429.92	427.32	426.10
35000	460.88	448.30	444.34	443.38	442.56	439.89	438.63
36000	474.05	461.10	457.04	456.05	455.20	452.46	451.17
37000	487.22	473.91	469.73	468.72	467.85	465.03	463.70
38000	500.39	486.72	482.43	481.39	480.49	477.59	476.23
39000	513.55	499.53	495.13	494.06	493.14	490.16	488.76
40000	526.72	512.34	507.82	506.72	505.78	502.73	501.29
45000	592.56	576.38	571.30	570.06	569.00	565.57	563.96
50000	658.40	640.42	634.77	633.40	632.23	628.41	626.62
55000	724.24	704.46	698.25	696.74	695.45	691.25	689.28
60000	790.08	768.50	761.73	760.08	758.67	754.09	751.94
65000	855.92	832.54	825.21	823.42	821.89	816.93	814.60
70000	921.76	896.59	888.68	886.76	885.12	879.77	877.26
75000	987.60	960.63	952.16	950.10	948.34	942.61	939.92
80000	1053.44	1024.67	1015.64	1013.44	1011.56	1005.46	1002.58
85000	1119.28	1088.71	1079.11	1076.78	1074.78	1068.30	1065.25
90000	1185.12	1152.75	1142.59	1140.12	1138.00	1131.14	1127.91
95000	1250.96	1216.79	1206.07	1203.46	1201.23	1193.98	1190.57
100000	1316.79	1280.84	1269.54	1266.80	1264.45	1256.82	1253.23

51

15.25% MONTHLY AMORTIZING PAYMENTS

AMOUNT OF LOAN	NUMBER OF YEARS IN TERM						
	1	2	3	4	5	10	15
$ 25	2.26	1.22	.87	.70	.60	.41	.36
50	4.52	2.44	1.74	1.40	1.20	.82	.71
75	6.78	3.65	2.61	2.10	1.80	1.23	1.07
100	9.04	4.87	3.48	2.80	2.40	1.63	1.42
200	18.08	9.73	6.96	5.60	4.79	3.26	2.84
300	27.12	14.59	10.44	8.39	7.18	4.89	4.26
400	36.16	19.45	13.92	11.19	9.57	6.52	5.67
500	45.19	24.31	17.40	13.98	11.97	8.15	7.09
600	54.23	29.17	20.88	16.78	14.36	9.78	8.51
700	63.27	34.03	24.36	19.58	16.75	11.41	9.92
800	72.31	38.89	27.84	22.37	19.14	13.03	11.34
900	81.34	43.75	31.31	25.17	21.53	14.66	12.76
1000	90.38	48.61	34.79	27.96	23.93	16.29	14.17
2000	180.76	97.22	69.58	55.92	47.85	32.58	28.34
2500	225.95	121.52	86.97	69.90	59.81	40.72	35.42
3000	271.13	145.82	104.37	83.88	71.77	48.87	42.51
4000	361.51	194.43	139.16	111.84	95.69	65.15	56.67
5000	451.89	243.03	173.94	139.79	119.61	81.44	70.84
6000	542.26	291.64	208.73	167.75	143.53	97.73	85.01
7000	632.64	340.24	243.52	195.71	167.45	114.01	99.18
8000	723.02	388.85	278.31	223.67	191.38	130.30	113.34
9000	813.39	437.45	313.10	251.62	215.30	146.59	127.51
10000	903.77	486.06	347.88	279.58	239.22	162.87	141.68
11000	994.14	534.67	382.67	307.54	263.14	179.16	155.85
12000	1084.52	583.27	417.46	335.50	287.06	195.45	170.01
13000	1174.90	631.88	452.25	363.45	310.98	211.74	184.18
14000	1265.27	680.48	487.04	391.41	334.90	228.02	198.35
15000	1355.65	729.09	521.82	419.37	358.83	244.31	212.52
16000	1446.03	777.69	556.61	447.33	382.75	260.60	226.68
17000	1536.40	826.30	591.40	475.28	406.67	276.88	240.85
18000	1626.78	874.90	626.19	503.24	430.59	293.17	255.02
19000	1717.16	923.51	660.97	531.20	454.51	309.46	269.19
20000	1807.53	972.12	695.76	559.16	478.43	325.74	283.35
21000	1897.91	1020.72	730.55	587.12	502.35	342.03	297.52
22000	1988.28	1069.33	765.34	615.07	526.27	358.32	311.69
23000	2078.66	1117.93	800.13	643.03	550.20	374.60	325.86
24000	2169.04	1166.54	834.91	670.99	574.12	390.89	340.02
25000	2259.41	1215.14	869.70	698.95	598.04	407.18	354.19
26000	2349.79	1263.75	904.49	726.90	621.96	423.47	368.36
27000	2440.17	1312.35	939.28	754.86	645.88	439.75	382.53
28000	2530.54	1360.96	974.07	782.82	669.80	456.04	396.69
29000	2620.92	1409.56	1008.85	810.78	693.72	472.33	410.86
30000	2711.29	1458.17	1043.64	838.73	717.65	488.61	425.03
31000	2801.67	1506.78	1078.43	866.69	741.57	504.90	439.20
32000	2892.05	1555.38	1113.22	894.65	765.49	521.19	453.36
33000	2982.42	1603.99	1148.01	922.61	789.41	537.47	467.53
34000	3072.80	1652.59	1182.79	950.56	813.33	553.76	481.70
35000	3163.18	1701.20	1217.58	978.52	837.25	570.05	495.87
36000	3253.55	1749.80	1252.37	1006.48	861.17	586.33	510.03
37000	3343.93	1798.41	1287.16	1034.44	885.10	602.62	524.20
38000	3434.31	1847.01	1321.94	1062.40	909.02	618.91	538.37
39000	3524.68	1895.62	1356.73	1090.35	932.94	635.20	552.54
40000	3615.06	1944.23	1391.52	1118.31	956.86	651.48	566.70
45000	4066.94	2187.25	1565.46	1258.10	1076.47	732.92	637.54
50000	4518.82	2430.28	1739.40	1397.89	1196.07	814.35	708.38
55000	4970.70	2673.31	1913.34	1537.68	1315.68	895.79	779.22
60000	5422.58	2916.34	2087.28	1677.46	1435.29	977.22	850.05
65000	5874.47	3159.36	2261.22	1817.25	1554.89	1058.66	920.89
70000	6326.35	3402.39	2435.16	1957.04	1674.50	1140.09	991.73
75000	6778.23	3645.42	2609.10	2096.83	1794.11	1221.53	1062.57
80000	7230.11	3888.45	2783.04	2236.62	1913.71	1302.96	1133.40
85000	7681.99	4131.47	2956.97	2376.40	2033.32	1384.39	1204.24
90000	8133.87	4374.50	3130.91	2516.19	2152.93	1465.83	1275.08
95000	8585.76	4617.53	3304.85	2655.98	2272.53	1547.26	1345.92
100000	9037.64	4860.56	3478.79	2795.77	2392.14	1628.70	1416.75

MONTHLY AMORTIZING PAYMENTS 15.25%

AMOUNT OF LOAN	NUMBER OF YEARS IN TERM						
	20	25	28	29	30	35	40
$ 25	.34	.33	.33	.33	.33	.32	.32
50	.67	.66	.65	.65	.65	.64	.64
75	1.01	.98	.97	.97	.97	.96	.96
100	1.34	1.31	1.29	1.29	1.29	1.28	1.28
200	2.68	2.61	2.58	2.58	2.57	2.56	2.55
300	4.01	3.91	3.87	3.87	3.86	3.84	3.83
400	5.35	5.21	5.16	5.15	5.14	5.11	5.10
500	6.68	6.51	6.45	6.44	6.43	6.39	6.37
600	8.02	7.81	7.74	7.73	7.71	7.67	7.65
700	9.35	9.11	9.03	9.01	9.00	8.95	8.92
800	10.69	10.41	10.32	10.30	10.28	10.22	10.20
900	12.02	11.71	11.61	11.59	11.57	11.50	11.47
1000	13.36	13.01	12.90	12.88	12.85	12.78	12.74
2000	26.71	26.01	25.79	25.74	25.69	25.55	25.48
2500	33.39	32.51	32.24	32.17	32.12	31.93	31.85
3000	40.06	39.01	38.69	38.61	38.54	38.32	38.22
4000	53.42	52.02	51.58	51.47	51.38	51.09	50.96
5000	66.77	65.02	64.47	64.34	64.23	63.86	63.70
6000	80.12	78.02	77.37	77.21	77.07	76.64	76.43
7000	93.48	91.02	90.26	90.08	89.92	89.41	89.17
8000	106.83	104.03	103.15	102.94	102.76	102.18	101.91
9000	120.18	117.03	116.05	115.81	115.61	114.95	114.65
10000	133.53	130.03	128.94	128.68	128.45	127.72	127.39
11000	146.89	143.03	141.83	141.54	141.30	140.50	140.12
12000	160.24	156.04	154.73	154.41	154.14	153.27	152.86
13000	173.59	169.04	167.62	167.28	166.98	166.04	165.60
14000	186.95	182.04	180.51	180.15	179.83	178.81	178.34
15000	200.30	195.04	193.41	193.01	192.67	191.58	191.08
16000	213.65	208.05	206.30	205.88	205.52	204.35	203.81
17000	227.01	221.05	219.19	218.75	218.36	217.13	216.55
18000	240.36	234.05	232.09	231.61	231.21	229.90	229.29
19000	253.71	247.05	244.98	244.48	244.05	242.67	242.03
20000	267.06	260.06	257.88	257.35	256.90	255.44	254.77
21000	280.42	273.06	270.77	270.22	269.74	268.21	267.50
22000	293.77	286.06	283.66	283.08	282.59	280.99	280.24
23000	307.12	299.06	296.56	295.95	295.43	293.76	292.98
24000	320.48	312.07	309.45	308.82	308.28	306.53	305.72
25000	333.83	325.07	322.34	321.68	321.12	319.30	318.46
26000	347.18	338.07	335.24	334.55	333.96	332.07	331.19
27000	360.54	351.07	348.13	347.42	346.81	344.84	343.93
28000	373.89	364.08	361.02	360.29	359.65	357.62	356.67
29000	387.24	377.08	373.92	373.15	372.50	370.39	369.41
30000	400.59	390.08	386.81	386.02	385.34	383.16	382.15
31000	413.95	403.09	399.70	398.89	398.19	395.93	394.88
32000	427.30	416.09	412.60	411.76	411.03	408.70	407.62
33000	440.65	429.09	425.49	424.62	423.88	421.48	420.36
34000	454.01	442.09	438.38	437.49	436.72	434.25	433.10
35000	467.36	455.10	451.28	450.36	449.57	447.02	445.84
36000	480.71	468.10	464.17	463.22	462.41	459.79	458.57
37000	494.07	481.10	477.07	476.09	475.25	472.56	471.31
38000	507.42	494.10	489.96	488.96	488.10	485.33	484.05
39000	520.77	507.11	502.85	501.82	500.94	498.11	496.79
40000	534.12	520.11	515.75	514.69	513.79	510.88	509.53
45000	600.89	585.12	580.21	579.03	578.01	574.74	573.22
50000	667.65	650.13	644.68	643.36	642.23	638.60	636.91
55000	734.42	715.15	709.15	707.70	706.46	702.46	700.60
60000	801.18	780.16	773.62	772.03	770.68	766.32	764.29
65000	867.95	845.17	838.08	836.37	834.90	830.17	827.98
70000	934.71	910.19	902.55	900.71	899.13	894.03	891.67
75000	1001.48	975.20	967.02	965.04	963.35	957.89	955.36
80000	1068.24	1040.21	1031.49	1029.38	1027.57	1021.75	1019.05
85000	1135.01	1105.22	1095.95	1093.71	1091.69	1085.61	1082.74
90000	1201.77	1170.24	1160.42	1158.05	1156.02	1149.47	1146.43
95000	1268.54	1235.25	1224.89	1222.38	1220.24	1213.33	1210.12
100000	1335.30	1300.26	1289.36	1286.72	1284.46	1277.19	1273.81

53

15.50% MONTHLY AMORTIZING PAYMENTS

AMOUNT OF LOAN	NUMBER OF YEARS IN TERM						
	1	2	3	4	5	10	15
$ 25	2.27	1.22	.88	.71	.61	.42	.36
50	4.53	2.44	1.75	1.41	1.21	.83	.72
75	6.79	3.66	2.62	2.11	1.81	1.24	1.08
100	9.05	4.88	3.50	2.81	2.41	1.65	1.44
200	18.10	9.75	6.99	5.62	4.82	3.29	2.87
300	27.15	14.62	10.48	8.43	7.22	4.94	4.31
400	36.20	19.49	13.97	11.24	9.63	6.58	5.74
500	45.25	24.37	17.46	14.05	12.03	8.23	7.17
600	54.30	29.24	20.95	16.86	14.44	9.87	8.61
700	63.35	34.11	24.44	19.66	16.84	11.51	10.04
800	72.40	38.98	27.93	22.47	19.25	13.16	11.48
900	81.45	43.86	31.42	25.28	21.65	14.80	12.91
1000	90.50	48.73	34.92	28.09	24.06	16.45	14.34
2000	180.99	97.45	69.83	56.17	48.11	32.89	28.68
2500	226.24	121.82	87.28	70.22	60.14	41.11	35.85
3000	271.49	146.18	104.74	84.26	72.16	49.33	43.02
4000	361.98	194.90	139.65	112.34	96.22	65.77	57.36
5000	452.48	243.63	174.56	140.43	120.27	82.21	71.70
6000	542.97	292.35	209.47	168.51	144.32	98.65	86.04
7000	633.47	341.08	244.38	196.60	168.38	115.09	100.38
8000	723.96	389.80	279.29	224.68	192.43	131.53	114.72
9000	814.45	438.53	314.20	252.77	216.48	147.97	129.06
10000	904.95	487.25	349.11	280.85	240.54	164.42	143.40
11000	995.44	535.97	384.02	308.94	264.59	180.86	157.74
12000	1085.94	584.70	418.93	337.02	288.64	197.30	172.08
13000	1176.43	633.42	453.84	365.11	312.70	213.74	186.42
14000	1266.93	682.15	488.75	393.19	336.75	230.18	200.76
15000	1357.42	730.87	523.67	421.28	360.80	246.62	215.10
16000	1447.92	779.60	558.58	449.36	384.86	263.06	229.44
17000	1538.41	828.32	593.49	477.45	408.91	279.50	243.78
18000	1628.90	877.05	628.40	505.53	432.96	295.94	258.12
19000	1719.40	925.77	663.31	533.62	457.02	312.39	272.46
20000	1809.89	974.50	698.22	561.70	481.07	328.83	286.80
21000	1900.39	1023.22	733.13	589.79	505.12	345.27	301.14
22000	1990.88	1071.94	768.04	617.87	529.18	361.71	315.48
23000	2081.38	1120.67	802.95	645.96	553.23	378.15	329.82
24000	2171.87	1169.39	837.86	674.04	577.28	394.59	344.16
25000	2262.37	1218.12	872.77	702.13	601.33	411.03	358.50
26000	2352.86	1266.84	907.68	730.21	625.39	427.47	372.84
27000	2443.35	1315.57	942.59	758.30	649.44	443.91	387.18
28000	2533.85	1364.29	977.50	786.38	673.49	460.35	401.52
29000	2624.34	1413.02	1012.41	814.47	697.55	476.80	415.86
30000	2714.84	1461.74	1047.33	842.55	721.60	493.24	430.20
31000	2805.33	1510.47	1082.24	870.64	745.65	509.68	444.54
32000	2895.83	1559.19	1117.15	898.72	769.71	526.12	458.88
33000	2986.32	1607.92	1152.06	926.81	793.76	542.56	473.22
34000	3076.82	1656.64	1186.97	954.89	817.81	559.00	487.56
35000	3167.31	1705.36	1221.88	982.98	841.87	575.44	501.90
36000	3257.80	1754.09	1256.79	1011.06	865.92	591.88	516.24
37000	3348.30	1802.81	1291.70	1039.14	889.97	608.32	530.58
38000	3438.79	1851.54	1326.61	1067.23	914.03	624.77	544.92
39000	3529.29	1900.26	1361.52	1095.31	938.08	641.21	559.26
40000	3619.78	1948.99	1396.43	1123.40	962.13	657.65	573.60
45000	4072.25	2192.61	1570.99	1263.82	1082.40	739.85	645.30
50000	4524.73	2436.23	1745.54	1404.25	1202.66	822.06	717.00
55000	4977.20	2679.85	1920.09	1544.67	1322.93	904.26	788.70
60000	5429.67	2923.48	2094.65	1685.10	1443.20	986.47	860.40
65000	5882.14	3167.10	2269.20	1825.52	1563.46	1068.67	932.10
70000	6334.61	3410.72	2443.75	1965.95	1683.73	1150.88	1003.80
75000	6787.09	3654.35	2618.31	2106.37	1803.99	1233.08	1075.50
80000	7239.56	3897.97	2792.86	2246.79	1924.26	1315.29	1147.20
85000	7692.03	4141.59	2967.41	2387.22	2044.53	1397.49	1218.90
90000	8144.50	4385.21	3141.97	2527.64	2164.79	1479.70	1290.60
95000	8596.97	4628.84	3316.52	2668.07	2285.06	1561.91	1362.30
100000	9049.45	4872.46	3491.07	2808.49	2405.32	1644.11	1434.00

54

MONTHLY AMORTIZING PAYMENTS 15.50%

AMOUNT OF LOAN	NUMBER OF YEARS IN TERM						
	20	25	28	29	30	35	40
$ 25	.34	.33	.33	.33	.33	.33	.33
50	.68	.66	.66	.66	.66	.65	.65
75	1.02	.99	.99	.99	.98	.98	.98
100	1.36	1.32	1.31	1.31	1.31	1.30	1.30
200	2.71	2.64	2.62	2.62	2.61	2.60	2.59
300	4.07	3.96	3.93	3.93	3.92	3.90	3.89
400	5.42	5.28	5.24	5.23	5.22	5.20	5.18
500	6.77	6.60	6.55	6.54	6.53	6.49	6.48
600	8.13	7.92	7.86	7.85	7.83	7.79	7.77
700	9.48	9.24	9.17	9.15	9.14	9.09	9.07
800	10.84	10.56	10.48	10.46	10.44	10.39	10.36
900	12.19	11.88	11.79	11.77	11.75	11.68	11.65
1000	13.54	13.20	13.10	13.07	13.05	12.98	12.95
2000	27.08	26.40	26.19	26.14	26.10	25.96	25.89
2500	33.85	33.00	32.74	32.67	32.62	32.44	32.36
3000	40.62	39.60	39.28	39.21	39.14	38.93	38.84
4000	54.16	52.79	52.37	52.27	52.19	51.91	51.78
5000	67.70	65.99	65.47	65.34	65.23	64.88	64.72
6000	81.24	79.19	78.56	78.41	78.28	77.86	77.67
7000	94.78	92.39	91.65	91.47	91.32	90.84	90.61
8000	108.32	105.58	104.74	104.54	104.37	103.81	103.56
9000	121.85	118.78	117.83	117.61	117.41	116.79	116.50
10000	135.39	131.98	130.93	130.67	130.46	129.76	129.44
11000	148.93	145.18	144.02	143.74	143.50	142.74	142.39
12000	162.47	59.37	157.11	156.81	156.55	155.72	155.33
13000	176.01	171.57	170.20	169.87	169.59	168.69	168.28
14000	189.55	184.77	183.30	182.94	182.64	181.67	181.22
15000	203.09	197.97	196.39	196.01	195.68	194.64	194.16
16000	216.63	211.16	209.48	209.07	208.73	207.62	207.11
17000	230.16	224.36	222.57	222.14	221.77	220.59	220.05
18000	243.70	237.56	235.66	235.21	234.82	233.57	233.00
19000	257.24	250.76	248.76	248.27	247.86	246.55	245.94
20000	270.78	263.95	261.85	261.34	260.91	259.52	258.88
21000	284.32	277.15	274.94	274.41	273.95	272.50	271.83
22000	297.86	290.35	288.03	287.47	287.00	285.47	284.77
23000	311.40	303.55	301.12	300.54	300.04	298.45	297.72
24000	324.94	316.74	314.22	313.61	313.09	311.43	310.66
25000	338.48	329.94	327.31	326.68	326.13	324.40	323.60
26000	352.01	343.14	340.40	339.74	339.18	337.38	336.55
27000	365.55	356.34	353.49	352.81	352.22	350.35	349.49
28000	379.09	369.53	366.59	365.88	365.27	363.33	362.44
29000	392.63	382.73	379.68	378.94	378.31	376.30	375.38
30000	406.17	395.93	392.77	392.01	391.36	389.28	388.32
31000	419.71	409.13	405.86	405.08	404.41	402.26	401.27
32000	433.25	422.32	418.95	418.14	417.45	415.23	414.21
33000	446.79	435.52	432.05	431.21	430.50	428.21	427.16
34000	460.32	448.72	445.14	444.28	443.54	441.18	440.10
35000	473.86	461.92	458.23	457.34	456.59	454.16	453.04
36000	487.40	475.11	471.32	470.41	469.63	467.14	465.99
37000	500.94	488.31	484.41	483.48	482.68	480.11	478.93
38000	514.48	501.51	497.51	496.54	495.72	493.09	491.88
39000	528.02	514.71	510.60	509.61	508.77	506.06	504.82
40000	541.56	527.90	523.69	522.68	521.81	519.04	517.76
45000	609.25	593.89	589.15	588.01	587.04	583.92	582.48
50000	676.95	659.88	654.61	653.35	652.26	648.80	647.20
55000	744.64	725.86	720.07	718.68	717.49	713.68	711.92
60000	812.33	791.85	785.53	784.01	782.72	778.56	776.64
65000	880.03	857.84	850.99	849.35	847.94	843.44	841.36
70000	947.72	923.83	916.46	914.68	913.17	908.31	906.08
75000	1015.42	989.81	981.92	980.02	978.39	973.19	970.80
80000	1083.11	1055.80	1047.38	1045.35	1043.62	1038.07	1035.52
85000	1150.80	1121.79	1112.84	1110.68	1108.84	1102.95	1100.24
90000	1218.50	1187.78	1178.30	1176.02	1174.07	1167.83	1164.96
95000	1286.19	1253.76	1243.76	1241.35	1239.30	1232.71	1229.68
100000	1353.89	1319.75	1309.22	1306.69	1304.52	1297.59	1294.40

15.75% MONTHLY AMORTIZING PAYMENTS

AMOUNT OF LOAN	NUMBER OF YEARS IN TERM						
	1	2	3	4	5	10	15
$ 25	2.27	1.23	.88	.71	.61	.42	.37
50	4.54	2.45	1.76	1.42	1.21	.83	.73
75	6.80	3.67	2.63	2.12	1.82	1.25	1.09
100	9.07	4.89	3.51	2.83	2.42	1.66	1.46
200	18.13	9.77	7.01	5.65	4.84	3.32	2.91
300	27.19	14.66	10.52	8.47	7.26	4.98	4.36
400	36.25	19.54	14.02	11.29	9.68	6.64	5.81
500	45.31	24.43	17.52	14.11	12.10	8.30	7.26
600	54.37	29.31	21.03	16.93	14.52	9.96	8.71
700	63.43	34.20	24.53	19.75	16.93	11.62	10.16
800	72.50	39.08	28.03	22.57	19.35	13.28	11.62
900	81.56	43.96	31.54	25.40	21.77	14.94	13.07
1000	90.62	48.85	35.04	28.22	24.19	16.60	14.52
2000	181.23	97.69	70.07	56.43	48.38	33.20	29.03
2500	226.54	122.11	87.59	70.54	60.47	41.49	36.29
3000	271.84	146.54	105.11	84.64	72.56	49.79	43.54
4000	362.46	195.38	140.14	112.85	96.75	66.39	58.06
5000	453.07	244.22	175.17	141.07	120.93	82.98	72.57
6000	543.68	293.07	210.21	169.28	145.12	99.58	87.08
7000	634.29	341.91	245.24	197.49	169.30	116.18	101.60
8000	724.91	390.75	280.27	225.70	193.49	132.77	116.11
9000	815.52	439.60	315.31	253.92	217.67	149.37	130.62
10000	906.13	488.44	350.34	282.13	241.86	165.96	145.14
11000	996.74	537.29	385.38	310.34	266.04	182.56	159.65
12000	1087.36	586.13	420.41	338.55	290.23	199.16	174.16
13000	1177.97	634.97	455.44	366.77	314.42	215.75	188.68
14000	1268.58	683.82	490.48	394.98	338.60	232.35	203.19
15000	1359.19	732.66	525.51	423.19	362.79	248.94	217.70
16000	1449.81	781.50	560.54	451.40	386.97	265.54	232.21
17000	1540.42	830.35	595.58	479.62	411.16	282.13	246.73
18000	1631.03	879.19	630.61	507.83	435.34	298.73	261.24
19000	1721.64	928.04	665.65	536.04	459.53	315.33	275.75
20000	1812.26	976.88	700.68	564.25	483.71	331.92	290.27
21000	1902.87	1025.72	735.71	592.47	507.90	348.52	304.78
22000	1993.48	1074.57	770.75	620.68	532.08	365.11	319.29
23000	2084.09	1123.41	805.78	648.89	556.27	381.71	333.81
24000	2174.71	1172.25	840.81	677.10	580.46	398.31	348.32
25000	2265.32	1221.10	875.85	705.32	604.64	414.90	362.83
26000	2355.93	1269.94	910.88	733.53	628.83	431.50	377.35
27000	2446.55	1318.79	945.92	761.74	653.01	448.09	391.86
28000	2537.16	1367.63	980.95	789.95	677.20	464.69	406.37
29000	2627.77	1416.47	1015.98	818.16	701.38	481.28	420.88
30000	2718.38	1465.32	1051.02	846.38	725.57	497.88	435.40
31000	2809.00	1514.16	1086.05	874.59	749.75	514.48	449.91
32000	2899.61	1563.00	1121.08	902.80	773.94	531.07	464.42
33000	2990.22	1611.85	1156.12	931.01	798.12	547.67	478.94
34000	3080.83	1660.69	1191.15	959.23	822.31	564.26	493.45
35000	3171.45	1709.54	1226.19	987.44	846.49	580.86	507.96
36000	3262.06	1758.38	1261.22	1015.65	870.68	597.46	522.48
37000	3352.67	1807.22	1296.25	1043.86	894.87	614.05	536.99
38000	3443.28	1856.07	1331.29	1072.08	919.05	630.65	551.50
39000	3533.90	1904.91	1366.32	1100.29	943.24	647.24	566.02
40000	3624.51	1953.75	1401.35	1128.50	967.42	663.84	580.53
45000	4077.57	2197.97	1576.52	1269.56	1088.35	746.82	653.09
50000	4530.63	2442.19	1751.69	1410.63	1209.28	829.80	725.66
55000	4983.70	2686.41	1926.86	1551.69	1330.20	912.78	798.22
60000	5436.76	2930.63	2102.03	1692.75	1451.13	995.76	870.79
65000	5889.82	3174.85	2277.20	1833.81	1572.06	1078.74	943.36
70000	6342.89	3419.07	2452.37	1974.87	1692.98	1161.71	1015.92
75000	6795.95	3663.29	2627.53	2115.94	1813.91	1244.69	1088.49
80000	7249.01	3907.50	2802.70	2257.00	1934.84	1327.67	1161.05
85000	7702.08	4151.72	2977.87	2398.06	2055.77	1410.65	1233.62
90000	8155.14	4395.94	3153.04	2539.12	2176.69	1493.63	1306.18
95000	8608.20	4640.16	3328.21	2680.18	2297.62	1576.61	1378.75
100000	9061.26	4884.38	3503.38	2821.25	2418.55	1659.59	1451.31

AMOUNT OF LOAN	NUMBER OF YEARS IN TERM						
	20	25	28	29	30	35	40
$ 25	.35	.34	.34	.34	.34	.33	.33
50	.69	.67	.67	.67	.67	.66	.66
75	1.03	1.01	1.00	1.00	1.00	.99	.99
100	1.38	1.34	1.33	1.33	1.33	1.32	1.32
200	2.75	2.68	2.66	2.66	2.65	2.64	2.64
300	4.12	4.02	3.99	3.99	3.98	3.96	3.95
400	5.50	5.36	5.32	5.31	5.30	5.28	5.27
500	6.87	6.70	6.65	6.64	6.63	6.60	6.58
600	8.24	8.04	7.98	7.97	7.95	7.91	7.90
700	9.61	9.38	9.31	9.29	9.28	9.23	9.21
800	10.99	10.72	10.64	10.62	10.60	10.55	10.53
900	12.36	12.06	11.97	11.95	11.93	11.87	11.84
1000	13.73	13.40	13.30	13.27	13.25	13.19	13.16
2000	27.46	26.79	26.59	26.54	26.50	26.37	26.31
2500	34.32	33.49	33.23	33.17	33.12	32.96	32.88
3000	41.18	40.18	39.88	39.81	39.74	39.55	39.46
4000	54.91	53.58	53.17	53.07	52.99	52.73	52.61
5000	68.63	66.97	66.46	66.34	66.24	65.91	65.76
6000	82.36	80.36	79.75	79.61	79.48	79.09	78.91
7000	96.08	93.76	93.04	92.87	92.73	92.27	92.06
8000	109.81	107.15	106.34	106.14	105.97	105.45	105.21
9000	123.53	120.54	119.63	119.41	119.22	118.63	118.36
10000	137.26	133.93	132.92	132.67	132.47	131.81	131.51
11000	150.98	147.33	146.21	145.94	145.71	144.99	144.66
12000	164.71	160.72	159.50	159.21	158.96	158.17	157.81
13000	178.43	174.11	172.79	172.47	172.21	171.35	170.96
14000	192.16	187.51	186.08	185.74	185.45	184.53	184.11
15000	205.89	200.90	199.37	199.01	198.70	197.71	197.26
16000	219.61	214.29	212.67	212.28	211.94	210.89	210.41
17000	233.34	227.68	225.96	225.54	225.19	224.07	223.56
18000	247.06	241.08	239.25	238.81	238.44	237.25	236.71
19000	260.79	254.47	252.54	252.08	251.68	250.43	249.86
20000	274.51	267.86	265.83	265.34	264.93	263.61	263.01
21000	288.24	281.26	279.12	278.61	278.17	276.79	276.16
22000	301.96	294.65	292.41	291.88	291.42	289.97	289.31
23000	315.69	308.04	305.70	305.14	304.67	303.15	302.46
24000	329.41	321.43	319.00	318.41	317.91	316.33	315.61
25000	343.14	334.83	332.29	331.68	331.16	329.51	328.76
26000	356.86	348.22	345.58	344.94	344.41	342.69	341.91
27000	370.59	361.61	358.87	358.21	357.65	355.87	355.06
28000	384.31	375.01	372.16	371.48	370.90	369.05	368.21
29000	398.04	388.40	385.45	384.75	384.14	382.23	381.36
30000	411.77	401.79	398.74	398.01	397.39	395.41	394.51
31000	425.49	415.18	412.03	411.28	410.64	408.59	407.66
32000	439.22	428.58	425.33	424.55	423.88	421.77	420.81
33000	452.94	441.97	438.62	437.81	437.13	434.95	433.96
34000	466.67	455.36	451.91	451.08	450.37	448.13	447.11
35000	480.39	468.75	465.20	464.35	463.62	461.31	460.26
36000	494.12	482.15	478.49	477.61	476.87	474.49	473.41
37000	507.84	495.54	491.78	490.88	490.11	487.67	486.56
38000	521.57	508.94	505.07	504.15	503.36	500.85	499.71
39000	535.29	522.33	518.36	517.41	516.61	514.03	512.86
40000	549.02	535.72	531.66	530.68	529.85	527.21	526.01
45000	617.65	602.69	598.11	597.02	596.08	593.11	591.76
50000	686.27	669.65	664.57	663.35	662.31	659.01	657.51
55000	754.90	736.61	731.02	729.69	728.54	724.91	723.26
60000	823.53	803.58	797.48	796.02	794.78	790.81	789.01
65000	892.15	870.54	863.94	862.35	861.01	856.71	854.77
70000	960.78	937.51	930.39	928.69	927.24	922.61	920.52
75000	1029.41	1004.47	996.85	995.02	993.47	988.52	986.27
80000	1098.03	1071.44	1063.31	1061.36	1059.70	1054.42	1052.02
85000	1166.66	1138.40	1129.76	1127.69	1125.93	1120.32	1117.77
90000	1235.29	1205.37	1196.22	1194.03	1192.16	1186.22	1183.52
95000	1303.91	1272.33	1262.67	1260.36	1258.39	1252.12	1249.27
100000	1372.54	1339.29	1329.13	1326.70	1324.62	1318.02	1315.02

16.00% MONTHLY AMORTIZING PAYMENTS

AMOUNT OF LOAN	NUMBER OF YEARS IN TERM						
	1	2	3	4	5	10	15
$ 25	2.27	1.23	.88	.71	.61	.42	.37
50	4.54	2.45	1.76	1.42	1.22	.84	.74
75	6.81	3.68	2.64	2.13	1.83	1.26	1.11
100	9.08	4.90	3.52	2.84	2.44	1.68	1.47
200	18.15	9.80	7.04	5.67	4.87	3.36	2.94
300	27.22	14.69	10.55	8.51	7.30	5.03	4.41
400	36.30	19.59	14.07	11.34	9.73	6.71	5.88
500	45.37	24.49	17.58	14.18	12.16	8.38	7.35
600	54.44	29.38	21.10	17.01	14.60	10.06	8.82
700	63.52	34.28	24.61	19.84	17.03	11.73	10.29
800	72.59	39.18	28.13	22.68	19.46	13.41	11.75
900	81.66	44.07	31.65	25.51	21.89	15.08	13.22
1000	90.74	48.97	35.16	28.35	24.32	16.76	14.69
2000	181.47	97.93	70.32	56.69	48.64	33.51	29.38
2500	226.83	122.41	87.90	70.86	60.80	41.88	36.72
3000	272.20	146.89	105.48	85.03	72.96	50.26	44.07
4000	362.93	195.86	140.63	113.37	97.28	67.01	58.75
5000	453.66	244.82	175.79	141.71	121.60	83.76	73.44
6000	544.39	293.78	210.95	170.05	145.91	100.51	88.13
7000	635.12	342.75	246.10	198.39	170.23	117.26	102.81
8000	725.85	391.71	281.26	226.73	194.55	134.02	117.50
9000	816.58	440.67	316.42	255.07	218.87	150.77	132.19
10000	907.31	489.64	351.58	283.41	243.19	167.52	146.88
11000	998.04	538.60	386.73	311.75	267.50	181.27	161.56
12000	1088.78	587.56	421.89	340.09	291.82	201.12	176.25
13000	1179.51	636.53	457.05	368.43	316.14	217.77	190.94
14000	1270.24	685.49	492.20	396.77	340.46	234.52	205.62
15000	1360.97	734.45	527.36	425.11	364.78	251.27	220.31
16000	1451.70	783.41	562.52	453.45	389.09	268.03	235.00
17000	1542.43	832.38	597.67	481.79	413.41	284.78	249.68
18000	1633.16	881.34	632.83	510.13	437.73	301.53	264.37
19000	1723.89	930.30	667.99	538.47	462.05	318.28	279.06
20000	1814.62	979.27	703.15	566.81	486.37	335.03	293.75
21000	1905.35	1028.23	738.30	595.15	510.68	351.78	308.43
22000	1996.08	1077.19	773.46	623.49	535.00	368.53	323.12
23000	2086.81	1126.16	808.62	651.83	559.32	385.29	337.81
24000	2177.55	1175.12	843.77	680.17	583.64	402.04	352.49
25000	2268.28	1224.08	878.93	708.51	607.96	418.79	367.18
26000	2359.01	1273.05	914.09	736.85	632.27	435.54	381.87
27000	2449.74	1322.01	949.24	765.19	656.59	452.29	396.55
28000	2540.47	1370.97	984.40	793.53	680.91	469.04	411.24
29000	2631.20	1419.94	1019.56	821.87	705.23	485.79	425.93
30000	2721.93	1468.90	1054.72	850.21	729.55	502.54	440.62
31000	2812.66	1517.86	1089.87	878.55	753.86	519.30	455.30
32000	2903.39	1566.82	1125.03	906.89	778.18	536.05	469.99
33000	2994.12	1615.79	1160.19	935.23	802.50	552.80	484.68
34000	3084.85	1664.75	1195.34	963.57	826.82	569.55	499.36
35000	3175.59	1713.71	1230.50	991.91	851.14	586.30	514.05
36000	3266.32	1762.68	1265.66	1020.26	875.46	603.05	528.74
37000	3357.05	1811.64	1300.82	1048.60	899.77	619.80	543.42
38000	3447.78	1860.60	1335.97	1076.94	924.09	636.55	558.11
39000	3538.51	1909.57	1371.13	1105.28	948.41	653.31	572.80
40000	3629.24	1958.53	1406.29	1133.62	972.73	670.06	587.49
45000	4082.89	2203.34	1582.07	1275.32	1094.32	753.81	660.92
50000	4536.55	2448.16	1757.86	1417.02	1215.91	837.57	734.36
55000	4990.20	2692.98	1933.64	1558.72	1337.50	921.33	807.79
60000	5443.86	2937.79	2109.43	1700.42	1459.09	1005.08	881.23
65000	5897.51	3182.61	2285.21	1842.12	1580.68	1088.84	954.66
70000	6351.17	3427.42	2461.00	1983.82	1702.27	1172.60	1028.10
75000	6804.82	3672.24	2636.78	2125.53	1823.86	1256.35	1101.53
80000	7258.47	3917.05	2812.57	2267.23	1945.45	1340.11	1174.97
85000	7712.13	4161.87	2988.35	2408.93	2067.04	1423.87	1248.40
90000	8165.78	4406.68	3164.14	2550.63	2188.63	1507.62	1321.84
95000	8619.44	4651.50	3339.92	2692.33	2310.22	1591.38	1395.27
100000	9073.09	4896.32	3515.71	2834.03	2431.81	1675.14	1468.71

58

MONTHLY AMORTIZING PAYMENTS 16.00%

AMOUNT OF LOAN	NUMBER OF YEARS IN TERM						
	20	25	28	29	30	35	40
$ 25	.35	.34	.34	.34	.34	.34	.34
50	.70	.68	.68	.68	.68	.67	.67
75	1.05	1.02	1.02	1.02	1.01	1.01	1.01
100	1.40	1.36	1.35	1.35	1.35	1.34	1.34
200	2.79	2.72	2.70	2.70	2.69	2.68	2.68
300	4.18	4.08	4.05	4.05	4.04	4.02	4.01
400	5.57	5.44	5.40	5.39	5.38	5.36	5.35
500	6.96	6.80	6.75	6.74	6.73	6.70	6.68
600	8.35	8.16	8.10	8.09	8.07	8.04	8.02
700	9.74	9.52	9.45	9.43	9.42	9.37	9.35
800	11.14	10.88	10.80	10.78	10.76	10.71	10.69
900	12.53	12.23	12.15	12.13	12.11	12.05	12.03
1000	13.92	13.59	13.50	13.47	13.45	13.39	13.36
2000	27.83	27.18	26.99	26.94	26.90	26.77	26.72
2500	34.79	33.98	33.73	33.67	33.62	33.47	33.40
3000	41.74	40.77	40.48	40.41	40.35	40.16	40.07
4000	55.66	54.36	53.97	53.87	53.80	53.54	53.43
5000	69.57	67.95	67.46	67.34	67.24	66.93	66.79
6000	83.48	81.54	80.95	80.81	80.69	80.31	80.14
7000	97.39	95.13	94.44	94.28	94.14	93.70	93.50
8000	111.31	108.72	107.93	107.74	107.59	107.08	106.86
9000	125.22	122.30	121.42	121.21	121.03	120.47	120.21
10000	139.13	135.89	134.91	134.68	134.48	133.85	133.57
11000	153.04	149.48	148.40	148.15	147.93	147.24	146.93
12000	166.96	163.07	161.89	161.61	161.38	160.62	160.28
13000	180.87	176.66	175.39	175.08	174.82	174.01	173.64
14000	194.78	190.25	188.88	188.55	188.27	187.39	187.00
15000	208.69	203.84	202.37	202.02	201.72	200.78	200.35
16000	222.61	217.43	215.86	215.48	215.17	214.16	213.71
17000	236.52	231.02	229.35	228.95	228.61	227.54	227.07
18000	250.43	244.60	242.84	242.42	242.06	240.93	240.42
19000	264.34	258.19	256.33	255.89	255.51	254.31	253.78
20000	278.26	271.78	269.82	269.35	268.96	267.70	267.13
21000	292.17	285.37	283.31	282.82	282.40	281.08	280.49
22000	306.08	298.96	296.80	296.29	295.85	294.47	293.85
23000	319.99	312.55	310.29	309.76	309.30	307.85	307.20
24000	333.91	326.14	323.78	323.22	322.75	321.24	320.56
25000	347.82	339.73	337.28	336.69	336.19	334.62	333.92
26000	361.73	353.32	350.77	350.16	349.64	348.01	347.27
27000	375.64	366.90	364.26	363.63	363.09	361.39	360.63
28000	389.56	380.49	377.75	377.09	376.54	374.78	373.99
29000	403.47	394.08	391.24	390.56	389.98	388.16	387.34
30000	417.38	407.67	404.73	404.03	403.43	401.55	400.70
31000	431.29	421.26	418.22	417.50	416.88	414.93	414.06
32000	445.21	434.85	431.71	430.96	430.33	428.32	427.41
33000	459.12	448.44	445.20	444.43	443.77	441.70	440.77
34000	473.03	462.03	458.69	457.90	457.22	455.08	454.13
35000	486.94	475.62	472.18	471.37	470.67	468.47	467.48
36000	500.86	489.20	485.67	484.83	484.12	481.85	480.84
37000	514.77	502.79	499.17	498.30	497.57	495.24	494.19
38000	528.68	516.38	512.66	511.77	511.01	508.62	507.55
39000	542.59	529.97	526.15	525.24	524.46	522.01	520.91
40000	556.51	543.56	539.64	538.70	537.91	535.39	534.26
45000	626.07	611.50	607.09	606.04	605.15	602.32	601.05
50000	695.63	679.45	674.55	673.38	672.38	669.24	667.83
55000	765.20	747.39	742.00	740.71	739.62	736.16	734.61
60000	834.76	815.34	809.45	808.05	806.86	803.09	801.39
65000	904.32	883.28	876.91	875.39	874.10	870.01	868.18
70000	973.88	951.23	944.36	942.73	941.33	936.93	934.96
75000	1043.45	1019.17	1011.82	1010.06	1008.57	1003.86	1001.74
80000	1113.01	1087.12	1079.27	1077.40	1075.81	1070.78	1068.52
85000	1182.57	1155.06	1146.73	1144.74	1143.05	1137.70	1135.31
90000	1252.14	1223.00	1214.18	1212.08	1210.29	1204.63	1202.09
95000	1321.70	1290.95	1281.63	1279.41	1277.52	1271.55	1268.87
100000	1391.26	1358.89	1349.09	1346.75	1344.76	1338.47	1335.65

16.25% MONTHLY AMORTIZING PAYMENTS

AMOUNT OF LOAN	NUMBER OF YEARS IN TERM						
	1	2	3	4	5	10	15
$ 25	2.28	1.23	.89	.72	.62	.43	.38
50	4.55	2.46	1.77	1.43	1.23	.85	.75
75	6.82	3.69	2.65	2.14	1.84	1.27	1.12
100	9.09	4.91	3.53	2.85	2.45	1.70	1.49
200	18.17	9.82	7.06	5.70	4.90	3.39	2.98
300	27.26	14.73	10.59	8.55	7.34	5.08	4.46
400	36.34	19.64	14.12	11.39	9.79	6.77	5.95
500	45.43	24.55	17.65	14.24	12.23	8.46	7.44
600	54.51	29.45	21.17	17.09	14.68	10.15	8.92
700	63.60	34.36	24.70	19.93	17.12	11.84	10.41
800	72.68	39.27	28.23	22.78	19.57	13.53	11.89
900	81.77	44.18	31.76	25.63	22.01	15.22	13.38
1000	90.85	49.09	35.29	28.47	24.46	16.91	14.87
2000	181.70	98.17	70.57	56.94	48.91	33.82	29.73
2500	227.13	122.71	88.21	71.18	61.13	42.27	37.16
3000	272.55	147.25	105.85	85.41	73.36	50.73	44.59
4000	363.40	196.34	141.13	113.88	97.81	67.63	59.45
5000	454.25	245.42	176.41	142.35	122.26	84.54	74.31
6000	545.10	294.50	211.69	170.82	146.71	101.45	89.18
7000	635.95	343.58	246.97	199.28	171.16	118.36	104.04
8000	726.80	392.67	282.25	227.75	195.61	135.26	118.90
9000	817.65	441.75	317.53	256.22	220.06	152.17	133.76
10000	908.50	490.83	352.81	284.69	244.52	169.08	148.62
11000	999.35	539.91	388.09	313.16	268.97	185.99	163.48
12000	1090.20	589.00	423.37	341.63	293.42	202.89	178.35
13000	1181.04	638.08	458.65	370.10	317.87	219.80	193.21
14000	1271.89	687.16	493.93	398.56	342.32	236.71	208.07
15000	1362.74	736.24	529.21	427.03	366.77	253.62	222.93
16000	1453.59	785.33	564.49	455.50	391.22	270.52	237.79
17000	1544.44	834.41	599.77	483.97	415.67	287.43	252.65
18000	1635.29	883.49	635.06	512.44	440.12	304.34	267.52
19000	1726.14	932.58	670.34	540.91	464.58	321.25	282.38
20000	1816.99	981.66	705.62	569.37	489.03	338.15	297.24
21000	1907.84	1030.74	740.90	597.84	513.48	355.06	312.10
22000	1998.69	1079.82	776.18	626.31	537.93	371.97	326.96
23000	2089.54	1128.91	811.46	654.78	562.38	388.88	341.82
24000	2180.39	1177.99	846.74	683.25	586.83	405.78	356.69
25000	2271.24	1227.07	882.02	711.72	611.28	422.69	371.55
26000	2362.08	1276.15	917.30	740.19	635.73	439.60	386.41
27000	2452.93	1325.24	952.58	768.65	660.18	456.51	401.27
28000	2543.78	1374.32	987.86	797.12	684.64	473.41	416.13
29000	2634.63	1423.40	1023.14	825.59	709.09	490.32	430.99
30000	2725.48	1472.48	1058.42	854.06	733.54	507.23	445.86
31000	2816.33	1521.57	1093.70	882.53	757.99	524.14	460.72
32000	2907.18	1570.65	1128.98	911.00	782.44	541.04	475.58
33000	2998.03	1619.73	1164.26	939.46	806.89	557.95	490.44
34000	3088.88	1668.81	1199.54	967.93	831.34	574.86	505.30
35000	3179.73	1717.90	1234.83	996.40	855.79	591.77	520.16
36000	3270.58	1766.98	1270.11	1024.87	880.24	608.67	535.03
37000	3361.43	1816.06	1305.39	1053.34	904.70	625.58	549.89
38000	3452.27	1865.15	1340.67	1081.81	929.15	642.49	564.75
39000	3543.12	1914.23	1375.95	1110.28	953.60	659.40	579.61
40000	3633.97	1963.31	1411.23	1138.74	978.05	676.30	594.47
45000	4088.22	2208.72	1587.63	1281.09	1100.30	760.84	668.78
50000	4542.47	2454.14	1764.03	1423.43	1222.56	845.38	743.09
55000	4996.71	2699.55	1940.44	1565.77	1344.81	929.91	817.40
60000	5450.96	2944.96	2116.84	1708.11	1467.07	1014.45	891.71
65000	5905.20	3190.38	2293.24	1850.46	1589.33	1098.99	966.01
70000	6359.45	3435.79	2469.65	1992.80	1711.58	1183.53	1040.32
75000	6813.70	3681.20	2646.05	2135.14	1833.84	1268.06	1114.63
80000	7267.94	3926.62	2822.45	2277.48	1956.09	1352.60	1188.94
85000	7722.19	4172.03	2998.85	2419.83	2078.35	1437.14	1263.25
90000	8176.43	4417.44	3175.26	2562.17	2200.60	1521.67	1337.56
95000	8630.68	4662.86	3351.66	2704.51	2322.86	1606.21	1411.86
100000	9084.93	4908.27	3528.06	2846.85	2445.11	1690.75	1486.17

AMOUNT OF LOAN	NUMBER OF YEARS IN TERM						
	20	25	28	29	30	35	40
$ 25	.36	.35	.35	.35	.35	.34	.34
50	.71	.69	.69	.69	.69	.68	.68
75	1.06	1.04	1.03	1.03	1.03	1.02	1.02
100	1.42	1.38	1.37	1.37	1.37	1.36	1.36
200	2.83	2.76	2.74	2.74	2.73	2.72	2.72
300	4.24	4.14	4.11	4.11	4.10	4.08	4.07
400	5.65	5.52	5.48	5.47	5.46	5.44	5.43
500	7.06	6.90	6.85	6.84	6.83	6.80	6.79
600	8.47	8.28	8.22	8.21	8.19	8.16	8.14
700	9.88	9.65	9.59	9.57	9.56	9.52	9.50
800	11.29	11.03	10.96	10.94	10.92	10.88	10.86
900	12.70	12.41	12.33	12.31	12.29	12.24	12.21
1000	14.11	13.79	13.70	13.67	13.65	13.59	13.57
2000	28.21	27.58	27.39	27.34	27.30	27.18	27.13
2500	35.26	34.47	34.23	34.18	34.13	33.98	33.91
3000	42.31	41.36	41.08	41.01	40.95	40.77	40.69
4000	56.41	55.15	54.77	54.68	54.60	54.36	54.26
5000	70.51	68.93	68.46	68.35	68.25	67.95	67.82
6000	84.61	82.72	82.15	82.02	81.90	81.54	81.38
7000	98.71	96.50	95.84	95.68	95.55	95.13	94.95
8000	112.81	110.29	109.53	109.35	109.20	108.72	108.51
9000	126.91	124.07	123.22	123.02	122.85	122.31	122.07
10000	141.01	137.86	136.91	136.69	136.50	135.90	135.63
11000	155.11	151.64	150.60	150.36	150.15	149.49	149.20
12000	169.21	165.43	164.29	164.03	163.80	163.08	162.76
13000	183.31	179.22	177.99	177.69	177.45	176.67	176.32
14000	197.41	193.00	191.68	191.36	191.10	190.26	189.89
15000	211.51	206.79	205.37	205.03	204.75	203.85	203.45
16000	225.61	220.57	219.06	218.70	218.39	217.44	217.01
17000	239.71	234.36	232.75	232.37	232.04	231.03	230.58
18000	253.81	248.14	246.44	246.04	245.69	244.62	244.14
19000	267.91	261.93	260.13	259.70	259.34	258.21	257.70
20000	282.01	275.71	273.82	273.37	272.99	271.79	271.26
21000	296.11	289.50	287.51	287.04	286.64	285.38	284.83
22000	310.22	303.28	301.20	300.71	300.29	298.97	298.39
23000	324.32	317.07	314.89	314.38	313.94	312.56	311.95
24000	338.42	330.85	328.58	328.05	327.59	326.15	325.52
25000	352.52	344.64	342.28	341.71	341.24	339.74	339.08
26000	366.62	358.43	355.97	355.38	354.89	353.33	352.64
27000	380.72	372.21	369.66	369.05	368.54	366.92	366.21
28000	394.82	386.00	383.35	382.72	382.19	380.51	379.77
29000	408.92	399.78	397.04	396.39	395.84	394.10	393.33
30000	423.02	413.57	410.73	410.06	409.49	407.69	406.89
31000	437.12	427.35	424.42	423.72	423.13	421.28	420.46
32000	451.22	441.14	438.11	437.39	436.78	434.87	434.02
33000	465.32	454.92	451.80	451.06	450.43	448.46	447.58
34000	479.42	468.71	465.49	464.73	464.08	462.05	461.15
35000	493.52	482.49	479.18	478.40	477.73	475.64	474.71
36000	507.62	496.28	492.87	492.07	491.38	489.23	488.27
37000	521.72	510.07	506.57	505.74	505.03	502.82	501.83
38000	535.82	523.85	520.26	519.40	518.68	516.41	515.40
39000	549.92	537.64	533.95	533.07	532.33	530.00	528.96
40000	564.02	551.42	547.64	546.74	545.98	543.58	542.52
45000	634.53	620.35	616.09	615.08	614.23	611.53	610.34
50000	705.03	689.28	684.55	683.42	682.47	679.48	678.15
55000	775.53	758.20	753.00	751.77	750.72	747.43	745.97
60000	846.03	827.13	821.45	820.11	818.97	815.37	813.78
65000	916.53	896.06	889.91	888.45	887.21	883.32	881.60
70000	987.04	964.98	958.36	956.79	955.46	951.27	949.41
75000	1057.54	1033.91	1026.82	1025.13	1023.71	1019.22	1017.23
80000	1128.04	1102.84	1095.27	1093.48	1091.95	1087.16	1085.04
85000	1198.54	1171.77	1163.73	1161.82	1160.20	1155.11	1152.86
90000	1269.05	1240.69	1232.18	1230.16	1228.45	1223.06	1220.67
95000	1339.55	1309.62	1300.63	1298.50	1296.69	1291.01	1288.49
100000	1410.05	1378.55	1369.09	1366.84	1364.94	1358.95	1356.30

16.50% MONTHLY AMORTIZING PAYMENTS

AMOUNT OF LOAN	NUMBER OF YEARS IN TERM						
	1	2	3	4	5	10	15
$ 25	2.28	1.24	.89	.72	.62	.43	.38
50	4.55	2.47	1.78	1.43	1.23	.86	.76
75	6.83	3.70	2.66	2.15	1.85	1.28	1.13
100	9.10	4.93	3.55	2.86	2.46	1.71	1.51
200	18.20	9.85	7.09	5.72	4.92	3.42	3.01
300	27.30	14.77	10.63	8.58	7.38	5.12	4.52
400	36.39	19.69	14.17	11.44	9.84	6.83	6.02
500	45.49	24.61	17.71	14.30	12.30	8.54	7.52
600	54.59	29.53	21.25	17.16	14.76	10.24	9.03
700	63.68	34.45	24.79	20.02	17.21	11.95	10.53
800	72.78	39.37	28.33	22.88	19.67	13.66	12.03
900	81.88	44.29	31.87	25.74	22.13	15.36	13.54
1000	90.97	49.21	35.41	28.60	24.59	17.07	15.04
2000	181.94	98.41	70.81	57.20	49.17	34.13	30.08
2500	227.42	123.01	88.52	71.50	61.47	42.67	37.60
3000	272.91	147.61	106.22	85.80	73.76	51.20	45.12
4000	363.88	196.81	141.62	114.39	98.34	68.26	60.15
5000	454.84	246.02	177.03	142.99	122.93	85.33	75.19
6000	545.81	295.22	212.43	171.59	147.51	102.39	90.23
7000	636.78	344.42	247.84	200.18	172.10	119.45	105.26
8000	727.75	393.62	283.24	228.78	196.68	136.52	120.30
9000	818.71	442.83	318.64	257.38	221.27	153.58	135.34
10000	909.68	492.03	354.05	285.98	245.85	170.65	150.38
11000	1000.65	541.23	389.45	314.57	270.43	187.71	165.41
12000	1091.62	590.43	424.86	343.17	295.02	204.78	180.45
13000	1182.58	639.64	460.26	371.77	319.60	221.84	195.49
14000	1273.55	688.84	495.67	400.36	344.19	238.90	210.52
15000	1364.52	738.04	531.07	428.96	368.77	255.97	225.56
16000	1455.49	787.24	566.48	457.56	393.36	273.03	240.60
17000	1546.45	836.44	601.88	486.15	417.94	290.10	255.64
18000	1637.42	885.65	637.28	514.75	442.53	307.16	270.67
19000	1728.39	934.85	672.69	543.35	467.11	324.23	285.71
20000	1819.36	984.05	708.09	571.95	491.70	341.29	300.75
21000	1910.33	1033.25	743.50	600.54	516.28	358.35	315.78
22000	2001.29	1082.46	778.90	629.14	540.86	375.42	330.82
23000	2092.26	1131.66	814.31	657.74	565.45	392.48	345.86
24000	2183.23	1180.86	849.71	686.33	590.03	409.55	360.90
25000	2274.20	1230.06	885.11	714.93	614.62	426.61	375.93
26000	2365.16	1279.27	920.52	743.53	639.20	443.67	390.97
27000	2456.13	1328.47	955.92	772.12	663.79	460.74	406.01
28000	2547.10	1377.67	991.33	800.72	688.37	477.80	421.04
29000	2638.07	1426.87	1026.73	829.32	712.96	494.87	436.08
30000	2729.03	1476.08	1062.14	857.92	737.54	511.93	451.12
31000	2820.00	1525.28	1097.54	886.51	762.13	529.00	466.15
32000	2910.97	1574.48	1132.95	915.11	786.71	546.06	481.19
33000	3001.94	1623.68	1168.35	943.71	811.29	563.12	496.23
34000	3092.90	1672.88	1203.75	972.30	835.88	580.19	511.27
35000	3183.87	1722.09	1239.16	1000.90	860.46	597.25	526.30
36000	3274.84	1771.29	1274.56	1029.50	885.05	614.32	541.34
37000	3365.81	1820.49	1309.97	1058.09	909.63	631.38	556.38
38000	3456.78	1869.69	1345.37	1086.69	934.22	648.45	571.41
39000	3547.74	1918.90	1380.78	1115.29	958.80	665.51	586.45
40000	3638.71	1968.10	1416.18	1143.89	983.39	682.57	601.49
45000	4093.55	2214.11	1593.20	1286.87	1106.31	767.90	676.67
50000	4548.39	2460.12	1770.22	1429.86	1229.23	853.22	751.86
55000	5003.23	2706.13	1947.25	1572.84	1352.15	938.54	827.04
60000	5458.06	2952.15	2124.27	1715.83	1475.08	1023.86	902.23
65000	5912.90	3198.16	2301.29	1858.81	1598.00	1109.18	977.42
70000	6367.74	3444.17	2478.31	2001.80	1720.92	1194.50	1052.60
75000	6822.58	3690.18	2655.33	2144.78	1843.84	1279.82	1127.79
80000	7277.42	3936.19	2832.36	2287.77	1966.77	1365.14	1202.97
85000	7732.25	4182.20	3009.38	2430.75	2089.69	1450.46	1278.16
90000	8187.09	4428.22	3186.40	2573.74	2212.61	1535.79	1353.34
95000	8641.93	4674.23	3363.42	2716.72	2335.53	1621.11	1428.53
100000	9096.77	4920.24	3540.44	2859.71	2458.46	1706.43	1503.71

AMOUNT OF LOAN	NUMBER OF YEARS IN TERM						
	20	25	28	29	30	35	40
$ 25	.36	.35	.35	.35	.35	.35	.35
50	.72	.70	.70	.70	.70	.69	.69
75	1.08	1.05	1.05	1.05	1.04	1.04	1.04
100	1.43	1.40	1.39	1.39	1.39	1.38	1.38
200	2.86	2.80	2.78	2.78	2.78	2.76	2.76
300	4.29	4.20	4.17	4.17	4.16	4.14	4.14
400	5.72	5.60	5.56	5.55	5.55	5.52	5.51
500	7.15	7.00	6.95	6.94	6.93	6.90	6.89
600	8.58	8.39	8.34	8.33	8.32	8.28	8.27
700	10.01	9.79	9.73	9.71	9.70	9.66	9.64
800	11.44	11.19	11.12	11.10	11.09	11.04	11.02
900	12.87	12.59	12.51	12.49	12.47	12.42	12.40
1000	14.29	13.99	13.90	13.87	13.86	13.80	13.77
2000	28.58	27.97	27.79	27.74	27.71	27.59	27.54
2500	35.73	34.96	34.73	34.68	34.63	34.49	34.43
3000	42.87	41.95	41.68	41.61	41.56	41.39	41.31
4000	57.16	55.93	55.57	55.48	55.41	55.18	55.08
5000	71.45	69.92	69.46	69.35	69.26	68.98	68.85
6000	85.74	83.90	83.35	83.22	83.11	82.77	82.62
7000	100.03	97.88	97.24	97.09	96.97	96.57	96.39
8000	114.32	111.86	111.13	110.96	110.82	110.36	110.16
9000	128.61	125.85	125.03	124.83	124.67	124.16	123.93
10000	142.90	139.83	138.92	138.70	138.52	137.95	137.70
11000	157.18	153.81	152.81	152.57	152.37	151.74	151.47
12000	171.47	167.79	166.70	166.44	166.22	165.54	165.24
13000	185.76	181.78	180.59	180.31	180.07	179.33	179.01
14000	200.05	195.76	194.48	194.18	193.93	193.13	192.78
15000	214.34	209.74	208.37	208.05	207.78	206.92	206.55
16000	228.63	223.72	222.26	221.92	221.63	220.72	220.32
17000	242.92	237.71	236.16	235.79	235.48	234.51	234.09
18000	257.21	251.69	250.05	249.66	249.33	248.31	247.86
19000	271.50	265.67	263.94	263.53	263.18	262.10	261.63
20000	285.79	279.65	277.83	277.40	277.03	275.90	275.40
21000	300.07	293.64	291.72	291.27	290.89	289.69	289.17
22000	314.36	307.62	305.61	305.14	304.74	303.48	302.94
23000	328.65	321.60	319.50	319.01	318.59	317.28	316.71
24000	342.94	335.58	333.39	332.88	332.44	331.07	330.48
25000	357.23	349.57	347.29	346.75	346.29	344.87	344.24
26000	371.52	363.55	361.18	360.62	360.14	358.66	358.01
27000	385.81	377.53	375.07	374.49	373.99	372.46	371.78
28000	400.10	391.51	388.96	388.36	387.85	386.25	385.55
29000	414.39	405.50	402.85	402.23	401.70	400.05	399.32
30000	428.68	419.48	416.74	416.10	415.55	413.84	413.09
31000	442.96	433.46	430.63	429.97	429.40	427.64	426.86
32000	457.25	447.44	444.52	443.84	443.25	441.43	440.63
33000	471.54	461.43	458.42	457.71	457.10	455.22	454.40
34000	485.83	475.41	472.31	471.58	470.96	469.02	468.17
35000	500.12	489.39	486.20	485.44	484.81	482.81	481.94
36000	514.41	503.37	500.09	499.31	498.66	496.61	495.71
37000	528.70	517.36	513.98	513.18	512.51	510.40	509.48
38000	542.99	531.34	527.87	527.05	526.36	524.20	523.25
39000	557.28	545.32	541.76	540.92	540.21	537.99	537.02
40000	571.57	559.30	555.65	554.79	554.06	551.79	550.79
45000	643.01	629.22	625.11	624.14	623.32	620.76	619.64
50000	714.46	699.13	694.57	693.49	692.58	689.73	688.48
55000	785.90	769.04	764.02	762.84	761.84	758.70	757.33
60000	857.35	838.95	833.48	832.19	831.09	827.68	826.18
65000	928.79	908.86	902.94	901.54	900.35	896.65	895.03
70000	1000.24	978.78	972.39	970.88	969.61	965.62	963.88
75000	1071.68	1048.69	1041.85	1040.23	1038.87	1034.60	1032.72
80000	1143.13	1118.60	1111.30	1109.58	1108.12	1103.57	1101.57
85000	1214.57	1188.51	1180.76	1178.93	1177.38	1172.54	1170.42
90000	1286.02	1258.43	1250.22	1248.28	1246.64	1241.51	1239.27
95000	1357.46	1328.34	1319.67	1317.63	1315.90	1310.49	1308.12
100000	1428.91	1398.25	1389.13	1386.98	1385.15	1379.46	1376.96

63

16.75% MONTHLY AMORTIZING PAYMENTS

AMOUNT OF LOAN	NUMBER OF YEARS IN TERM						
	1	2	3	4	5	10	15
$ 25	2.28	1.24	.89	.72	.62	.44	.39
50	4.56	2.47	1.78	1.44	1.24	.87	.77
75	6.84	3.70	2.67	2.16	1.86	1.30	1.15
100	9.11	4.94	3.56	2.88	2.48	1.73	1.53
200	18.22	9.87	7.11	5.75	4.95	3.45	3.05
300	27.33	14.80	10.66	8.62	7.42	5.17	4.57
400	36.44	19.73	14.22	11.50	9.89	6.89	6.09
500	45.55	24.67	17.77	14.37	12.36	8.62	7.61
600	54.66	29.60	21.32	17.24	14.84	10.34	9.13
700	63.77	34.53	24.87	20.11	17.31	12.06	10.65
800	72.87	39.46	28.43	22.99	19.78	13.78	12.18
900	81.98	44.40	31.98	25.86	22.25	15.50	13.70
1000	91.09	49.33	35.53	28.73	24.72	17.23	15.22
2000	182.18	98.65	71.06	57.46	49.44	34.45	30.43
2500	227.72	123.31	88.83	71.82	61.80	43.06	38.04
3000	273.26	147.97	106.59	86.18	74.16	51.67	45.64
4000	364.35	197.29	142.12	114.91	98.88	68.89	60.86
5000	455.44	246.62	177.65	143.63	123.60	86.11	76.07
6000	546.52	295.94	213.18	172.36	148.32	103.34	91.28
7000	637.61	345.26	248.70	201.09	173.03	120.56	106.50
8000	728.69	394.58	284.23	229.81	197.75	137.78	121.71
9000	819.78	443.91	319.76	258.54	222.47	155.00	136.92
10000	910.87	493.23	355.29	287.26	247.19	172.22	152.14
11000	1001.95	542.55	390.82	315.99	271.91	189.44	167.35
12000	1093.04	591.87	426.35	344.72	296.63	206.67	182.56
13000	1184.12	641.19	461.87	373.44	321.34	223.89	197.78
14000	1275.21	690.52	497.40	402.17	346.06	241.11	212.99
15000	1366.30	739.84	532.93	430.89	370.78	258.33	228.20
16000	1457.38	789.16	568.46	459.62	395.50	275.55	243.42
17000	1548.47	838.48	603.99	488.34	420.22	292.77	258.63
18000	1639.56	887.81	639.52	517.07	444.94	310.00	273.84
19000	1730.64	937.13	675.05	545.80	469.65	327.22	289.06
20000	1821.73	986.45	710.57	574.52	494.37	344.44	304.27
21000	1912.81	1035.77	746.10	603.25	519.09	361.66	319.48
22000	2003.90	1085.09	781.63	631.97	543.81	378.88	334.70
23000	2094.99	1134.42	817.16	660.70	568.53	396.10	349.91
24000	2186.07	1183.74	852.69	689.43	593.25	413.33	365.12
25000	2277.16	1233.06	888.22	718.15	617.96	430.55	380.34
26000	2368.24	1282.38	923.74	746.88	642.68	447.77	395.55
27000	2459.33	1331.71	959.27	775.60	667.40	464.99	410.76
28000	2550.42	1381.03	994.80	804.33	692.12	482.21	425.97
29000	2641.50	1430.35	1030.33	833.06	716.84	499.43	441.19
30000	2732.59	1479.67	1065.86	861.78	741.56	516.66	456.40
31000	2823.68	1528.99	1101.39	890.51	766.27	533.88	471.61
32000	2914.76	1578.32	1136.91	919.23	790.99	551.10	486.83
33000	3005.85	1627.64	1172.44	947.96	815.71	568.32	502.04
34000	3096.93	1676.96	1207.97	976.68	840.43	585.54	517.25
35000	3188.02	1726.28	1243.50	1005.41	865.15	602.76	532.47
36000	3279.11	1775.61	1279.03	1034.14	889.87	619.99	547.68
37000	3370.19	1824.93	1314.56	1062.86	914.58	637.21	562.89
38000	3461.28	1874.25	1350.09	1091.59	939.30	654.43	578.11
39000	3552.36	1923.57	1385.61	1120.31	964.02	671.65	593.32
40000	3643.45	1972.89	1421.14	1149.04	988.74	688.87	608.53
45000	4098.88	2219.51	1598.78	1292.67	1112.33	774.98	684.60
50000	4554.31	2466.12	1776.43	1436.30	1235.92	861.09	760.67
55000	5009.74	2712.73	1954.07	1579.93	1359.51	947.20	836.73
60000	5465.17	2959.34	2131.71	1723.56	1483.11	1033.31	912.80
65000	5920.60	3205.95	2309.35	1867.19	1606.70	1119.41	988.86
70000	6376.04	3452.56	2487.00	2010.82	1730.29	1205.52	1064.93
75000	6831.47	3699.17	2664.64	2154.44	1853.88	1291.63	1141.00
80000	7286.90	3945.78	2842.28	2298.07	1977.47	1377.74	1217.06
85000	7742.33	4192.39	3019.92	2441.70	2101.06	1463.85	1293.13
90000	8197.76	4439.01	3197.56	2585.33	2224.66	1549.96	1369.19
95000	8653.19	4685.62	3375.21	2728.96	2348.25	1636.06	1445.26
100000	9108.62	4932.23	3552.85	2872.59	2471.84	1722.17	1521.33

64

MONTHLY AMORTIZING PAYMENTS 16.75%

AMOUNT OF LOAN	NUMBER OF YEARS IN TERM						
	20	25	28	29	30	35	40
$ 25	.37	.36	.36	.36	.36	.35	.35
50	.73	.71	.71	.71	.71	.70	.70
75	1.09	1.07	1.06	1.06	1.06	1.05	1.05
100	1.45	1.42	1.41	1.41	1.41	1.40	1.40
200	2.90	2.84	2.82	2.82	2.82	2.80	2.80
300	4.35	4.26	4.23	4.23	4.22	4.20	4.20
400	5.80	5.68	5.64	5.63	5.63	5.60	5.60
500	7.24	7.09	7.05	7.04	7.03	7.00	6.99
600	8.69	8.51	8.46	8.45	8.44	8.40	8.39
700	10.14	9.93	9.87	9.85	9.84	9.80	9.79
800	11.59	11.35	11.28	11.26	11.25	11.20	11.19
900	13.04	12.77	12.69	12.67	12.65	12.60	12.58
1000	14.48	14.18	14.10	14.08	14.06	14.00	13.98
2000	28.96	28.36	28.19	28.15	28.11	28.00	27.96
2500	36.20	35.45	35.24	35.18	35.14	35.00	34.95
3000	43.44	42.54	42.28	42.22	42.17	42.00	41.93
4000	57.92	56.72	56.37	56.29	56.22	56.00	55.91
5000	72.40	70.90	70.47	70.36	70.27	70.00	69.89
6000	86.87	85.08	84.56	84.43	84.33	84.00	83.86
7000	101.35	99.26	98.65	98.50	98.38	98.00	97.84
8000	115.83	113.44	112.74	112.58	112.44	112.00	111.82
9000	130.31	127.62	126.83	126.65	126.49	126.00	125.79
10000	144.79	141.80	140.93	140.72	140.54	140.00	139.77
11000	159.27	155.98	155.02	154.79	154.60	154.00	153.74
12000	173.74	170.16	169.11	168.86	168.65	168.00	167.72
13000	188.22	184.34	183.20	182.93	182.71	182.00	181.70
14000	202.70	198.52	197.29	197.00	196.76	196.00	195.67
15000	217.18	212.70	211.39	211.08	210.81	210.00	209.65
16000	231.66	226.88	225.48	225.15	224.87	224.00	223.63
17000	246.13	241.06	239.57	239.22	238.92	238.00	237.60
18000	260.61	255.24	253.66	253.29	252.98	252.00	251.58
19000	275.09	269.42	267.75	267.36	267.03	266.00	265.56
20000	289.57	283.60	281.85	281.43	281.08	280.00	279.53
21000	304.05	297.78	295.94	295.50	295.14	294.00	293.51
22000	318.53	311.96	310.03	309.58	309.19	308.00	307.48
23000	333.00	326.14	324.12	323.65	323.25	322.00	321.46
24000	347.48	340.32	338.21	337.72	337.30	336.00	335.44
25000	361.96	354.50	352.31	351.79	351.35	350.00	349.41
26000	376.44	368.68	366.40	365.86	365.41	364.00	363.39
27000	390.92	382.86	380.49	379.93	379.46	378.00	377.37
28000	405.39	397.04	394.58	394.00	393.52	392.00	391.34
29000	419.87	411.22	408.67	408.08	407.57	406.00	405.32
30000	434.35	425.40	422.77	422.15	421.62	420.00	419.30
31000	448.83	439.58	436.86	436.22	435.68	434.00	433.27
32000	463.31	453.76	450.95	450.29	449.73	448.00	447.25
33000	477.79	467.94	465.04	464.36	463.79	462.00	461.22
34000	492.26	482.12	479.14	478.43	477.84	476.00	475.20
35000	506.74	496.30	493.23	492.50	491.89	490.00	489.18
36000	521.22	510.48	507.32	506.58	505.95	504.00	503.15
37000	535.70	524.66	521.41	520.65	520.00	518.00	517.13
38000	550.18	538.84	535.50	534.72	534.06	532.00	531.11
39000	564.65	553.02	549.60	548.79	548.11	546.00	545.08
40000	579.13	567.20	563.69	562.86	562.16	560.00	559.06
45000	651.52	638.10	634.15	633.22	632.43	630.00	628.94
50000	723.91	709.00	704.61	703.58	702.70	699.99	698.82
55000	796.31	779.90	775.07	773.93	772.97	769.99	768.70
60000	868.70	850.80	845.53	844.29	843.24	839.99	838.59
65000	941.09	921.70	915.99	914.65	913.51	909.99	908.47
70000	1013.48	992.60	986.45	985.00	983.78	979.99	978.35
75000	1085.87	1063.50	1056.91	1055.36	1054.05	1049.99	1048.23
80000	1158.26	1134.40	1127.37	1125.72	1124.32	1119.99	1118.11
85000	1230.65	1205.30	1197.83	1196.07	1194.59	1189.99	1187.99
90000	1303.04	1276.20	1268.29	1266.43	1264.86	1259.99	1257.88
95000	1375.43	1347.10	1338.75	1336.79	1335.13	1329.99	1327.76
100000	1447.82	1418.00	1409.21	1407.15	1405.40	1399.98	1397.64

17.00% MONTHLY AMORTIZING PAYMENTS

AMOUNT OF LOAN	NUMBER OF YEARS IN TERM						
	1	2	3	4	5	10	15
$ 25	2.29	1.24	.90	.73	.63	.44	.39
50	4.57	2.48	1.79	1.45	1.25	.87	.77
75	6.85	3.71	2.68	2.17	1.87	1.31	1.16
100	9.13	4.95	3.57	2.89	2.49	1.74	1.54
200	18.25	9.89	7.14	5.78	4.98	3.48	3.08
300	27.37	14.84	10.70	8.66	7.46	5.22	4.62
400	36.49	19.78	14.27	11.55	9.95	6.96	6.16
500	45.61	24.73	17.83	14.43	12.43	8.69	7.70
600	54.73	29.67	21.40	17.32	14.92	10.43	9.24
700	63.85	34.61	24.96	20.20	17.40	12.17	10.78
800	72.97	39.56	28.53	23.09	19.89	13.91	12.32
900	82.09	44.50	32.09	25.97	22.37	15.65	13.86
1000	91.21	49.45	35.66	28.86	24.86	17.38	15.40
2000	182.41	98.89	71.31	57.72	49.71	34.76	30.79
2500	228.02	123.61	89.14	72.14	62.14	43.45	38.48
3000	273.62	148.33	106.96	86.57	74.56	52.14	46.18
4000	364.82	197.77	142.62	115.43	99.42	69.52	61.57
5000	456.03	247.22	178.27	144.28	124.27	86.90	76.96
6000	547.23	296.66	213.92	173.14	149.12	104.28	92.35
7000	638.44	346.10	249.57	201.99	173.97	121.66	107.74
8000	729.64	395.54	285.23	230.85	198.83	139.04	123.13
9000	820.85	444.99	320.88	259.70	223.68	156.42	138.52
10000	912.05	494.43	356.53	288.56	248.53	173.80	153.91
11000	1003.26	543.87	392.19	317.41	273.38	191.18	169.30
12000	1094.46	593.31	427.84	346.27	298.24	208.56	184.69
13000	1185.67	642.75	463.49	375.12	323.09	225.94	200.08
14000	1276.87	692.20	499.14	403.98	347.94	243.32	215.47
15000	1368.08	741.64	534.80	432.83	372.79	260.70	230.86
16000	1459.28	791.08	570.45	461.69	397.65	278.08	246.25
17000	1550.49	840.52	606.10	490.54	422.50	295.46	261.64
18000	1641.69	889.97	641.75	519.40	447.35	312.84	277.03
19000	1732.90	939.41	677.41	548.25	472.20	330.22	292.42
20000	1824.10	988.85	713.06	577.11	497.06	347.60	307.81
21000	1915.30	1038.29	748.71	605.96	521.91	364.98	323.20
22000	2006.51	1087.73	784.37	634.82	546.76	382.36	338.59
23000	2097.71	1137.18	820.02	663.67	571.61	399.74	353.98
24000	2188.92	1186.62	855.67	692.53	596.47	417.12	369.37
25000	2280.12	1236.06	891.32	721.38	621.32	434.50	384.76
26000	2371.33	1285.50	926.98	750.24	646.17	451.88	400.15
27000	2462.53	1334.95	962.63	779.09	671.02	469.26	415.54
28000	2553.74	1384.39	998.28	807.95	695.88	486.64	430.93
29000	2644.94	1433.83	1033.93	836.80	720.73	504.02	446.32
30000	2736.15	1483.27	1069.59	865.66	745.58	521.40	461.71
31000	2827.35	1532.72	1105.24	894.51	770.43	538.78	477.10
32000	2918.56	1582.16	1140.89	923.37	795.29	556.16	492.49
33000	3009.76	1631.60	1176.55	952.22	820.14	573.54	507.88
34000	3100.97	1681.04	1212.20	981.08	844.99	590.92	523.27
35000	3192.17	1730.48	1247.85	1009.93	869.85	608.30	538.66
36000	3283.38	1779.93	1283.50	1038.79	894.70	625.68	554.05
37000	3374.58	1829.37	1319.16	1067.64	919.55	643.06	569.44
38000	3465.79	1878.81	1354.81	1096.50	944.40	660.44	584.83
39000	3556.99	1928.25	1390.46	1125.35	969.26	677.82	600.22
40000	3648.20	1977.70	1426.11	1154.21	994.11	695.20	615.61
45000	4104.22	2224.91	1604.38	1298.48	1118.37	782.09	692.56
50000	4560.24	2472.12	1782.64	1442.76	1242.63	868.99	769.51
55000	5016.27	2719.33	1960.91	1587.03	1366.90	955.89	846.46
60000	5472.29	2966.54	2139.17	1731.31	1491.16	1042.79	923.41
65000	5928.31	3213.75	2317.43	1875.58	1615.42	1129.69	1000.36
70000	6384.34	3460.96	2495.70	2019.86	1739.69	1216.59	1077.31
75000	6840.36	3708.17	2673.96	2164.13	1863.95	1303.49	1154.26
80000	7296.39	3955.39	2852.22	2308.41	1988.21	1390.38	1231.21
85000	7752.41	4202.60	3030.49	2452.68	2112.47	1477.28	1308.16
90000	8208.43	4449.81	3208.75	2596.96	2236.74	1564.18	1385.11
95000	8664.46	4697.02	3387.01	2741.23	2361.00	1651.08	1462.06
100000	9120.48	4944.23	3565.28	2885.51	2485.26	1737.98	1539.01

AMOUNT OF LOAN	NUMBER OF YEARS IN TERM						
	20	25	28	29	30	35	40
$ 25	.37	.36	.36	.36	.36	.36	.36
50	.74	.72	.72	.72	.72	.72	.71
75	1.11	1.08	1.08	1.08	1.07	1.07	1.07
100	1.47	1.44	1.43	1.43	1.43	1.43	1.42
200	2.94	2.88	2.86	2.86	2.86	2.85	2.84
300	4.41	4.32	4.29	4.29	4.28	4.27	4.26
400	5.87	5.76	5.72	5.71	5.71	5.69	5.68
500	7.34	7.19	7.15	7.14	7.13	7.11	7.10
600	8.81	8.63	8.58	8.57	8.56	8.53	8.51
700	10.27	10.07	10.01	10.00	9.98	9.95	9.93
800	11.74	11.51	11.44	11.42	11.41	11.37	11.35
900	13.21	12.95	12.87	12.85	12.84	12.79	12.77
1000	14.67	14.38	14.30	14.28	14.26	14.21	14.19
2000	29.34	28.76	28.59	28.55	28.52	28.42	28.37
2500	36.68	35.95	35.74	35.69	35.65	35.52	35.46
3000	44.01	43.14	42.88	42.83	42.78	42.62	42.55
4000	58.68	57.52	57.18	57.10	57.03	56.83	56.74
5000	73.35	71.89	71.47	71.37	71.29	71.03	70.92
6000	88.01	86.27	85.76	85.65	85.55	85.24	85.10
7000	102.68	100.65	100.06	99.92	99.80	99.44	99.29
8000	117.35	115.03	114.35	114.19	114.06	113.65	113.47
9000	132.02	129.41	128.64	128.47	128.32	127.85	127.65
10000	146.69	143.78	142.94	142.74	142.57	142.06	141.84
11000	161.35	158.16	157.23	157.01	156.83	156.26	156.02
12000	176.02	172.54	171.52	171.29	171.09	170.47	170.20
13000	190.69	186.92	185.82	185.56	185.34	184.67	184.39
14000	205.36	201.30	200.11	199.83	199.60	198.88	198.57
15000	220.03	215.67	214.40	214.11	213.86	213.08	212.75
16000	234.69	230.05	228.70	228.38	228.11	227.29	226.94
17000	249.36	244.43	242.99	242.65	242.37	241.49	241.12
18000	264.03	258.81	257.28	256.93	256.63	255.70	255.30
19000	278.70	273.19	271.58	271.20	270.88	269.90	269.49
20000	293.37	287.56	285.87	285.47	285.14	284.11	283.67
21000	308.03	301.94	300.16	299.75	299.40	298.32	297.85
22000	322.70	316.32	314.46	314.02	313.65	312.52	312.04
23000	337.37	330.70	328.75	328.29	327.91	326.73	326.22
24000	352.04	345.08	343.04	342.57	342.17	340.93	340.40
25000	366.71	359.45	357.34	356.84	356.42	355.14	354.59
26000	381.37	373.83	371.63	371.11	370.68	369.34	368.77
27000	396.04	388.21	385.92	385.39	384.94	383.55	382.95
28000	410.71	402.59	400.22	399.66	399.19	397.75	397.14
29000	425.38	416.97	414.51	413.93	413.45	411.96	411.32
30000	440.05	431.34	428.80	428.21	427.71	426.16	425.50
31000	454.71	445.72	443.10	442.48	441.96	440.37	439.69
32000	469.38	460.10	457.39	456.76	456.22	454.57	453.87
33000	484.05	474.48	471.68	471.03	470.48	468.78	468.05
34000	498.72	488.86	485.98	485.30	484.73	482.98	482.24
35000	513.39	503.23	500.27	499.58	498.99	497.19	496.42
36000	528.05	517.61	514.56	513.85	513.25	511.39	510.60
37000	542.72	531.99	528.86	528.12	527.50	525.60	524.78
38000	557.39	546.37	543.15	542.40	541.76	539.80	538.97
39000	572.06	560.75	557.44	556.67	556.02	554.01	553.15
40000	586.73	575.12	571.74	570.94	570.28	568.22	567.33
45000	660.07	647.01	643.20	642.31	641.56	639.24	638.25
50000	733.41	718.90	714.67	713.68	712.84	710.27	709.17
55000	806.75	790.79	786.13	785.04	784.13	781.29	780.08
60000	880.09	862.68	857.60	856.41	855.41	852.32	851.00
65000	953.43	934.57	929.07	927.78	926.69	923.35	921.92
70000	1026.77	1006.46	1000.53	999.15	997.98	994.37	992.83
75000	1100.11	1078.35	1072.00	1070.51	1069.26	1065.40	1063.75
80000	1173.45	1150.24	1143.47	1141.88	1140.55	1136.43	1134.66
85000	1246.79	1222.13	1214.93	1213.25	1211.83	1207.45	1205.58
90000	1320.13	1294.02	1286.40	1284.62	1283.11	1278.48	1276.50
95000	1393.47	1365.91	1357.86	1355.98	1354.40	1349.50	1347.41
100000	1466.81	1437.80	1429.33	1427.35	1425.68	1420.53	1418.33

17.25% MONTHLY AMORTIZING PAYMENTS

AMOUNT OF LOAN	NUMBER OF YEARS IN TERM						
	1	2	3	4	5	10	15
$ 25	2.29	1.24	.90	.73	.63	.44	.39
50	4.57	2.48	1.79	1.45	1.25	.88	.78
75	6.85	3.72	2.69	2.18	1.88	1.32	1.17
100	9.14	4.96	3.58	2.90	2.50	1.76	1.56
200	18.27	9.92	7.16	5.80	5.00	3.51	3.12
300	27.40	14.87	10.74	8.70	7.50	5.27	4.68
400	36.53	19.83	14.32	11.60	10.00	7.02	6.23
500	45.67	24.79	17.89	14.50	12.50	8.77	7.79
600	54.80	29.74	21.47	17.40	15.00	10.53	9.35
700	63.93	34.70	25.05	20.29	17.50	12.28	10.90
800	73.06	39.65	28.63	23.19	19.99	14.04	12.46
900	82.20	44.61	32.20	26.09	22.49	15.79	14.02
1000	91.33	49.57	35.78	28.99	24.99	17.54	15.57
2000	182.65	99.13	71.56	57.97	49.98	35.08	31.14
2500	228.31	123.91	89.45	72.47	62.47	43.85	38.92
3000	273.98	148.69	107.34	86.96	74.97	52.62	46.71
4000	365.30	198.25	143.11	115.94	99.95	70.16	62.28
5000	456.62	247.82	178.89	144.93	124.94	87.70	77.84
6000	547.95	297.38	214.67	173.91	149.93	105.24	93.41
7000	639.27	346.94	250.45	202.90	174.92	122.77	108.98
8000	730.59	396.50	286.22	231.88	199.90	140.31	124.55
9000	821.92	446.07	322.00	260.87	224.89	157.85	140.11
10000	913.24	495.63	357.78	289.85	249.88	175.39	155.68
11000	1004.56	545.19	393.55	318.84	274.86	192.93	171.25
12000	1095.89	594.75	429.33	347.82	299.85	210.47	186.82
13000	1187.21	644.32	465.11	376.80	324.84	228.01	202.38
14000	1278.53	693.88	500.89	405.79	349.83	245.54	217.95
15000	1369.86	743.44	536.66	434.77	374.81	263.08	233.52
16000	1461.18	793.00	572.44	463.76	399.80	280.62	249.09
17000	1552.50	842.57	608.22	492.74	424.79	298.16	264.65
18000	1643.83	892.13	644.00	521.73	449.77	315.70	280.22
19000	1735.15	941.69	679.77	550.71	474.76	333.24	295.79
20000	1826.47	991.25	715.55	579.70	499.75	350.78	311.36
21000	1917.80	1040.82	751.33	608.68	524.74	368.31	326.92
22000	2009.12	1090.38	787.10	637.67	549.72	385.85	342.49
23000	2100.44	1139.94	822.88	666.65	574.71	403.39	358.06
24000	2191.77	1189.50	858.66	695.63	599.70	420.93	373.63
25000	2283.09	1239.07	894.44	724.62	624.68	438.47	389.19
26000	2374.41	1288.63	930.21	753.60	649.67	456.01	404.76
27000	2465.74	1338.19	965.99	782.59	674.66	473.54	420.33
28000	2557.06	1387.75	1001.77	811.57	699.65	491.08	435.90
29000	2648.38	1437.32	1037.55	840.56	724.63	508.62	451.46
30000	2739.71	1486.88	1073.32	869.54	749.62	526.16	467.03
31000	2831.03	1536.44	1109.10	898.53	774.61	543.70	482.60
32000	2922.35	1586.00	1144.88	927.51	799.60	561.24	498.17
33000	3013.68	1635.57	1180.65	956.50	824.58	578.78	513.73
34000	3105.00	1685.13	1216.43	985.48	849.57	596.31	529.30
35000	3196.33	1734.69	1252.21	1014.46	874.56	613.85	544.87
36000	3287.65	1784.25	1287.99	1043.45	899.54	631.39	560.44
37000	3378.97	1833.82	1323.76	1072.43	924.53	648.93	576.01
38000	3470.30	1883.38	1359.54	1101.42	949.52	666.47	591.57
39000	3561.62	1932.94	1395.32	1130.40	974.51	684.01	607.14
40000	3652.94	1982.50	1431.10	1159.39	999.49	701.55	622.71
45000	4109.56	2230.32	1609.98	1304.31	1124.43	789.24	700.55
50000	4566.18	2478.13	1788.87	1449.23	1249.36	876.93	778.38
55000	5022.79	2725.94	1967.75	1594.16	1374.30	964.62	856.22
60000	5479.41	2973.75	2146.64	1739.08	1499.24	1052.32	934.06
65000	5936.03	3221.57	2325.53	1884.00	1624.17	1140.01	1011.90
70000	6392.65	3469.38	2504.41	2028.92	1749.11	1227.70	1089.73
75000	6849.26	3717.19	2683.30	2173.85	1874.04	1315.39	1167.57
80000	7305.88	3965.00	2862.19	2318.77	1998.98	1403.09	1245.41
85000	7762.50	4212.82	3041.07	2463.69	2123.92	1490.78	1323.25
90000	8219.11	4460.63	3219.96	2608.61	2248.85	1578.47	1401.09
95000	8675.73	4708.44	3398.85	2753.54	2373.79	1666.16	1478.92
100000	9132.35	4956.25	3577.73	2898.46	2498.72	1753.86	1556.76

MONTHLY AMORTIZING PAYMENTS 17.25%

AMOUNT OF LOAN	NUMBER OF YEARS IN TERM						
	20	25	28	29	30	35	40
$ 25	.38	.37	.37	.37	.37	.37	.36
50	.75	.73	.73	.73	.73	.73	.72
75	1.12	1.10	1.09	1.09	1.09	1.09	1.08
100	1.49	1.46	1.45	1.45	1.45	1.45	1.44
200	2.98	2.92	2.90	2.90	2.90	2.89	2.88
300	4.46	4.38	4.35	4.35	4.34	4.33	4.32
400	5.95	5.84	5.80	5.80	5.79	5.77	5.76
500	7.43	7.29	7.25	7.24	7.23	7.21	7.20
600	8.92	8.75	8.70	8.69	8.68	8.65	8.64
700	10.41	10.21	10.15	10.14	10.13	10.09	10 09
800	11.89	11.67	11.60	11.59	11.57	11.53	11.52
900	13.38	13.12	13.05	13.03	13.02	12.97	12.96
1000	14.86	14.58	14.50	14.48	14.46	14.42	14.40
2000	29.72	29.16	28.99	28.96	28.92	28.83	28.79
2500	37.15	36.45	36.24	36.19	36.16	36.03	35.98
3000	44.58	43.73	43.49	43.43	43.38	43.24	43.18
4000	59.44	58.31	57.98	57.91	57.84	57.65	57.57
5000	74.30	72.89	72.48	72.38	72.30	72.06	71.96
6000	89.16	87.46	86.97	86.86	86.76	86.47	86.35
7000	104.01	102.04	101.47	101.34	101.22	100.88	100.74
8000	118.87	116.62	115.96	115.81	115.68	115.29	115.13
9000	133.73	131.19	130.46	130.29	130.14	129.70	129.52
10000	148.59	145.77	144.95	144.76	144.60	144.11	143.91
11000	163.45	160.35	159.45	159.24	159.06	158.53	158.30
12000	178.31	174.92	173.94	173.71	173.52	172.94	172.69
13000	193.16	189.50	188.44	188.19	187.98	187.35	187.08
14000	208.02	204.07	202.93	202.67	202.44	201.76	201.47
15000	222.88	218.65	217.43	217.14	216.90	216.17	215.86
16000	237.74	233.23	231.92	231.62	231.36	230.58	230.25
17000	252.60	247.80	246.42	246.09	245.82	244.99	244.64
18000	267.46	262.38	260.91	260.57	260.28	259.40	259.03
19000	282.31	276.96	275.41	275.05	274.74	273.81	273.42
20000	297.17	291.53	289.90	289.52	289.20	288.22	287.81
21000	312.03	306.11	304.40	304.00	303.66	302.63	302.20
22000	326.89	320.69	318.89	318.47	318.12	317.05	316.59
23000	341.75	335.26	333.39	332.95	332.58	331.46	330.98
24000	356.61	349.84	347.88	347.42	347.04	345.87	345.37
25000	371.47	364.42	362.38	361.90	361.50	360.28	359.76
26000	386.32	378.99	376.87	376.38	375.96	374.69	374.15
27000	401.18	393.57	391.36	390.85	390.42	389.10	388.54
28000	416.04	408.14	405.86	405.33	404.88	403.51	402.93
29000	430.90	422.72	420.35	419.80	419.34	417.92	417.32
30000	445.76	437.30	434.85	434.28	433.80	432.33	431.71
31000	460.62	451.87	449.34	448.76	448.26	446.74	446.10
32000	475.47	466.45	463.84	463.23	462.72	461.15	460.49
33000	490.33	481.03	478.33	477.71	477.18	475.57	474.88
34000	505.19	495.60	492.83	492.18	491.64	489.98	489.27
35000	520.05	510.18	507.32	506.66	506.10	504.39	503.66
36000	534.91	524.76	521.82	521.13	520.56	518.80	518.05
37000	549.77	539.33	536.31	535.61	535.02	533.21	532.44
38000	564.62	553.91	550.81	550.09	549.48	547.62	546.83
39000	579.48	568.49	565.30	564.56	563.94	562.03	561.22
40000	594.34	583.06	579.80	579.04	578.40	576.44	575.61
45000	668.63	655.94	652.27	651.42	650.70	648.50	647.57
50000	742.93	728.83	724.75	723.80	723.00	720.55	719.52
55000	817.22	801.71	797.22	796.18	795.30	792.61	791.47
60000	891.51	874.59	869.69	868.55	867.60	864.66	863.42
65000	965.80	947.47	942.17	940.93	939.90	936.71	935.37
70000	1040.09	1020.35	1014.64	1013.31	1012.20	1008.77	1007.32
75000	1114.39	1093.24	1087.12	1085.69	1084.49	1080.82	1079.27
80000	1188.68	1166.12	1159.59	1158.07	1156.79	1152.88	1151.22
85000	1262.97	1239.00	1232.06	1230.45	1229.09	1224.93	1223.17
90000	1337.26	1311.88	1304.54	1302.83	1301.39	1296.99	1295.13
95000	1411.55	1384.76	1377.01	1375.21	1373.69	1369.04	1367.08
100000	1485.85	1457.65	1449.49	1447.59	1445.99	1441.10	1439.03

69

17.50% MONTHLY AMORTIZING PAYMENTS

AMOUNT OF LOAN	NUMBER OF YEARS IN TERM						
	1	2	3	4	5	10	15
$ 25	2.29	1.25	.90	.73	.63	.45	.40
50	4.58	2.49	1.80	1.46	1.26	.89	.79
75	6.86	3.73	2.70	2.19	1.89	1.33	1.19
100	9.15	4.97	3.60	2.92	2.52	1.77	1.58
200	18.29	9.94	7.19	5.83	5.03	3.54	3.15
300	27.44	14.91	10.78	8.74	7.54	5.31	4.73
400	36.58	19.88	14.37	11.65	10.05	7.08	6.30
500	45.73	24.85	17.96	14.56	12.57	8.85	7.88
600	54.87	29.81	21.55	17.47	15.08	10.62	9.45
700	64.01	34.78	25.14	20.39	17.59	12.39	11.03
800	73.16	39.75	28.73	23.30	20.10	14.16	12.60
900	82.30	44.72	32.32	26.21	22.61	15.93	14.18
1000	91.45	49.69	35.91	29.12	25.13	17.70	15.75
2000	182.89	99.37	71.81	58.23	50.25	35.40	31.50
2500	228.61	124.21	89.76	72.79	62.81	44.25	39.37
3000	274.33	149.05	107.71	87.35	75.37	53.10	47.24
4000	365.77	198.74	143.61	116.46	100.49	70.80	62.99
5000	457.22	248.42	179.52	145.58	125.62	88.49	78.73
6000	548.66	298.10	215.42	174.69	150.74	106.19	94.48
7000	640.10	347.78	251.32	203.81	175.86	123.89	110.23
8000	731.54	397.47	287.22	232.92	200.98	141.59	125.97
9000	822.98	447.15	323.12	262.03	226.10	159.29	141.72
10000	914.43	496.83	359.03	291.15	251.23	176.98	157.46
11000	1005.87	546.52	394.93	320.26	276.35	194.68	173.21
12000	1097.31	596.20	430.83	349.38	301.47	212.38	188.95
13000	1188.75	645.88	466.73	378.49	326.59	230.08	204.70
14000	1280.20	695.56	502.63	407.61	351.72	247.78	220.45
15000	1371.64	745.25	538.54	436.72	376.84	265.47	236.19
16000	1463.08	794.93	574.44	465.83	401.96	283.17	251.94
17000	1554.52	844.61	610.34	494.95	427.08	300.87	267.68
18000	1645.96	894.30	646.24	524.06	452.20	318.57	283.43
19000	1737.41	943.98	682.14	553.18	477.33	336.26	299.17
20000	1828.85	993.66	718.05	582.29	502.45	353.96	314.92
21000	1920.29	1043.34	753.95	611.41	527.57	371.66	330.67
22000	2011.73	1093.03	789.85	640.52	552.69	389.36	346.41
23000	2103.18	1142.71	825.75	669.64	577.82	407.06	362.16
24000	2194.62	1192.39	861.65	698.75	602.94	424.75	377.90
25000	2286.06	1242.08	897.56	727.86	628.06	442.45	393.65
26000	2377.50	1291.76	933.46	756.98	653.18	460.15	409.40
27000	2468.94	1341.44	969.36	786.09	678.30	477.85	425.14
28000	2560.39	1391.12	1005.26	815.21	703.43	495.55	440.89
29000	2651.83	1440.81	1041.16	844.32	728.55	513.24	456.63
30000	2743.27	1490.49	1077.07	873.44	753.67	530.94	472.38
31000	2834.71	1540.17	1112.97	902.55	778.79	548.64	488.12
32000	2926.16	1589.86	1148.87	931.66	803.92	566.34	503.87
33000	3017.60	1639.54	1184.77	960.78	829.04	584.03	519.62
34000	3109.04	1689.22	1220.68	989.89	854.16	601.73	535.36
35000	3200.48	1738.90	1256.58	1019.01	879.28	619.43	551.11
36000	3291.92	1788.59	1292.48	1048.12	904.40	637.13	566.85
37000	3383.37	1838.27	1328.38	1077.24	929.53	654.83	582.60
38000	3474.81	1887.95	1364.28	1106.35	954.65	672.52	598.34
39000	3566.25	1937.64	1400.19	1135.47	979.77	690.22	614.09
40000	3657.69	1987.32	1436.09	1164.58	1004.89	707.92	629.84
45000	4114.90	2235.73	1615.60	1310.15	1130.51	796.41	708.57
50000	4572.12	2484.15	1795.11	1455.72	1256.12	884.90	787.29
55000	5029.33	2732.56	1974.62	1601.30	1381.73	973.39	866.02
60000	5486.54	2980.98	2154.13	1746.87	1507.34	1061.88	944.75
65000	5943.75	3229.39	2333.64	1892.44	1632.95	1150.37	1023.48
70000	6400.96	3477.80	2513.15	2038.01	1758.56	1238.86	1102.21
75000	6858.17	3726.22	2692.66	2183.58	1884.17	1327.35	1180.94
80000	7315.38	3974.63	2872.17	2329.15	2009.78	1415.84	1259.67
85000	7772.59	4223.05	3051.68	2474.73	2135.39	1504.32	1338.40
90000	8229.80	4471.46	3231.19	2620.30	2261.00	1592.81	1417.13
95000	8687.01	4719.88	3410.70	2765.87	2386.62	1681.30	1495.85
100000	9144.23	4968.29	3590.21	2911.44	2512.23	1769.79	1574.58

70

AMOUNT OF LOAN	NUMBER OF YEARS IN TERM						
	20	25	28	29	30	35	40
$ 25	.38	.37	.37	.37	.37	.37	.37
50	.76	.74	.74	.74	.74	.74	.73
75	1.13	1.11	1.11	1.11	1.10	1.10	1.10
100	1.51	1.48	1.47	1.47	1.47	1.47	1.46
200	3.01	2.96	2.94	2.94	2.94	2.93	2.92
300	4.52	4.44	4.41	4.41	4.40	4.39	4.38
400	6.02	5.92	5.88	5.88	5.87	5.85	5.84
500	7.53	7.39	7.35	7.34	7.34	7.31	7.30
600	9.03	8.87	8.82	8.81	8.80	8.78	8.76
700	10.54	10.35	10.29	10.28	10.27	10.24	10.22
800	12.04	11.83	11.76	11.75	11.74	11.70	11.68
900	13.55	13.30	13.23	13.22	13.20	13.16	13.14
1000	15.05	14.78	14.70	14.68	14.67	14.62	14.60
2000	30.10	29.56	29.40	29.36	29.33	29.24	29.20
2500	37.63	36.94	36.75	36.70	36.66	36.55	36.50
3000	45.15	44.33	44.10	44.04	43.99	43.86	43.80
4000	60.20	59.11	58.79	58.72	58.66	58.47	58.39
5000	75.25	73.88	73.49	73.40	73.32	73.09	72.99
6000	90.30	88.66	88.19	88.08	87.98	87.71	87.59
7000	105.35	103.43	102.88	102.75	102.65	102.32	102.19
8000	120.40	118.21	117.58	117.43	117.31	116.94	116.78
9000	135.45	132.98	132.28	132.11	131.97	131.56	131.38
10000	150.50	147.76	146.97	146.79	146.64	146.17	145.98
11000	165.55	162.53	161.67	161.47	161.30	160.79	160.58
12000	180.60	177.31	176.37	176.15	175.96	175.41	175.17
13000	195.65	192.08	191.06	190.83	190.63	190.02	189.77
14000	210.70	206.86	205.76	205.50	205.29	204.64	204.37
15000	225.75	221.63	220.46	220.18	219.95	219.26	218.97
16000	240.80	236.41	235.15	234.86	234.62	233.87	233.56
17000	255.85	251.19	249.85	249.54	249.28	248.49	248.16
18000	270.89	265.96	264.55	264.22	263.94	263.11	262.76
19000	285.94	280.74	279.24	278.90	278.61	277.72	277.35
20000	300.99	295.51	293.94	293.58	293.27	292.34	291.95
21000	316.04	310.29	308.64	308.25	307.93	306.96	306.55
22000	331.09	325.06	323.33	322.93	322.60	321.57	321.15
23000	346.14	339.84	338.03	337.61	337.26	336.19	335.74
24000	361.19	354.61	352.73	352.29	351.92	350.81	350.34
25000	376.24	369.39	367.42	366.97	366.59	365.42	364.94
26000	391.29	384.16	382.12	381.65	381.25	380.04	379.54
27000	406.34	398.94	396.82	396.32	395.91	394.66	394.13
28000	421.39	413.71	411.51	411.00	410.58	409.27	408.73
29000	436.44	428.49	426.21	425.68	425.24	423.89	423.33
30000	451.49	443.26	440.91	440.36	439.90	438.51	437.93
31000	466.54	458.04	455.60	455.04	454.57	453.12	452.52
32000	481.59	472.81	470.30	469.72	469.23	467.74	467.12
33000	496.64	487.59	485.00	484.40	483.89	482.36	481.72
34000	511.69	502.37	499.69	499.07	498.56	496.97	496.31
35000	526.73	517.14	514.39	513.75	513.22	511.59	510.91
36000	541.78	531.92	529.09	528.43	527.88	526.21	525.51
37000	556.83	546.69	543.78	543.11	542.55	540.82	540.11
38000	571.88	561.47	558.48	557.79	557.21	555.44	554.70
39000	586.93	576.24	573.18	572.47	571.87	570.06	569.30
40000	601.98	591.02	587.87	587.15	586.54	584.68	583.90
45000	677.23	664.89	661.36	660.54	659.85	657.76	656.89
50000	752.48	738.77	734.84	733.93	733.17	730.84	729.87
55000	827.72	812.65	808.32	807.32	806.48	803.93	802.86
60000	902.97	886.52	881.81	880.72	879.80	877.01	875.85
65000	978.22	960.40	955.29	954.11	953.12	950.09	948.83
70000	1053.46	1034.28	1028.78	1027.50	1026.43	1023.18	1021.82
75000	1128.71	1108.15	1102.26	1100.89	1099.75	1096.26	1094.81
80000	1203.96	1182.03	1175.74	1174.29	1173.07	1169.35	1167.79
85000	1279.21	1255.91	1249.23	1247.68	1246.38	1242.43	1240.78
90000	1354.45	1329.78	1322.71	1321.07	1319.70	1315.51	1313.77
95000	1429.70	1403.66	1396.19	1394.46	1393.01	1388.60	1386.75
100000	1504.95	1477.53	1469.68	1467.86	1466.33	1461.68	1459.74

17.75% MONTHLY AMORTIZING PAYMENTS

AMOUNT OF LOAN	NUMBER OF YEARS IN TERM						
	1	2	3	4	5	10	15
$ 25	2.29	1.25	.91	.74	.64	.45	.40
50	4.58	2.50	1.81	1.47	1.27	.90	.80
75	6.87	3.74	2.71	2.20	1.90	1.34	1.20
100	9.16	4.99	3.61	2.93	2.53	1.79	1.60
200	18.32	9.97	7.21	5.85	5.06	3.58	3.19
300	27.47	14.95	10.81	8.78	7.58	5.36	4.78
400	36.63	19.93	14.42	11.70	10.11	7.15	6.37
500	45.79	24.91	18.02	14.63	12.63	8.93	7.97
600	54.94	29.89	21.62	17.55	15.16	10.72	9.56
700	64.10	34.87	25.22	20.48	17.69	12.51	11.15
800	73.25	39.85	28.83	23.40	20.21	14.29	12.74
900	82.41	44.83	32.43	26.33	22.74	16.08	14.34
1000	91.57	49.81	36.03	29.25	25.26	17.86	15.93
2000	183.13	99.61	72.06	58.49	50.52	35.72	31.85
2500	228.91	124.51	90.07	73.12	63.15	44.65	39.82
3000	274.69	149.42	108.09	87.74	75.78	53.58	47.78
4000	366.25	199.22	144.11	116.98	101.04	71.44	63.70
5000	457.81	249.02	180.14	146.23	126.29	89.29	79.63
6000	549.37	298.83	216.17	175.47	151.55	107.15	95.55
7000	640.93	348.63	252.19	204.72	176.81	125.01	111.48
8000	732.49	398.43	288.22	233.96	202.07	142.87	127.40
9000	824.05	448.24	324.25	263.21	227.32	160.73	143.33
10000	915.62	498.04	360.28	292.45	252.58	178.58	159.25
11000	1007.18	547.84	396.30	321.69	277.84	196.44	175.18
12000	1098.74	597.65	432.33	350.94	303.10	214.30	191.10
13000	1190.30	647.45	468.36	380.18	328.35	232.16	207.03
14000	1281.86	697.25	504.38	409.43	353.61	250.02	222.95
15000	1373.42	747.06	540.41	438.67	378.87	267.87	238.87
16000	1464.98	796.86	576.44	467.92	404.13	285.73	254.80
17000	1556.54	846.66	612.47	497.16	429.38	303.59	270.72
18000	1648.10	896.47	648.49	526.41	454.64	321.45	286.65
19000	1739.67	946.27	684.52	555.65	479.90	339.30	302.57
20000	1831.23	996.07	720.55	584.90	505.16	357.16	318.50
21000	1922.79	1045.88	756.57	614.14	530.42	375.02	334.42
22000	2014.35	1095.68	792.60	643.38	555.67	392.88	350.35
23000	2105.91	1145.48	828.63	672.63	580.93	410.74	366.27
24000	2197.48	1195.29	864.66	701.87	606.19	428.59	382.20
25000	2289.03	1245.09	900.68	731.12	631.45	446.45	398.12
26000	2380.59	1294.89	936.71	760.36	656.70	464.31	414.05
27000	2472.15	1344.70	972.74	789.61	681.96	482.17	429.97
28000	2563.71	1394.50	1008.76	818.85	707.22	500.03	445.90
29000	2655.28	1444.30	1044.79	848.10	732.48	517.88	461.82
30000	2746.84	1494.11	1080.82	877.34	757.73	535.74	477.74
31000	2838.40	1543.91	1116.85	906.59	782.99	553.60	493.67
32000	2929.96	1593.71	1152.87	935.83	808.25	571.46	509.59
33000	3021.52	1643.52	1188.90	965.07	833.51	589.32	525.52
34000	3113.08	1693.32	1224.93	994.32	858.76	607.17	541.44
35000	3204.64	1743.12	1260.95	1023.56	884.02	625.03	557.37
36000	3296.20	1792.93	1296.98	1052.81	909.28	642.89	573.29
37000	3387.76	1842.73	1333.01	1082.05	934.54	660.75	589.22
38000	3479.33	1892.53	1369.04	1111.30	959.79	678.60	605.14
39000	3570.89	1942.34	1405.06	1140.54	985.05	696.46	621.07
40000	3662.45	1992.14	1441.09	1169.79	1010.31	714.32	636.99
45000	4120.25	2241.16	1621.22	1316.01	1136.60	803.61	716.61
50000	4578.06	2490.17	1801.36	1462.23	1262.89	892.90	796.24
55000	5035.86	2739.19	1981.50	1608.45	1389.17	982.19	875.86
60000	5493.67	2988.21	2161.63	1754.68	1515.46	1071.48	955.48
65000	5951.47	3237.23	2341.77	1900.90	1641.75	1160.77	1035.11
70000	6409.28	3486.24	2521.90	2047.12	1768.04	1250.06	1114.73
75000	6867.08	3735.26	2702.04	2193.34	1894.33	1339.35	1194.35
80000	7324.89	3984.28	2882.17	2339.57	2020.61	1428.64	1273.98
85000	7782.69	4233.29	3062.31	2485.79	2146.90	1517.93	1353.60
90000	8240.50	4482.31	3242.44	2632.01	2273.19	1607.21	1433.22
95000	8698.31	4731.33	3422.58	2778.23	2399.48	1696.50	1512.85
100000	9156.11	4980.34	3602.72	2924.46	2525.77	1785.79	1592.47

AMOUNT OF LOAN	NUMBER OF YEARS IN TERM						
	20	25	28	29	30	35	40
$ 25	.39	.38	.38	.38	.38	.38	.38
50	.77	.75	.75	.75	.75	.75	.75
75	1.15	1.13	1.12	1.12	1.12	1.12	1.12
100	1.53	1.50	1.49	1.49	1.49	1.49	1.49
200	3.05	3.00	2.98	2.98	2.98	2.97	2.97
300	4.58	4.50	4.47	4.47	4.47	4.45	4.45
400	6.10	5.99	5.96	5.96	5.95	5.93	5.93
500	7.63	7.49	7.45	7.45	7.44	7.42	7.41
600	9.15	8.99	8.94	8.93	8.93	8.90	8.89
700	10.67	10.49	10.43	10.42	10.41	10.38	10.37
800	12.20	11.98	11.92	11.91	11.90	11.86	11.85
900	13.72	13.48	13.41	13.40	13.39	13.35	13.33
1000	15.25	14.98	14.90	14.89	14.87	14.83	14.81
2000	30.49	29.95	29.80	29.77	29.74	29.65	29.61
2500	38.11	37.44	37.25	37.21	37.17	37.06	37.02
3000	45.73	44.93	44.70	44.65	44.61	44.47	44.42
4000	60.97	59.90	59.60	59.53	59.47	59.30	59.22
5000	76.21	74.88	74.50	74.41	74.34	74.12	74.03
6000	91.45	89.85	89.40	89.29	89.21	88.94	88.83
7000	106.69	104.83	104.30	104.18	104.07	103.76	103.64
8000	121.93	119.80	119.20	119.06	118.94	118.59	118.44
9000	137.17	134.78	134.10	133.94	133.81	133.41	133.25
10000	152.41	149.75	148.99	148.82	148.67	148.23	148.05
11000	167.66	164.73	163.89	163.70	163.54	163.06	162.85
12000	182.90	179.70	178.79	178.58	178.41	177.88	177.66
13000	198.14	194.67	193.69	193.46	193.27	192.70	192.46
14000	213.38	209.65	208.59	208.35	208.14	207.52	207.27
15000	228.62	224.62	223.49	223.23	223.01	222.35	222.07
16000	243.86	239.60	238.39	238.11	237.88	237.17	236.88
17000	259.10	254.57	253.29	252.99	252.74	251.99	251.68
18000	274.34	269.55	268.19	267.87	267.61	266.81	266.49
19000	289.58	284.52	283.08	282.75	282.48	281.64	281.29
20000	304.82	299.50	297.98	297.64	297.34	296.46	296.10
21000	320.07	314.47	312.88	312.52	312.21	311.28	310.90
22000	335.31	329.45	327.78	327.40	327.08	326.11	325.70
23000	350.55	344.42	342.68	342.28	341.94	340.93	340.51
24000	365.79	359.40	357.58	357.16	356.81	355.75	355.31
25000	381.03	374.37	372.48	372.04	371.68	370.57	370.12
26000	396.27	389.34	387.38	386.92	386.54	385.40	384.92
27000	411.51	404.32	402.28	401.81	401.41	400.22	399.73
28000	426.75	419.29	417.18	416.69	416.28	415.04	414.53
29000	441.99	434.27	432.07	431.57	431.15	429.86	429.34
30000	457.23	449.24	446.97	446.45	446.01	444.69	444.14
31000	472.48	464.22	461.87	461.33	460.88	459.51	458.95
32000	487.72	479.19	476.77	476.21	475.75	474.33	473.75
33000	502.96	494.17	491.67	491.09	490.61	489.16	488.55
34000	518.20	509.14	506.57	505.98	505.48	503.98	503.36
35000	533.44	524.12	521.47	520.86	520.35	518.80	518.16
36000	548.68	539.09	536.37	535.74	535.21	533.62	532.97
37000	563.92	554.07	551.27	550.62	550.08	548.45	547.77
38000	579.16	569.04	566.16	565.50	564.95	563.27	562.58
39000	594.40	584.01	581.06	580.38	579.81	578.09	577.38
40000	609.64	598.99	595.96	595.27	594.68	592.92	592.19
45000	685.85	673.86	670.46	669.67	669.02	667.03	666.21
50000	762.05	748.73	744.95	744.08	743.35	741.14	740.23
55000	838.26	823.61	819.45	818.49	817.69	815.26	814.25
60000	914.46	898.48	893.94	892.90	892.02	889.37	888.28
65000	990.67	973.35	968.44	967.30	966.35	963.48	962.30
70000	1066.87	1048.23	1042.93	1041.71	1040.69	1037.60	1036.32
75000	1143.08	1123.10	1117.43	1116.12	1115.02	1111.71	1110.35
80000	1219.28	1197.97	1191.92	1190.53	1189.36	1185.83	1184.37
85000	1295.49	1272.85	1266.42	1264.93	1263.69	1259.94	1258.39
90000	1371.69	1347.72	1340.91	1339.34	1338.03	1334.05	1332.41
95000	1447.90	1422.59	1415.40	1413.75	1412.36	1408.17	1406.44
100000	1524.10	1497.46	1489.90	1488.16	1486.70	1482.28	1480.46

18.00% MONTHLY AMORTIZING PAYMENTS

AMOUNT OF LOAN	NUMBER OF YEARS IN TERM						
	1	2	3	4	5	10	15
$ 25	2.30	1.25	.91	.74	.64	.46	.41
50	4.59	2.50	1.81	1.47	1.27	.91	.81
75	6.88	3.75	2.72	2.21	1.91	1.36	1.21
100	9.17	5.00	3.62	2.94	2.54	1.81	1.62
200	18.34	9.99	7.24	5.88	5.08	3.61	3.23
300	27.51	14.98	10.85	8.82	7.62	5.41	4.84
400	36.68	19.97	14.47	11.75	10.16	7.21	6.45
500	45.84	24.97	18.08	14.69	12.70	9.01	8.06
600	55.01	29.96	21.70	17.63	15.24	10.82	9.67
700	64.18	34.95	25.31	20.57	17.78	12.62	11.28
800	73.35	39.94	28.93	23.50	20.32	14.42	12.89
900	82.52	44.94	32.54	26.44	22.86	16.22	14.50
1000	91.68	49.93	36.16	29.38	25.40	18.02	16.11
2000	183.36	99.85	72.31	58.75	50.79	36.04	32.21
2500	229.20	124.82	90.39	73.44	63.49	45.05	40.27
3000	275.04	149.78	108.46	88.13	76.19	54.06	48.32
4000	366.72	199.70	144.61	117.50	101.58	72.08	64.42
5000	458.40	249.63	180.77	146.88	126.97	90.10	80.53
6000	550.08	299.55	216.92	176.25	152.37	108.12	96.63
7000	641.76	349.47	253.07	205.63	177.76	126.13	112.73
8000	733.44	399.40	289.22	235.00	203.15	144.15	128.84
9000	825.12	449.32	325.38	264.38	228.55	162.17	144.94
10000	916.80	499.25	361.53	293.75	253.94	180.19	161.05
11000	1008.48	549.17	397.68	323.13	279.33	198.21	177.15
12000	1100.16	599.09	433.83	352.50	304.73	216.23	193.26
13000	1191.84	649.02	469.99	381.88	330.12	234.25	209.36
14000	1283.52	698.94	506.14	411.25	355.51	252.26	225.46
15000	1375.20	748.87	542.29	440.63	380.91	270.28	241.57
16000	1466.88	798.79	578.44	470.00	406.30	288.30	257.67
17000	1558.56	848.71	614.60	499.38	431.69	306.32	273.78
18000	1650.24	898.64	650.75	528.75	457.09	324.34	289.88
19000	1741.92	948.56	686.90	558.13	482.48	342.36	305.98
20000	1833.60	998.49	723.05	587.50	507.87	360.38	322.09
21000	1925.28	1048.41	759.21	616.88	533.27	378.39	338.19
22000	2016.96	1098.34	795.36	646.25	558.66	396.41	354.30
23000	2108.64	1148.26	831.51	675.63	584.05	414.43	370.40
24000	2200.32	1198.18	867.66	705.00	609.45	432.45	386.51
25000	2292.00	1248.11	903.81	734.38	634.84	450.47	402.61
26000	2383.68	1298.03	939.97	763.75	660.23	468.49	418.71
27000	2475.36	1347.96	976.12	793.13	685.63	486.51	434.82
28000	2567.04	1397.88	1012.27	822.50	711.02	504.52	450.92
29000	2658.72	1447.80	1048.42	851.88	736.41	522.54	467.03
30000	2750.40	1497.73	1084.58	881.25	761.81	540.56	483.13
31000	2842.08	1547.65	1120.73	910.63	787.20	558.58	499.24
32000	2933.76	1597.58	1156.88	940.00	812.59	576.60	515.34
33000	3025.44	1647.50	1193.03	969.38	837.99	594.62	531.44
34000	3117.12	1697.42	1229.19	998.75	863.38	612.63	547.55
35000	3208.80	1747.35	1265.34	1028.13	888.77	630.65	563.65
36000	3300.48	1797.27	1301.49	1057.50	914.17	648.67	579.76
37000	3392.16	1847.20	1337.64	1086.88	939.56	666.69	595.86
38000	3483.84	1897.12	1373.80	1116.25	964.96	684.71	611.96
39000	3575.52	1947.04	1409.95	1145.63	990.35	702.73	628.07
40000	3667.20	1996.97	1446.10	1175.00	1015.74	720.75	644.17
45000	4125.60	2246.59	1626.86	1321.88	1142.71	810.84	724.69
50000	4584.00	2496.21	1807.62	1468.75	1269.68	900.93	805.22
55000	5042.40	2745.83	1988.39	1615.63	1396.64	991.02	885.74
60000	5500.80	2995.45	2169.15	1762.50	1523.61	1081.12	966.26
65000	5959.20	3245.07	2349.91	1909.38	1650.58	1171.21	1046.78
70000	6417.60	3494.69	2530.67	2056.25	1777.54	1261.30	1127.30
75000	6876.00	3744.31	2711.43	2203.13	1904.51	1351.39	1207.82
80000	7334.40	3993.93	2892.20	2350.00	2031.48	1441.49	1288.34
85000	7792.80	4243.55	3072.96	2496.88	2158.45	1531.58	1368.86
90000	8251.20	4493.17	3253.72	2643.75	2285.41	1621.67	1449.38
95000	8709.60	4742.79	3434.48	2790.63	2412.38	1711.76	1529.90
100000	9168.00	4992.42	3615.24	2937.50	2539.35	1801.86	1610.43

74

AMOUNT OF LOAN	NUMBER OF YEARS IN TERM						
	20	25	28	29	30	35	40
$ 25	.39	.38	.38	.38	.38	.38	.38
50	.78	.76	.76	.76	.76	.76	.76
75	1.16	1.14	1.14	1.14	1.14	1.13	1.13
100	1.55	1.52	1.52	1.51	1.51	1.51	1.51
200	3.09	3.04	3.03	3.02	3.02	3.01	3.01
300	4.63	4.56	4.54	4.53	4.53	4.51	4.51
400	6.18	6.07	6.05	6.04	6.03	6.02	6.01
500	7.72	7.59	7.56	7.55	7.54	7.52	7.51
600	9.26	9.11	9.07	9.06	9.05	9.02	9.01
700	10.81	10.63	10.58	10.56	10.55	10.53	10.51
800	12.35	12.14	12.09	12.07	12.06	12.03	12.01
900	13.89	13.66	13.60	13.58	13.57	13.53	13.52
1000	15.44	15.18	15.11	15.09	15.08	15.03	15.02
2000	30.87	30.35	30.21	30.17	30.15	30.06	30.03
2500	38.59	37.94	37.76	37.72	37.68	37.58	37.53
3000	46.30	45.53	45.31	45.26	45.22	45.09	45.04
4000	61.74	60.70	60.41	60.34	60.29	60.12	60.05
5000	77.17	75.88	75.51	75.43	75.36	75.15	75.06
6000	92.60	91.05	90.61	90.51	90.43	90.18	90.08
7000	108.04	106.23	105.72	105.60	105.50	105.21	105.09
8000	123.47	121.40	120.82	120.68	120.57	120.24	120.10
9000	138.90	136.57	135.92	135.77	135.64	135.27	135.11
10000	154.34	151.75	151.02	150.85	150.71	150.29	150.12
11000	169.77	166.92	166.12	165.94	165.78	165.32	165.14
12000	185.20	182.10	181.22	181.02	180.86	180.35	180.15
13000	200.64	197.27	196.32	196.11	195.93	195.38	195.16
14000	216.07	212.45	211.43	211.19	211.00	210.41	210.17
15000	231.50	227.62	226.53	226.28	226.07	225.44	225.18
16000	246.93	242.79	241.63	241.36	241.14	240.47	240.19
17000	262.37	257.97	256.73	256.45	256.21	255.50	255.21
18000	277.80	273.14	271.83	271.53	271.28	270.53	270.22
19000	293.23	288.32	286.93	286.62	286.35	285.55	285.23
20000	308.67	303.49	302.03	301.70	301.42	300.58	300.24
21000	324.10	318.67	317.14	316.79	316.49	315.61	315.25
22000	339.53	333.84	332.24	331.87	331.56	330.64	330.27
23000	354.97	349.01	347.34	346.96	346.63	345.67	345.28
24000	370.40	364.19	362.44	362.04	361.71	360.70	360.29
25000	385.83	379.36	377.54	377.12	376.78	375.73	375.30
26000	401.27	394.54	392.64	392.21	391.85	390.76	390.31
27000	416.70	409.71	407.75	407.29	406.92	405.79	405.32
28000	432.13	424.89	422.85	422.38	421.99	420.81	420.34
29000	447.57	440.06	437.95	437.46	437.06	435.84	435.35
30000	463.00	455.23	453.05	452.55	452.13	450.87	450.36
31000	478.43	470.41	468.15	467.63	467.20	465.90	465.37
32000	493.86	485.58	483.25	482.72	482.27	480.93	480.38
33000	509.30	500.76	498.35	497.80	497.34	495.96	495.40
34000	524.73	515.93	513.46	512.89	512.41	510.99	510.41
35000	540.16	531.11	528.56	527.97	527.48	526.02	525.42
36000	555.60	546.28	543.66	543.06	542.56	541.05	540.43
37000	571.03	561.45	558.76	558.14	557.63	556.08	555.44
38000	586.46	576.63	573.86	573.23	572.70	571.10	570.45
39000	601.90	591.80	588.96	588.31	587.77	586.13	585.47
40000	617.33	606.98	604.06	603.40	602.84	601.16	600.48
45000	694.50	682.85	679.57	678.82	678.19	676.31	675.54
50000	771.66	758.72	755.08	754.24	753.55	751.45	750.60
55000	848.83	834.59	830.59	829.67	828.90	826.60	825.66
60000	925.99	910.46	906.09	905.09	904.26	901.74	900.71
65000	1003.16	986.33	981.60	980.52	979.61	976.88	975.77
70000	1080.32	1062.21	1057.11	1055.94	1054.96	1052.03	1050.83
75000	1157.49	1138.08	1132.62	1131.36	1130.32	1127.17	1125.89
80000	1234.65	1213.95	1208.12	1206.79	1205.67	1202.32	1200.95
85000	1311.82	1289.82	1283.63	1282.21	1281.03	1277.46	1276.01
90000	1388.99	1365.69	1359.14	1357.64	1356.38	1352.61	1351.07
95000	1466.15	1441.56	1434.65	1433.06	1431.74	1427.75	1426.13
100000	1543.32	1517.43	1510.15	1508.48	1507.09	1502.90	1501.19

18.25% MONTHLY AMORTIZING PAYMENTS

AMOUNT OF LOAN	NUMBER OF YEARS IN TERM						
	1	2	3	4	5	10	15
$ 25	2.30	1.26	.91	.74	.64	.46	.41
50	4.59	2.51	1.82	1.48	1.28	.91	.82
75	6.89	3.76	2.73	2.22	1.92	1.37	1.23
100	9.18	5.01	3.63	2.96	2.56	1.82	1.63
200	18.36	10.01	7.26	5.91	5.11	3.64	3.26
300	27.54	15.02	10.89	8.86	7.66	5.46	4.89
400	36.72	20.02	14.52	11.81	10.22	7.28	6.52
500	45.90	25.03	18.14	14.76	12.77	9.09	8.15
600	55.08	30.03	21.77	17.71	15.32	10.91	9.78
700	64.26	35.04	25.40	20.66	17.88	12.73	11.40
800	73.44	40.04	29.03	23.61	20.43	14.55	13.03
900	82.62	45.05	32.66	26.56	22.98	16.37	14.66
1000	91.80	50.05	36.28	29.51	25.53	18.18	16.29
2000	183.60	100.09	72.56	59.02	51.06	36.36	32.57
2500	229.50	125.12	90.70	73.77	63.83	45.45	40.72
3000	275.40	150.14	108.84	88.52	76.59	54.54	48.86
4000	367.20	200.18	145.12	118.03	102.12	72.72	65.14
5000	459.00	250.23	181.39	147.53	127.65	90.90	81.43
6000	550.80	300.27	217.67	177.04	153.18	109.08	97.71
7000	642.60	350.32	253.95	206.55	178.71	127.26	114.00
8000	734.40	400.36	290.23	236.05	204.24	145.44	130.28
9000	826.20	450.41	326.51	265.56	229.77	163.62	146.56
10000	918.00	500.45	362.78	295.06	255.30	181.80	162.85
11000	1009.79	550.50	399.06	324.57	280.83	199.98	179.13
12000	1101.59	600.54	435.34	354.07	306.36	218.16	195.42
13000	1193.39	650.59	471.62	383.58	331.89	236.34	211.70
14000	1285.19	700.63	507.90	413.09	357.42	254.52	227.99
15000	1376.99	750.68	544.17	442.59	382.95	272.70	244.27
16000	1468.79	800.72	580.45	472.10	408.48	290.88	260.56
17000	1560.59	850.77	616.73	501.60	434.01	309.06	276.84
18000	1652.39	900.81	653.01	531.11	459.54	327.24	293.12
19000	1744.19	950.86	689.29	560.62	485.07	345.42	309.41
20000	1835.99	1000.90	725.56	590.12	510.60	363.60	325.69
21000	1927.78	1050.95	761.84	619.63	536.13	381.78	341.98
22000	2019.58	1100.99	798.12	649.13	561.66	399.96	358.26
23000	2111.38	1151.04	834.40	678.64	587.19	418.14	374.55
24000	2203.18	1201.08	870.68	708.14	612.72	436.32	390.83
25000	2294.98	1251.13	906.95	737.65	638.25	454.50	407.12
26000	2386.78	1301.17	943.23	767.16	663.78	472.68	423.40
27000	2478.58	1351.22	979.51	796.66	689.30	490.86	439.68
28000	2570.38	1401.26	1015.79	826.17	714.83	509.04	455.97
29000	2662.18	1451.31	1052.07	855.67	740.36	527.22	472.25
30000	2753.98	1501.35	1088.34	885.18	765.89	545.40	488.54
31000	2845.77	1551.40	1124.62	914.68	791.42	563.58	504.82
32000	2937.57	1601.44	1160.90	944.19	816.95	581.76	521.11
33000	3029.37	1651.49	1197.18	973.70	842.48	599.94	537.39
34000	3121.17	1701.53	1233.45	1003.20	868.01	618.12	553.67
35000	3212.97	1751.58	1269.73	1032.71	893.54	636.30	569.96
36000	3304.77	1801.62	1306.01	1062.21	919.07	654.48	586.24
37000	3396.57	1851.67	1342.29	1091.72	944.60	672.66	602.53
38000	3488.37	1901.71	1378.57	1121.23	970.13	690.84	618.81
39000	3580.17	1951.76	1414.84	1150.73	995.66	709.02	635.10
40000	3671.97	2001.80	1451.12	1180.24	1021.19	727.20	651.38
45000	4130.96	2252.03	1632.51	1327.77	1148.84	818.10	732.80
50000	4589.96	2502.25	1813.90	1475.29	1276.49	908.99	814.23
55000	5048.95	2752.48	1995.29	1622.82	1404.13	999.89	895.65
60000	5507.95	3002.70	2176.68	1770.35	1531.78	1090.89	977.07
65000	5966.94	3252.93	2358.07	1917.88	1659.43	1181.69	1058.49
70000	6425.94	3503.15	2539.46	2065.41	1787.08	1272.59	1139.91
75000	6884.93	3753.38	2720.85	2212.94	1914.73	1363.49	1221.34
80000	7343.93	4003.60	2902.24	2360.47	2042.37	1454.39	1302.76
85000	7802.92	4253.83	3083.63	2508.00	2170.02	1545.29	1384.18
90000	8261.92	4504.05	3265.02	2655.53	2297.67	1636.19	1465.60
95000	8720.91	4754.28	3446.41	2803.06	2425.32	1727.08	1547.02
100000	9179.91	5004.50	3627.80	2950.58	2552.97	1817.98	1628.45

AMOUNT OF LOAN	NUMBER OF YEARS IN TERM						
	20	**25**	**28**	**29**	**30**	**35**	**40**
$ 25	.40	.39	.39	.39	.39	.39	.39
50	.79	.77	.77	.77	.77	.77	.77
75	1.18	1.16	1.15	1.15	1.15	1.15	1.15
100	1.57	1.54	1.54	1.53	1.53	1.53	1.53
200	3.13	3.08	3.07	3.06	3.06	3.05	3.05
300	4.69	4.62	4.60	4.59	4.59	4.58	4.57
400	6.26	6.15	6.13	6.12	6.12	6.10	6.09
500	7.82	7.69	7.66	7.65	7.64	7.62	7.61
600	9.38	9.23	9.19	9.18	9.17	9.15	9.14
700	10.94	10.77	10.72	10.71	10.70	10.67	10.66
800	12.51	12.30	12.25	12.24	12.23	12.20	12.18
900	14.07	13.84	13.78	13.76	13.75	13.72	13.70
1000	15.63	15.38	15.31	15.29	15.28	15.24	15.22
2000	31.26	30.75	30.61	30.58	30.56	30.48	30.44
2500	39.07	38.44	38.27	38.23	38.19	38.09	38.05
3000	46.88	46.13	45.92	45.87	45.83	45.71	45.66
4000	62.51	61.50	61.22	61.16	61.11	60.95	60.88
5000	78.13	76.88	76.53	76.45	76.38	76.18	76.10
6000	93.76	92.25	91.83	91.74	91.66	91.42	91.32
7000	109.39	107.63	107.14	107.02	106.93	106.65	106.54
8000	125.01	123.00	122.44	122.31	122.21	121.89	121.76
9000	140.64	138.37	137.74	137.60	137.48	137.12	136.98
10000	156.26	153.75	153.05	152.89	152.76	152.36	152.20
11000	171.89	169.12	168.35	168.18	168.03	167.59	167.42
12000	187.51	184.50	183.66	183.47	183.31	182.83	182.64
13000	203.14	199.87	198.96	198.75	198.58	198.06	197.85
14000	218.77	215.25	214.27	214.04	213.86	213.30	213.07
15000	234.39	230.62	229.57	229.33	229.13	228.53	228.29
16000	250.02	246.00	244.87	244.62	244.41	243.77	243.51
17000	265.64	261.37	260.18	259.91	259.68	259.00	258.73
18000	281.27	276.74	275.48	275.20	274.96	274.24	273.95
19000	296.89	292.12	290.79	290.48	290.23	289.47	289.17
20000	312.52	307.49	306.09	305.77	305.51	304.71	304.39
21000	328.15	322.87	321.40	321.06	320.78	319.94	319.61
22000	343.77	338.24	336.70	336.35	336.06	335.18	334.83
23000	359.40	353.62	352.00	351.64	351.33	350.42	350.05
24000	375.02	368.99	367.31	366.93	366.61	365.65	365.27
25000	390.65	384.36	382.61	382.21	381.88	380.89	380.48
26000	406.28	399.74	397.92	397.50	397.16	396.12	395.70
27000	421.90	415.11	413.22	412.79	412.43	411.36	410.92
28000	437.53	430.49	428.53	428.08	427.71	426.59	426.14
29000	453.15	445.86	443.83	443.37	442.98	441.83	441.36
30000	468.78	461.24	459.14	458.66	458.26	457.06	456.58
31000	484.40	476.61	474.44	473.94	473.53	472.30	471.80
32000	500.03	491.99	489.74	489.23	488.81	487.53	487.02
33000	515.66	507.36	505.05	504.52	504.08	502.77	502.24
34000	531.28	522.73	520.35	519.81	519.36	518.00	517.46
35000	546.91	538.11	535.66	535.10	534.63	533.24	532.68
36000	562.53	553.48	550.96	550.39	549.91	548.47	547.90
37000	578.16	568.86	566.27	565.67	565.18	563.71	563.12
38000	593.78	584.23	581.57	580.96	580.46	578.94	578.33
39000	609.41	599.61	596.87	596.25	595.73	594.18	593.55
40000	625.04	614.98	612.18	611.54	611.01	609.41	608.77
45000	703.17	691.85	688.70	687.98	687.38	685.59	684.87
50000	781.29	768.72	765.22	764.42	763.76	761.77	760.96
55000	859.42	845.60	841.74	840.86	840.13	837.94	837.06
60000	937.55	922.47	918.27	917.31	916.51	914.12	913.16
65000	1015.68	999.34	994.79	993.75	992.88	990.29	989.25
70000	1093.81	1076.21	1071.31	1070.19	1069.26	1066.47	1065.35
75000	1171.94	1153.08	1147.83	1146.63	1145.63	1142.65	1141.44
80000	1250.07	1229.96	1224.35	1223.07	1222.01	1218.82	1217.54
85000	1328.20	1306.83	1300.87	1299.51	1298.38	1295.00	1293.64
90000	1406.33	1383.70	1377.40	1375.96	1374.76	1371.18	1369.73
95000	1484.45	1460.57	1453.92	1452.40	1451.13	1447.35	1445.83
100000	1562.58	1537.44	1530.44	1528.84	1527.51	1523.53	1521.92

18.50% MONTHLY AMORTIZING PAYMENTS

AMOUNT OF LOAN	NUMBER OF YEARS IN TERM						
	1	2	3	4	5	10	15
$ 25	2.30	1.26	.92	.75	.65	.46	.42
50	4.60	2.51	1.83	1.49	1.29	.92	.83
75	6.90	3.77	2.74	2.23	1.93	1.38	1.24
100	9.20	5.02	3.65	2.97	2.57	1.84	1.65
200	18.39	10.04	7.29	5.93	5.14	3.67	3.30
300	27.58	15.05	10.93	8.90	7.70	5.51	4.94
400	36.77	20.07	14.57	11.86	10.27	7.34	6.59
500	45.96	25.09	18.21	14.82	12.84	9.18	8.24
600	55.16	30.10	21.85	17.79	15.40	11.01	9.88
700	64.35	35.12	25.49	20.75	17.97	12.84	11.53
800	73.54	40.14	29.13	23.71	20.54	14.68	13.18
900	82.73	45.15	32.77	26.68	23.10	16.51	14.82
1000	91.92	50.17	36.41	29.64	25.67	18.35	16.47
2000	183.84	100.34	72.81	59.28	51.34	36.69	32.94
2500	229.80	125.42	91.01	74.10	64.17	45.86	41.17
3000	275.76	150.50	109.22	88.92	77.00	55.03	49.40
4000	367.68	200.67	145.62	118.55	102.67	73.37	65.87
5000	459.60	250.84	182.02	148.19	128.34	91.71	82.33
6000	551.51	301.00	218.43	177.83	154.00	110.05	98.80
7000	643.43	351.17	254.83	207.46	179.67	128.40	115.26
8000	735.35	401.33	291.23	237.10	205.33	146.74	131.73
9000	827.27	451.50	327.64	266.74	231.00	165.08	148.19
10000	919.19	501.67	364.04	296.37	256.67	183.42	164.66
11000	1011.10	551.83	400.45	326.01	282.33	201.76	181.12
12000	1103.02	602.00	436.85	355.65	308.00	220.10	197.59
13000	1194.94	652.16	473.25	385.28	333.67	238.45	214.05
14000	1286.86	702.33	509.66	414.92	359.33	256.79	230.52
15000	1378.78	752.50	546.06	444.56	385.00	275.13	246.98
16000	1470.69	802.66	582.46	474.20	410.66	293.47	263.45
17000	1562.61	852.83	618.87	503.83	436.33	311.81	279.91
18000	1654.53	902.99	655.27	533.47	462.00	330.15	296.38
19000	1746.45	953.16	691.68	563.11	487.66	348.50	312.84
20000	1838.37	1003.33	728.08	592.74	513.33	366.84	329.31
21000	1930.29	1053.49	764.48	622.38	539.00	385.18	345.77
22000	2022.21	1103.66	800.89	652.02	564.66	403.52	362.24
23000	2114.12	1153.82	837.29	681.65	590.33	421.86	378.71
24000	2206.04	1203.99	873.69	711.29	615.99	440.20	395.17
25000	2297.96	1254.16	910.10	740.93	641.66	458.55	411.64
26000	2389.88	1304.32	946.50	770.56	667.33	476.89	428.10
27000	2481.79	1354.49	982.91	800.20	692.99	495.23	444.57
28000	2573.71	1404.65	1019.31	829.84	718.66	513.57	461.03
29000	2665.63	1454.82	1055.71	859.48	744.33	531.91	477.50
30000	2757.55	1504.99	1092.12	889.11	769.99	550.25	493.96
31000	2849.47	1555.15	1128.52	918.75	795.66	568.60	510.43
32000	2941.38	1605.32	1164.92	948.39	821.32	586.94	526.89
33000	3033.30	1655.48	1201.33	978.02	846.99	605.28	543.36
34000	3125.22	1705.65	1237.73	1007.66	872.66	623.62	559.82
35000	3217.14	1755.82	1274.13	1037.30	898.32	641.96	576.29
36000	3309.06	1805.98	1310.54	1066.93	923.99	660.30	592.75
37000	3400.98	1856.15	1346.94	1096.57	949.65	678.65	609.22
38000	3492.89	1906.31	1383.35	1126.21	975.32	696.99	625.68
39000	3584.81	1956.48	1419.75	1155.84	1000.99	715.33	642.15
40000	3676.73	2006.65	1456.15	1185.48	1026.65	733.67	658.61
45000	4136.32	2257.48	1638.17	1333.67	1154.99	825.38	740.94
50000	4595.91	2508.31	1820.19	1481.85	1283.32	917.09	823.27
55000	5055.50	2759.14	2002.21	1630.04	1411.65	1008.80	905.59
60000	5515.09	3009.97	2184.23	1778.22	1539.98	1100.50	987.92
65000	5974.68	3260.80	2366.25	1926.40	1668.31	1192.21	1070.25
70000	6434.27	3511.63	2548.27	2074.59	1796.64	1283.92	1152.57
75000	6893.86	3762.46	2730.28	2222.77	1924.97	1375.63	1234.90
80000	7353.45	4013.29	2912.30	2370.95	2053.30	1467.34	1317.22
85000	7813.04	4264.12	3094.32	2519.14	2181.63	1559.05	1399.55
90000	8272.64	4514.95	3276.34	2667.33	2309.96	1650.75	1481.88
95000	8732.23	4765.78	3458.36	2815.51	2438.29	1742.46	1564.20
100000	9191.82	5016.61	3640.38	2963.70	2566.63	1834.17	1646.53

AMOUNT OF LOAN	NUMBER OF YEARS IN TERM						
	20	25	28	29	30	35	40
$ 25	.40	.39	.39	.39	.39	.39	.39
50	.80	.78	.78	.78	.78	.78	.78
75	1.19	1.17	1.17	1.17	1.17	1.16	1.16
100	1.59	1.56	1.56	1.55	1.55	1.55	1.55
200	3.17	3.12	3.11	3.10	3.10	3.09	3.09
300	4.75	4.68	4.66	4.65	4.65	4.64	4.63
400	6.33	6.23	6.21	6.20	6.20	6.18	6.18
500	7.91	7.79	7.76	7.75	7.74	7.73	7.72
600	9.50	9.35	9.31	9.30	9.29	9.27	9.26
700	11.08	10.91	10.86	10.85	10.84	10.81	10.80
800	12.66	12.46	12.41	12.40	12.39	12.36	12.35
900	14.24	14.02	13.96	13.95	13.94	13.90	13.89
1000	15.82	15.58	15.51	15.50	15.48	15.45	15.43
2000	31.64	31.15	31.02	30.99	30.96	30.89	30.86
2500	39.55	38.94	38.77	38.74	38.70	38.61	38.57
3000	47.46	46.73	46.53	46.48	46.44	46.33	46.28
4000	63.28	62.30	62.03	61.97	61.92	61.77	61.71
5000	79.10	77.88	77.54	77.47	77.40	77.21	77.14
6000	94.92	93.45	93.05	92.96	92.88	92.66	92.56
7000	110.74	109.03	108.56	108.45	108.36	108.10	107.99
8000	126.56	124.60	124.06	123.94	123.84	123.54	123.42
9000	142.38	140.18	139.57	139.43	139.32	138.98	138.84
10000	158.19	155.75	155.08	154.93	154.80	154.42	154.27
11000	174.01	171.33	170.59	170.42	170.28	169.86	169.70
12000	189.83	186.90	186.09	185.91	185.76	185.31	185.12
13000	205.65	202.48	201.60	201.40	201.24	200.75	200.55
14000	221.47	218.05	217.11	216.90	216.72	216.19	215.98
15000	237.29	233.63	232.62	232.39	232.20	231.63	231.40
16000	253.11	249.20	248.12	247.88	247.68	247.07	246.83
17000	268.93	264.78	263.63	263.37	263.16	262.51	262.26
18000	284.75	280.35	279.14	278.87	278.64	277.96	277.68
19000	300.57	295.93	294.65	294.36	294.11	293.40	293.11
20000	316.38	311.50	310.15	309.85	309.59	308.84	308.54
21000	332.20	327.08	325.66	325.34	325.07	324.28	323.96
22000	348.02	342.65	341.17	340.83	340.55	339.72	339.39
23000	363.84	358.23	356.68	356.32	356.03	355.16	354.82
24000	379.66	373.80	372.18	371.82	371.51	370.61	370.24
25000	395.48	389.38	387.69	387.31	386.99	386.05	385.67
26000	411.30	404.95	403.20	402.80	402.47	401.49	401.10
27000	427.12	420.53	418.71	418.29	417.95	416.93	416.52
28000	442.94	436.10	434.21	433.79	433.43	432.37	431.95
29000	458.76	451.68	449.72	449.28	448.91	447.81	447.38
30000	474.57	467.25	465.23	464.77	464.39	463.26	462.80
31000	490.39	482.83	480.74	480.26	479.87	478.70	478.23
32000	506.21	498.40	496.24	495.75	4 5.35	494.14	493.66
33000	522.03	513.97	511.75	511.25	510.83	509.58	509.08
34000	537.85	529.55	527.26	526.74	526.31	525.02	524.51
35000	553.67	545.12	542.77	542.23	541.79	540.46	539.94
36000	569.49	560.70	558.27	557.72	557.27	555.91	555.36
37000	585.31	576.27	573.78	573.21	572.74	571.35	570.79
38000	601.13	591.85	589.29	588.71	588.22	586.79	586.22
39000	616.94	607.42	604.80	604.20	603.70	602.23	601.64
40000	632.76	623.00	620.30	619.69	619.18	617.67	617.07
45000	711.86	700.87	697.84	697.15	696.58	694.88	694.20
50000	790.95	778.75	775.38	774.61	773.98	772.09	771.34
55000	870.05	856.62	852.92	852.07	851.37	849.30	848.47
60000	949.14	934.50	930.45	929.53	928.77	926.51	925.60
65000	1028.24	1012.37	1007.99	1007.00	1006.17	1003.71	1002.74
70000	1107.33	1090.24	1085.53	1084.46	1083.57	1080.92	1079.87
75000	1186.43	1168.12	1163.06	1161.92	1160.96	1158.13	1157.00
80000	1265.52	1245.99	1240.60	1239.38	1238.36	1235.34	1234.14
85000	1344.62	1323.87	1318.14	1316.84	1315.76	1312.55	1311.27
90000	1423.71	1401.74	1395.68	1394.30	1393.16	1389.76	1388.40
95000	1502.81	1479.61	1473.21	1471.76	1470.55	1466.96	1465.54
100000	1581.90	1557.49	1550.75	1549.22	1547.95	1544.17	1542.67

18.75% MONTHLY AMORTIZING PAYMENTS

AMOUNT OF LOAN	NUMBER OF YEARS IN TERM						
	1	2	3	4	5	10	15
$ 25	2.31	1.26	.92	.75	.65	.47	.42
50	4.61	2.52	1.83	1.49	1.30	.93	.84
75	6.91	3.78	2.74	2.24	1.94	1.39	1.25
100	9.21	5.03	3.66	2.98	2.59	1.86	1.67
200	18.41	10.06	7.31	5.96	5.17	3.71	3.33
300	27.62	15.09	10.96	8.94	7.75	5.56	5.00
400	36.82	20.12	14.62	11.91	10.33	7.41	6.66
500	46.02	25.15	18.27	14.89	12.91	9.26	8.33
600	55.23	30.18	21.92	17.87	15.49	11.11	9.99
700	64.43	35.21	25.58	20.84	18.07	12.96	11.66
800	73.63	40.23	29.23	23.82	20.65	14.81	13.32
900	82.84	45.26	32.88	26.80	23.23	16.66	14.99
1000	92.04	50.29	36.53	29.77	25.81	18.51	16.65
2000	184.08	100.58	73.06	59.54	51.61	37.01	33.30
2500	230.10	125.72	91.33	74.43	64.51	46.27	41.62
3000	276.12	150.87	109.59	89.31	77.41	55.52	49.95
4000	368.15	201.15	146.12	119.08	103.22	74.02	66.59
5000	460.19	251.44	182.65	148.85	129.02	92.53	83.24
6000	552.23	301.73	219.18	178.62	154.82	111.03	99.89
7000	644.27	352.02	255.71	208.38	180.63	129.53	116.53
8000	736.30	402.30	292.24	238.15	206.43	148.04	133.18
9000	828.34	452.59	328.77	267.92	232.23	166.54	149.83
10000	920.38	502.88	365.30	297.69	258.04	185.05	166.47
11000	1012.42	553.16	401.83	327.46	283.84	203.55	183.12
12000	1104.45	603.45	438.36	357.23	309.64	222.05	199.77
13000	1196.49	653.74	474.89	386.99	335.45	240.56	216.41
14000	1288.53	704.03	511.42	416.76	361.25	259.06	233.06
15000	1380.56	754.31	547.95	446.53	387.05	277.57	249.71
16000	1472.60	804.60	584.48	476.30	412.86	296.07	266.35
17000	1564.64	854.89	621.01	506.07	438.66	314.58	283.00
18000	1656.68	905.18	657.54	535.84	464.46	333.08	299.65
19000	1748.71	955.46	694.07	565.60	490.27	351.58	316.29
20000	1840.75	1005.75	730.60	595.37	516.07	370.09	332.94
21000	1932.79	1056.04	767.13	625.14	541.87	388.59	349.59
22000	2024.83	1106.32	803.66	654.91	567.68	407.10	366.23
23000	2116.86	1156.61	840.19	684.68	593.48	425.60	382.88
24000	2208.90	1206.90	876.72	714.45	619.28	444.10	399.53
25000	2300.94	1257.19	913.25	744.21	645.08	462.61	416.17
26000	2392.97	1307.47	949.78	773.98	670.89	481.11	432.82
27000	2485.01	1357.76	986.31	803.75	696.69	499.62	449.47
28000	2577.05	1408.05	1022.84	833.52	722.49	518.12	466.11
29000	2669.09	1458.33	1059.37	863.29	748.30	536.63	482.76
30000	2761.12	1508.62	1095.90	893.06	774.10	555.13	499.41
31000	2853.16	1558.91	1132.43	922.82	799.90	573.63	516.05
32000	2945.20	1609.20	1168.96	952.59	825.71	592.14	532.70
33000	3037.24	1659.48	1205.49	982.36	851.51	610.64	549.35
34000	3129.27	1709.77	1242.02	1012.13	877.31	629.15	565.99
35000	3221.31	1760.06	1278.55	1041.90	903.12	647.65	582.64
36000	3313.35	1810.35	1315.08	1071.67	928.92	666.15	599.29
37000	3405.39	1860.63	1351.61	1101.43	954.72	684.66	615.93
38000	3497.42	1910.92	1388.14	1131.20	980.53	703.16	632.58
39000	3589.46	1961.21	1424.67	1160.97	1006.33	721.67	649.23
40000	3681.50	2011.49	1461.19	1190.74	1032.13	740.17	665.87
45000	4141.68	2262.93	1643.84	1339.58	1161.15	832.69	749.11
50000	4601.87	2514.37	1826.49	1488.42	1290.16	925.21	832.34
55000	5062.06	2765.80	2009.14	1637.26	1419.18	1017.73	915.57
60000	5522.24	3017.24	2191.79	1786.11	1548.20	1110.25	998.81
65000	5982.43	3268.68	2374.44	1934.95	1677.21	1202.77	1082.04
70000	6442.62	3520.11	2557.09	2083.79	1806.23	1295.29	1165.27
75000	6902.80	3771.55	2739.74	2232.63	1935.24	1387.82	1248.51
80000	7362.99	4022.98	2922.38	2381.47	2064.26	1480.34	1331.74
85000	7823.18	4274.42	3105.03	2530.32	2193.28	1572.86	1414.97
90000	8283.36	4525.86	3287.68	2679.16	2322.29	1665.38	1498.21
95000	8743.55	4777.29	3470.33	2828.00	2451.31	1757.90	1581.44
100000	9203.74	5028.73	3652.98	2976.84	2580.32	1850.42	1664.67

AMOUNT OF LOAN	NUMBER OF YEARS IN TERM						
	20	25	28	29	30	35	40
$ 25	.41	.40	.40	.40	40	.40	.40
50	.81	.79	.79	.79	79	.79	.79
75	1.21	1.19	1.18	1.18	1.18	1.18	1.18
100	1.61	1.58	1.58	1.57	1.57	1.57	1.57
200	3.21	3.16	3.15	3.14	3.14	3.13	3.13
300	4.81	4.74	4.72	4.71	4.71	4.70	4.70
400	6.41	6.32	6.29	6.28	6.28	6.26	6.26
500	8.01	7.89	7.86	7.85	7.85	7.83	7.82
600	9.61	9.47	9.43	9.42	9.42	9.39	9.39
700	11.21	11.05	11.00	10.99	10.98	10.96	10.95
800	12.82	12.63	12.57	12.56	12.55	12.52	12.51
900	14.42	14.20	14.14	14.13	14.12	14.09	14.08
1000	16.02	15.78	15.72	15.70	15.69	15.65	15.64
2000	32.03	31.56	31.43	31.40	31.37	31.30	31.27
2500	40.04	39.44	39.28	39.25	39.22	39.13	39.09
3000	48.04	47.33	47.14	47.09	47.06	46.95	46.91
4000	64.06	63.11	62.85	62.79	62.74	62.60	62.54
5000	80.07	78.88	78.56	78.49	78.43	78.25	78.18
6000	96.08	94.66	94.27	94.18	94.11	93.89	93.81
7000	112.09	110.43	109.98	109.88	109.80	109.54	109.44
8000	128.11	126.21	125.69	125.57	125.48	125.19	125.08
9000	144.12	141.99	141.40	141.27	141.16	140.84	140.71
10000	160.13	157.76	157.11	156.97	156.85	156.49	156.35
11000	176.14	173.54	172.82	172.66	172.53	172.14	171.98
12000	192.16	189.31	188.54	188.36	188.21	187.78	187.61
13000	208.17	205.09	204.25	204.06	203.90	203.43	203.25
14000	224.18	220.86	219.96	219.75	219.58	219.08	218.88
15000	240.19	236.64	235.67	235.45	235.27	234.73	234.52
16000	256.21	252.42	251.38	251.14	250.95	250.38	250.15
17000	272.22	268.19	267.09	266.84	266.63	266.03	265.79
18000	288.23	283.97	282.80	282.54	282.32	281.67	281.42
19000	304.25	299.74	298.51	298.23	298.00	297.32	297.05
20000	320.26	315.52	314.22	313.93	313.69	312.97	312.69
21000	336.27	331.29	329.93	329.63	329.37	328.62	328.32
22000	352.28	347.07	345.64	345.32	345.05	344.27	343.96
23000	368.30	362.84	361.35	361.02	360.74	359.91	359.59
24000	384.31	378.62	377.07	376.71	376.42	375.56	375.22
25000	400.32	394.40	392.78	392.41	392.11	391.21	390.86
26000	416.33	410.17	408.49	408.11	407.79	406.86	406.49
27000	432.35	425.95	424.20	423.80	423.48	422.51	422.13
28000	448.36	441.72	439.91	439.50	439.16	438.16	437.76
29000	464.37	457.50	455.62	455.20	454.84	453.80	453.40
30000	480.38	473.27	471.33	470.89	470.53	469.45	469.03
31000	496.40	489.05	487.04	486.59	486.21	485.10	484.66
32000	512.41	504.83	502.75	502.28	501.90	500.75	500.30
33000	528.42	520.60	518.46	517.98	517.58	516.40	515.93
34000	544.44	536.38	534.17	533.68	533.26	532.05	531.57
35000	560.45	552.15	549.89	549.37	548.95	547.69	547.20
36000	576.46	567.93	565.60	565.07	564.63	563.34	562.83
37000	592.47	583.70	581.31	580.76	580.32	578.99	578.47
38000	608.49	599.48	597.02	596.46	596.00	594.64	594.10
39000	624.50	615.26	612.73	612.16	611.68	610.29	609.74
40000	640.51	631.03	628.44	627.85	627.37	625.94	625.37
45000	720.57	709.91	706.99	706.33	705.79	704.18	703.54
50000	800.64	788.79	785.55	784.82	784.21	782.42	781.71
55000	880.70	867.67	864.10	863.30	862.63	860.66	859.88
60000	960.76	946.54	942.66	941.78	941.05	938.90	938.05
65000	1040.83	1025.42	1021.21	1020.26	1019.47	1017.14	1016.23
70000	1120.89	1104.30	1099.77	1098.74	1097.89	1095.38	1094.40
75000	1200.95	1183.18	1178.32	1177.22	1176.31	1173.62	1172.57
80000	1281.02	1262.06	1256.87	1255.70	1254.73	1251.87	1250.74
85000	1361.08	1340.94	1335.43	1334.18	1333.15	1330.11	1328.91
90000	1441.14	1419.81	1413.98	1412.66	1411.57	1408.35	1407.08
95000	1521.21	1498.69	1492.54	1491.15	1489.99	1486.59	1485.25
100000	1601.27	1577.57	1571.09	1569.63	1568.41	1564.83	1563.42

19.00% MONTHLY AMORTIZING PAYMENTS

AMOUNT OF LOAN	NUMBER OF YEARS IN TERM						
	1	2	3	4	5	10	15
$ 25	2.31	1.27	.92	.75	.65	.47	.43
50	4.61	2.53	1.84	1.50	1.30	.94	.85
75	6.92	3.79	2.75	2.25	1.95	1.41	1.27
100	9.22	5.05	3.67	3.00	2.60	1.87	1.69
200	18.44	10.09	7.34	5.99	5.19	3.74	3.37
300	27.65	15.13	11.00	8.98	7.79	5.61	5.05
400	36.87	20.17	14.67	11.97	10.38	7.47	6.74
500	46.08	25.21	18.33	14.96	12.98	9.34	8.42
600	55.30	30.25	22.00	17.95	15.57	11.21	10.10
700	64.51	35.29	25.66	20.94	18.16	13.07	11.79
800	73.73	40.33	29.33	23.93	20.76	14.94	13.47
900	82.95	45.37	33.00	26.92	23.35	16.81	15.15
1000	92.16	50.41	36.66	29.91	25.95	18.67	16.83
2000	184.32	100.82	73.32	59.81	51.89	37.34	33.66
2500	230.40	126.03	91.65	74.76	64.86	46.67	42.08
3000	276.47	151.23	109.97	89.71	77.83	56.01	50.49
4000	368.63	201.64	146.63	119.61	103.77	74.67	67.32
5000	460.79	252.05	183.29	149.51	129.71	93.34	84.15
6000	552.94	302.46	219.94	179.41	155.65	112.01	100.98
7000	645.10	352.87	256.60	209.31	181.59	130.68	117.81
8000	737.26	403.27	293.25	239.21	207.53	149.34	134.64
9000	829.41	453.68	329.91	269.11	233.47	168.01	151.46
10000	921.57	504.09	366.57	299.01	259.41	186.68	168.29
11000	1013.73	554.50	403.22	328.91	285.35	205.34	185.12
12000	1105.88	604.91	439.88	358.81	311.29	224.01	201.95
13000	1198.04	655.32	476.53	388.71	337.23	242.68	218.78
14000	1290.20	705.73	513.19	418.61	363.17	261.35	235.61
15000	1382.35	756.13	549.85	448.51	389.11	280.01	252.44
16000	1474.51	806.54	586.50	478.41	415.05	298.68	269.27
17000	1566.67	856.95	623.16	508.31	440.99	317.35	286.09
18000	1658.82	907.36	659.81	538.21	466.93	336.02	302.92
19000	1750.98	957.77	696.47	568.11	492.88	354.68	319.75
20000	1843.14	1008.18	733.13	598.01	518.82	373.35	336.58
21000	1935.29	1058.59	769.78	627.91	544.76	392.02	353.41
22000	2027.45	1108.99	806.44	657.81	570.70	410.68	370.24
23000	2119.61	1159.40	843.09	687.71	596.64	429.35	387.07
24000	2211.76	1209.81	879.75	717.61	622.58	448.02	403.90
25000	2303.92	1260.22	916.41	747.51	648.52	466.69	420.72
26000	2396.08	1310.63	953.06	777.41	674.46	485.35	437.55
27000	2488.23	1361.04	989.72	807.31	700.40	504.02	454.38
28000	2580.39	1411.45	1026.37	837.21	726.34	522.69	471.21
29000	2672.55	1461.85	1063.03	867.11	752.28	541.35	488.04
30000	2764.70	1512.26	1099.69	897.01	778.22	560.02	504.87
31000	2856.86	1562.67	1136.34	926.91	804.16	578.69	521.70
32000	2949.02	1613.08	1173.00	956.81	830.10	597.36	538.53
33000	3041.17	1663.49	1209.65	986.71	856.04	616.02	555.35
34000	3133.33	1713.90	1246.31	1016.61	881.98	634.69	572.18
35000	3225.49	1764.31	1282.97	1046.51	907.92	653.36	589.01
36000	3317.64	1814.72	1319.62	1076.41	933.86	672.03	605.84
37000	3409.80	1865.12	1356.28	1106.31	959.81	690.69	622.67
38000	3501.95	1915.53	1392.93	1136.21	985.75	709.36	639.50
39000	3594.11	1965.94	1429.59	1166.11	1011.69	728.03	656.33
40000	3686.27	2016.35	1466.25	1196.01	1037.63	746.69	673.16
45000	4147.55	2268.39	1649.53	1345.51	1167.33	840.03	757.30
50000	4607.83	2520.44	1832.81	1495.01	1297.03	933.37	841.44
55000	5068.62	2772.48	2016.09	1644.51	1426.74	1026.70	925.59
60000	5529.40	3024.52	2199.37	1794.01	1556.44	1120.04	1009.73
65000	5990.18	3276.57	2382.65	1943.51	1686.14	1213.38	1093.87
70000	6450.97	3528.61	2565.93	2093.01	1815.84	1306.71	1178.02
75000	6911.75	3780.65	2749.21	2242.51	1945.55	1400.05	1262.16
80000	7372.53	4032.69	2932.49	2392.01	2075.25	1493.38	1346.31
85000	7833.31	4284.74	3115.77	2541.52	2204.95	1586.72	1430.45
90000	8294.10	4536.78	3299.05	2691.02	2334.65	1680.06	1514.59
95000	8754.88	4788.82	3482.33	2840.52	2464.36	1773.39	1598.74
100000	9215.66	5040.87	3665.61	2990.02	2594.06	1866.73	1682.88

AMOUNT OF LOAN	NUMBER OF YEARS IN TERM						
	20	25	28	29	30	35	40
$ 25	.41	.40	.40	.40	.40	.40	.40
50	.82	.80	.80	.80	.80	.80	.80
75	1.22	1.20	1.20	1.20	1.20	1.19	1.19
100	1.63	1.60	1.60	1.60	1.59	1.59	1.59
200	3.25	3.20	3.19	3.19	3.18	3.18	3.17
300	4.87	4.80	4.78	4.78	4.77	4.76	4.76
400	6.49	6.40	6.37	6.37	6.36	6.35	6.34
500	8.11	7.99	7.96	7.96	7.95	7.93	7.93
600	9.73	9.59	9.55	9.55	9.54	9.52	9.51
700	11.35	11.19	11.15	11.14	11.13	11.10	11.09
800	12.97	12.79	12.74	12.73	12.72	12.69	12.68
900	14.59	14.38	14.33	14.32	14.31	14.27	14.26
1000	16.21	15.98	15.92	15.91	15.89	15.86	15.85
2000	32.42	31.96	31.83	31.81	31.78	31.71	31.69
2500	40.52	39.95	39.79	39.76	39.73	39.64	39.61
3000	48.63	47.94	47.75	47.71	47.67	47.57	47.53
4000	64.83	63.91	63.66	63.61	63.56	63.42	63.37
5000	81.04	79.89	79.58	79.51	79.45	79.28	79.21
6000	97.25	95.87	95.49	95.41	95.34	95.13	95.06
7000	113.45	111.84	111.41	111.31	111.23	110.99	110.90
8000	129.66	127.82	127.32	127.21	127.12	126.84	126.74
9000	145.87	143.80	143.24	143.11	143.01	142.70	142.58
10000	162.07	159.77	159.15	159.01	158.89	158.55	158.42
11000	178.28	175.75	175.06	174.91	174.78	174.41	174.26
12000	194.49	191.73	190.98	190.81	190.67	190.26	190.11
13000	210.69	207.70	206.89	206.71	206.56	206.12	205.95
14000	226.90	223.68	222.81	222.61	222.45	221.97	221.79
15000	243.11	239.66	238.72	238.51	238.34	237.83	237.63
16000	259.31	255.63	254.64	254.41	254.23	253.68	253.47
17000	275.52	271.61	270.55	270.31	270.12	269.54	269.31
18000	291.73	287.59	286.47	286.21	286.01	285.39	285.16
19000	307.94	303.56	302.38	302.11	301.89	301.25	301.00
20000	324.14	319.54	318.30	318.02	317.78	317.10	316.84
21000	340.35	335.52	334.21	333.92	333.67	332.96	332.68
22000	356.56	351.49	350.12	349.82	349.56	348.81	348.52
23000	372.76	367.47	366.04	365.72	365.45	364.67	364.37
24000	388.97	383.45	381.95	381.62	381.34	380.52	380.21
25000	405.18	399.43	397.87	397.52	397.23	396.38	396.05
26000	421.38	415.40	413.78	413.42	413.12	412.23	411.89
27000	437.59	431.38	429.70	429.32	429.01	428.09	427.73
28000	453.80	447.36	445.61	445.22	444.89	443.94	443.57
29000	470.00	463.33	461.53	461.12	460.78	459.80	459.42
30000	486.21	479.31	477.44	477.02	476.67	475.65	475.26
31000	502.42	495.29	493.35	492.92	492.56	491.51	491.10
32000	518.62	511.26	509.27	508.82	508.45	507.36	506.94
33000	534.83	527.24	525.18	524.72	524.34	523.22	522.78
34000	551.04	543.22	541.10	540.62	540.23	539.07	538.62
35000	567.24	559.19	557.01	556.52	556.12	554.93	554.47
36000	583.45	575.17	572.93	572.42	572.01	570.78	570.31
37000	599.66	591.15	588.84	588.32	587.90	586.64	586.15
38000	615.87	607.12	604.76	604.22	603.78	602.49	601.99
39000	632.07	623.10	620.67	620.12	619.67	618.35	617.83
40000	648.28	639.08	636.59	636.03	635.56	634.20	633.67
45000	729.31	718.96	716.16	715.53	715.01	713.48	712.88
50000	810.35	798.85	795.73	795.03	794.45	792.75	792.09
55000	891.38	878.73	875.30	874.53	873.90	872.03	871.30
60000	972.42	958.61	954.88	954.04	953.34	951.30	950.51
65000	1053.45	1038.50	1034.45	1033.54	1032.79	1030.58	1029.72
70000	1134.48	1118.38	1114.02	1113.04	1112.23	1109.85	1108.93
75000	1215.52	1198.27	1193.59	1192.54	1191.67	1189.13	1188.14
80000	1296.55	1278.15	1273.17	1272.05	1271.12	1268.40	1267.34
85000	1377.59	1358.03	1352.74	1351.55	1350.56	1347.68	1346.55
90000	1458.62	1437.92	1432.31	1431.05	1430.01	1426.95	1425.76
95000	1539.66	1517.80	1511.88	1510.55	1509.45	1506.22	1504.97
100000	1620.69	1597.69	1591.46	1590.06	1588.90	1585.50	1584.18

19.25% MONTHLY AMORTIZING PAYMENTS

AMOUNT OF LOAN	NUMBER OF YEARS IN TERM						
	1	2	3	4	5	10	15
$ 25	2.31	1.27	.92	.76	.66	.48	.43
50	4.62	2.53	1.84	1.51	1.31	.95	.86
75	6.93	3.79	2.76	2.26	1.96	1.42	1.28
100	9.23	5.06	3.68	3.01	2.61	1.89	1.71
200	18.46	10.11	7.36	6.01	5.22	3.77	3.41
300	27.69	15.16	11.04	9.01	7.83	5.65	5.11
400	36.92	20.22	14.72	12.02	10.44	7.54	6.81
500	46.14	25.27	18.40	15.02	13.04	9.42	8.51
600	55.37	30.32	22.07	18.02	15.65	11.30	10.21
700	64.60	35.38	25.75	21.03	18.26	13.19	11.91
800	73.83	40.43	29.43	24.03	20.87	15.07	13.61
900	83.05	45.48	33.11	27.03	23.48	16.95	15.32
1000	92.28	50.54	36.79	30.04	26.08	18.84	17.02
2000	184.56	101.07	73.57	60.07	52.16	37.67	34.03
2500	230.69	126.33	91.96	75.09	65.20	47.08	42.53
3000	276.83	151.60	110.35	90.10	78.24	56.50	51.04
4000	369.11	202.13	147.14	120.13	104.32	75.33	68.05
5000	461.38	252.66	183.92	150.17	130.40	94.16	85.06
6000	553.66	303.19	220.70	180.20	156.47	112.99	102.07
7000	645.94	353.72	257.48	210.23	182.55	131.82	119.09
8000	738.21	404.25	294.27	240.26	208.63	150.65	136.10
9000	830.49	454.78	331.05	270.29	234.71	169.48	153.11
10000	922.76	505.31	367.83	300.33	260.79	188.31	170.12
11000	1015.04	555.84	404.61	330.36	286.87	207.15	187.13
12000	1107.32	606.37	441.40	360.39	312.94	225.98	204.14
13000	1199.59	656.90	478.18	390.42	339.02	244.81	221.15
14000	1291.87	707.43	514.96	420.46	365.10	263.64	238.17
15000	1384.14	757.96	551.74	450.49	391.18	282.47	255.18
16000	1476.42	808.49	588.53	480.52	417.26	301.30	272.19
17000	1568.70	859.02	625.31	510.55	443.34	320.13	289.20
18000	1660.97	909.55	662.09	540.58	469.41	338.96	306.21
19000	1753.25	960.08	698.87	570.62	495.49	357.79	323.22
20000	1845.52	1010.61	735.66	600.65	521.57	376.62	340.23
21000	1937.80	1061.14	772.44	630.68	547.65	395.45	357.25
22000	2030.08	1111.67	809.22	660.71	573.73	414.29	374.26
23000	2122.35	1162.20	846.00	690.75	599.81	433.12	391.27
24000	2214.63	1212.73	882.79	720.78	625.88	451.95	408.28
25000	2306.90	1263.26	919.57	750.81	651.96	470.78	425.29
26000	2399.18	1313.79	956.35	780.84	678.04	489.61	442.30
27000	2491.46	1364.32	993.13	810.87	704.12	508.44	459.31
28000	2583.73	1414.85	1029.92	840.91	730.20	527.27	476.33
29000	2676.01	1465.38	1066.70	870.94	756.28	546.10	493.34
30000	2768.28	1515.91	1103.48	900.97	782.35	564.93	510.35
31000	2860.56	1566.44	1140.26	931.00	808.43	583.76	527.36
32000	2952.83	1616.97	1177.05	961.04	834.51	602.59	544.37
33000	3045.11	1667.50	1213.83	991.07	860.59	621.43	561.38
34000	3137.39	1718.03	1250.61	1021.10	886.67	640.26	578.39
35000	3229.66	1768.56	1287.39	1051.13	912.75	659.09	595.41
36000	3321.94	1819.09	1324.18	1081.16	938.82	677.92	612.42
37000	3414.21	1869.62	1360.96	1111.20	964.90	696.75	629.43
38000	3506.49	1920.15	1397.74	1141.23	990.98	715.58	646.44
39000	3598.77	1970.68	1434.52	1171.26	1017.06	734.41	663.45
40000	3691.04	2021.21	1471.31	1201.29	1043.14	753.24	680.46
45000	4152.42	2273.86	1655.22	1351.45	1173.53	847.40	765.52
50000	4613.80	2526.51	1839.13	1501.62	1303.92	941.55	850.58
55000	5075.18	2779.16	2023.04	1651.78	1434.31	1035.71	935.63
60000	5536.56	3031.81	2206.96	1801.94	1564.70	1129.86	1020.69
65000	5997.94	3284.47	2390.87	1952.10	1695.09	1224.02	1105.75
70000	6459.32	3537.12	2574.78	2102.26	1825.49	1318.17	1190.81
75000	6920.70	3789.77	2758.70	2252.42	1955.88	1412.32	1275.86
80000	7382.08	4042.42	2942.61	2402.58	2086.27	1506.48	1360.92
85000	7843.46	4295.07	3126.52	2552.74	2216.66	1600.63	1445.98
90000	8304.84	4547.72	3310.43	2702.90	2347.05	1694.79	1531.03
95000	8766.22	4800.37	3494.35	2853.06	2477.44	1788.94	1616.09
100000	9227.60	5053.02	3678.26	3003.23	2607.84	1883.10	1701.15

MONTHLY AMORTIZING PAYMENTS 19.25%

AMOUNT OF LOAN	NUMBER OF YEARS IN TERM						
	20	25	28	29	30	35	40
$ 25	.42	.41	.41	.41	.41	.41	.41
50	.83	.81	.81	.81	.81	.81	.81
75	1.24	1.22	1.21	1.21	1.21	1.21	1.21
100	1.65	1.62	1.62	1.62	1.61	1.61	1.61
200	3.29	3.24	3.23	3.23	3.22	3.22	3.21
300	4.93	4.86	4.84	4.84	4.83	4.82	4.82
400	6.57	6.48	6.45	6.45	6.44	6.43	6.42
500	8.21	8.09	8.06	8.06	8.05	8.04	8.03
600	9.85	9.71	9.68	9.67	9.66	9.64	9.63
700	11.49	11.33	11.29	11.28	11.27	11.25	11.24
800	13.13	12.95	12.90	12.89	12.88	12.85	12.84
900	14.77	14.57	14.51	14.50	14.49	14.46	14.45
1000	16.41	16.18	16.12	16.11	16.10	16.07	16.05
2000	32.81	32.36	32.24	32.22	32.19	32.13	32.10
2500	41.01	40.45	40.30	40.27	40.24	40.16	40.13
3000	49.21	48.54	48.36	48.32	48.29	48.19	48.15
4000	65.61	64.72	64.48	64.43	64.38	64.25	64.20
5000	82.01	80.90	80.60	80.53	80.47	80.31	80.25
6000	98.41	97.07	96.72	96.64	96.57	96.38	96.30
7000	114.82	113.25	112.83	112.74	112.66	112.44	112.35
8000	131.22	129.43	128.95	128.85	128.76	128.50	128.40
9000	147.62	145.61	145.07	144.95	144.85	144.56	144.45
10000	164.02	161.79	161.19	161.06	160.94	160.62	160.50
11000	180.42	177.97	177.31	177.16	177.04	176.68	176.55
12000	196.82	194.14	193.43	193.27	193.13	192.75	192.60
13000	213.22	210.32	209.54	209.37	209.23	208.81	208.65
14000	229.63	226.50	225.66	225.48	225.32	224.87	224.70
15000	246.03	242.68	241.78	241.58	241.41	240.93	240.75
16000	262.43	258.86	257.90	257.69	257.51	256.99	256.80
17000	278.83	275.04	274.02	273.79	273.60	273.05	272.84
18000	295.23	291.21	290.14	289.90	289.70	289.12	288.89
19000	311.63	307.39	306.25	306.00	305.79	305.18	304.94
20000	328.04	323.57	322.37	322.11	321.88	321.24	320.99
21000	344.44	339.75	338.49	338.21	337.98	337.30	337.04
22000	360.84	355.93	354.61	354.32	354.07	353.36	353.09
23000	377.24	372.11	370.73	370.42	370.17	369.43	369.14
24000	393.64	388.28	386.85	386.53	386.26	385.49	385.19
25000	410.04	404.46	402.97	402.63	402.35	401.55	401.24
26000	426.44	420.64	419.08	418.74	418.45	417.61	417.29
27000	442.85	436.82	435.20	434.84	434.54	433.67	433.34
28000	459.25	453.00	451.32	450.95	450.64	449.73	449.39
29000	475.65	469.17	467.44	467.05	466.73	465.80	465.44
30000	492.05	485.35	483.56	483.16	482.82	481.86	481.49
31000	508.45	501.53	499.68	499.26	498.92	497.92	497.54
32000	524.85	517.71	515.79	515.37	515.01	513.98	513.59
33000	541.25	533.89	531.91	531.47	531.11	530.04	529.63
34000	557.66	550.07	548.03	547.58	547.20	546.10	545.68
35000	574.06	566.24	564.15	563.68	563.29	562.17	561.73
36000	590.46	582.42	580.27	579.79	579.39	578.23	577.78
37000	606.86	598.60	596.39	595.89	595.48	594.29	593.83
38000	623.26	614.78	612.50	612.00	611.58	610.35	609.88
39000	639.66	630.96	628.62	628.10	627.67	626.41	625.93
40000	656.07	647.14	644.74	644.21	643.76	642.48	641.98
45000	738.07	728.03	725.33	724.73	724.23	722.78	722.23
50000	820.08	808.92	805.93	805.26	804.70	803.09	802.47
55000	902.09	889.81	886.52	885.78	885.17	883.40	882.72
60000	984.10	970.70	967.11	966.31	965.64	963.71	962.97
65000	1066.10	1051.59	1047.70	1046.83	1046.11	1044.02	1043.22
70000	1148.11	1132.48	1128.29	1127.36	1126.58	1124.33	1123.46
75000	1230.12	1213.38	1208.89	1207.88	1207.05	1204.64	1203.71
80000	1312.13	1294.27	1289.48	1288.41	1287.52	1284.95	1283.96
85000	1394.13	1375.16	1370.07	1368.93	1367.99	1365.25	1364.20
90000	1476.14	1456.05	1450.66	1449.46	1448.46	1445.56	1444.45
95000	1558.15	1536.94	1531.25	1529.98	1528.93	1525.87	1524.70
100000	1640.16	1617.83	1611.85	1610.51	1609.40	1606.18	1604.94

85

19.50% MONTHLY AMORTIZING PAYMENTS

AMOUNT OF LOAN	NUMBER OF YEARS IN TERM						
	1	2	3	4	5	10	15
$ 25	2.31	1.27	.93	.76	.66	.48	.43
50	4.62	2.54	1.85	1.51	1.32	.95	.86
75	6.93	3.80	2.77	2.27	1.97	1.43	1.29
100	9.24	5.07	3.70	3.02	2.63	1.90	1.72
200	18.48	10.14	7.39	6.04	5.25	3.80	3.44
300	27.72	15.20	11.08	9.05	7.87	5.70	5.16
400	36.96	20.27	14.77	12.07	10.49	7.60	6.88
500	46.20	25.33	18.46	15.09	13.11	9.50	8.60
600	55.44	30.40	22.15	18.10	15.73	11.40	10.32
700	64.68	35.46	25.84	21.12	18.36	13.30	12.04
800	73.92	40.53	29.53	24.14	20.98	15.20	13.76
900	83.16	45.59	33.22	27.15	23.60	17.10	15.48
1000	92.40	50.66	36.91	30.17	26.22	19.00	17.20
2000	184.80	101.31	73.82	60.33	52.44	38.00	34.39
2500	230.99	126.63	92.28	75.42	65.55	47.49	42.99
3000	277.19	151.96	110.73	90.50	78.65	56.99	51.59
4000	369.59	202.61	147.64	120.66	104.87	75.99	68.78
5000	461.98	253.26	184.55	150.83	131.09	94.98	85.98
6000	554.38	303.92	221.46	180.99	157.30	113.98	103.17
7000	646.77	354.57	258.37	211.16	183.52	132.97	120.37
8000	739.17	405.22	295.28	241.32	209.74	151.97	137.56
9000	831.56	455.87	332.19	271.49	235.95	170.96	154.76
10000	923.96	506.52	369.10	301.65	262.17	189.96	171.95
11000	1016.35	557.18	406.01	331.82	288.39	208.95	189.15
12000	1108.75	607.83	442.92	361.98	314.60	227.95	206.34
13000	1201.14	658.48	479.83	392.14	340.82	246.94	223.54
14000	1293.54	709.13	516.74	422.31	367.04	265.94	240.73
15000	1385.94	759.78	553.64	452.47	393.25	284.93	257.93
16000	1478.33	810.44	590.55	482.64	419.47	303.93	275.12
17000	1570.73	861.09	627.46	512.80	445.68	322.92	292.31
18000	1663.12	911.74	664.37	542.97	471.90	341.92	309.51
19000	1755.52	962.39	701.28	573.13	498.12	360.91	326.70
20000	1847.91	1013.04	738.19	603.30	524.33	379.91	343.90
21000	1940.31	1063.69	775.10	633.46	550.55	398.90	361.09
22000	2032.70	1114.35	812.01	663.63	576.77	417.90	378.29
23000	2125.10	1165.00	848.92	693.79	602.98	436.90	395.48
24000	2217.49	1215.65	885.83	723.96	629.20	455.89	412.68
25000	2309.89	1266.30	922.74	754.12	655.42	474.89	429.87
26000	2402.28	1316.95	959.65	784.28	681.63	493.88	447.07
27000	2494.68	1367.61	996.56	814.45	707.85	512.88	464.26
28000	2587.08	1418.26	1033.47	844.61	734.07	531.87	481.46
29000	2679.47	1468.91	1070.38	874.78	760.28	550.87	498.65
30000	2771.87	1519.56	1107.28	904.94	786.50	569.86	515.85
31000	2864.26	1570.21	1144.19	935.11	812.71	588.86	533.04
32000	2956.66	1620.87	1181.10	965.27	838.93	607.85	550.24
33000	3049.05	1671.52	1218.01	995.44	865.15	626.85	567.43
34000	3141.45	1722.17	1254.92	1025.60	891.36	645.84	584.62
35000	3233.84	1772.82	1291.83	1055.77	917.58	664.84	601.82
36000	3326.24	1823.47	1328.74	1085.93	943.80	683.83	619.01
37000	3418.63	1874.13	1365.65	1116.10	970.01	702.83	636.21
38000	3511.03	1924.78	1402.56	1146.26	996.23	721.82	653.40
39000	3603.42	1975.43	1439.47	1176.42	1022.45	740.82	670.60
40000	3695.82	2026.08	1476.38	1206.59	1048.66	759.81	687.79
45000	4157.80	2279.34	1660.92	1357.41	1179.75	854.79	773.77
50000	4619.77	2532.60	1845.47	1508.24	1310.83	949.77	859.74
55000	5081.75	2785.86	2030.02	1659.06	1441.91	1044.74	945.71
60000	5543.73	3039.12	2214.56	1809.88	1572.99	1139.72	1031.69
65000	6005.70	3292.38	2399.11	1960.70	1704.07	1234.69	1117.66
70000	6467.68	3545.64	2583.66	2111.53	1835.16	1329.67	1203.63
75000	6929.66	3798.90	2768.20	2262.35	1966.24	1424.65	1289.61
80000	7391.63	4052.16	2952.75	2413.17	2097.32	1519.62	1375.58
85000	7853.61	4305.41	3137.30	2564.00	2228.40	1614.60	1461.55
90000	8315.59	4558.67	3321.84	2714.82	2359.49	1709.57	1547.53
95000	8777.57	4811.93	3506.39	2865.64	2490.57	1804.55	1633.50
100000	9239.54	5065.19	3690.94	3016.47	2621.65	1899.53	1719.48

86

MONTHLY AMORTIZING PAYMENTS 19.50%

AMOUNT OF LOAN	NUMBER OF YEARS IN TERM						
	20	25	28	29	30	35	40
$ 25	.42	.41	.41	.41	.41	.41	.41
50	.83	.82	.82	.82	.82	.82	.82
75	1.25	1.23	1.23	1.23	1.23	1.23	1.22
100	1.66	1.64	1.64	1.64	1.63	1.63	1.63
200	3.32	3.28	3.27	3.27	3.26	3.26	3.26
300	4.98	4.92	4.90	4.90	4.89	4.89	4.88
400	6.64	6.56	6.53	6.53	6.52	6.51	6.51
500	8.30	8.20	8.17	8.16	8.15	8.14	8.13
600	9.96	9.83	9.80	9.79	9.78	9.77	9.76
700	11.62	11.47	11.43	11.42	11.41	11.39	11.38
800	13.28	13.11	13.06	13.05	13.04	13.02	13.01
900	14.94	14.75	14.70	14.68	14.67	14.65	14.64
1000	16.60	16.39	16.33	16.31	16.30	16.27	16.26
2000	33.20	32.77	32.65	32.62	32.60	32.54	32.52
2500	41.50	40.96	40.81	40.78	40.75	40.68	40.65
3000	49.79	49.15	48.97	48.93	48.90	48.81	48.78
4000	66.39	65.53	65.30	65.24	65.20	65.08	65.03
5000	82.99	81.91	81.62	81.55	81.50	81.35	81.29
6000	99.58	98.29	97.94	97.86	97.80	97.62	97.55
7000	116.18	114.67	114.26	114.17	114.10	113.89	113.80
8000	132.78	131.05	130.59	130.48	130.40	130.15	130.06
9000	149.37	147.43	146.91	146.79	146.70	146.42	146.32
10000	165.97	163.81	163.23	163.10	163.00	162.69	162.58
11000	182.57	180.19	179.55	179.41	179.30	178.96	178.83
12000	199.16	196.57	195.88	195.72	195.60	195.23	195.09
13000	215.76	212.95	212.20	212.03	211.89	211.50	211.35
14000	232.36	229.33	228.52	228.34	228.19	227.77	227.60
15000	248.95	245.71	244.84	244.65	244.49	244.04	243.86
16000	265.55	262.09	261.17	260.96	260.79	260.30	260.12
17000	282.15	278.47	277.49	277.27	277.09	276.57	276.38
18000	298.74	294.85	293.81	293.58	293.39	292.84	292.63
19000	315.34	311.23	310.13	309.89	309.69	309.11	308.89
20000	331.94	327.61	326.46	326.20	325.99	325.38	325.15
21000	348.53	343.99	342.78	342.51	342.29	341.65	341.40
22000	365.13	360.37	359.10	358.82	358.59	357.92	357.66
23000	381.73	376.75	375.42	375.13	374.89	374.18	373.92
24000	398.32	393.13	391.75	391.44	391.19	390.45	390.18
25000	414.92	409.51	408.07	407.75	407.48	406.72	406.43
26000	431.52	425.89	424.39	424.06	423.78	422.99	422.69
27000	448.11	442.27	440.72	440.37	440.08	439.26	438.95
28000	464.71	458.65	457.04	456.68	456.38	455.53	455.20
29000	481.31	475.03	473.36	472.99	472.68	471.80	471.46
30000	497.90	491.41	489.68	489.30	488.98	488.07	487.72
31000	514.50	507.79	506.00	505.61	505.28	504.33	503.97
32000	531.10	524.17	522.33	521.92	521.58	520.60	520.23
33000	547.69	540.55	538.65	538.23	537.88	536.87	536.49
34000	564.29	556.93	554.97	554.54	554.18	553.14	552.75
35000	580.89	573.31	571.29	570.85	570.48	569.41	569.00
36000	597.48	589.69	587.62	587.16	586.78	585.68	585.26
37000	614.08	606.07	603.94	603.47	603.08	601.95	601.52
38000	630.68	622.45	620.26	619.78	619.37	618.21	617.77
39000	647.27	638.83	636.58	636.08	635.67	634.48	634.03
40000	663.87	655.21	652.91	652.39	651.97	650.75	650.29
45000	746.85	737.11	734.52	733.94	733.47	732.10	731.57
50000	829.84	819.01	816.13	815.49	814.96	813.44	812.86
55000	912.82	900.91	897.74	897.04	896.46	894.78	894.15
60000	995.80	982.81	979.36	978.59	977.96	976.13	975.43
65000	1078.79	1064.71	1060.97	1060.14	1059.45	1057.47	1056.72
70000	1161.77	1146.61	1142.58	1141.69	1140.95	1138.81	1138.00
75000	1244.75	1228.51	1224.20	1223.24	1222.44	1220.16	1219.29
80000	1327.74	1310.41	1305.81	1304.78	1303.94	1301.50	1300.57
85000	1410.72	1392.31	1387.42	1386.33	1385.44	1382.84	1381.86
90000	1493.70	1474.21	1469.03	1467.88	1466.93	1464.19	1463.14
95000	1576.69	1556.11	1550.65	1549.43	1548.43	1545.53	1544.43
100000	1659.67	1638.01	1632.26	1630.98	1629.93	1626.87	1625.71

19.75% MONTHLY AMORTIZING PAYMENTS

AMOUNT OF LOAN	NUMBER OF YEARS IN TERM						
	1	2	3	4	5	10	15
$ 25	2.32	1.27	.93	.76	.66	.48	.44
50	4.63	2.54	1.86	1.52	1.32	.96	.87
75	6.94	3.81	2.78	2.28	1.98	1.44	1.31
100	9.26	5.08	3.71	3.03	2.64	1.92	1.74
200	18.51	10.16	7.41	6.06	5.28	3.84	3.48
300	27.76	15.24	11.12	9.09	7.91	5.75	5.22
400	37.01	20.31	14.82	12.12	10.55	7.67	6.96
500	46.26	25.39	18.52	15.15	13.18	9.59	8.69
600	55.51	30.47	22.23	18.18	15.82	11.50	10.43
700	64.77	35.55	25.93	21.21	18.45	13.42	12.17
800	74.02	40.62	29.63	24.24	21.09	15.33	13.91
900	83.27	45.70	33.34	27.27	23.72	17.25	15.65
1000	92.52	50.78	37.04	30.30	26.36	19.17	17.38
2000	185.03	101.55	74.08	60.60	52.71	38.33	34.76
2500	231.29	126.94	92.60	75.75	65.89	47.91	43.45
3000	277.55	152.33	111.11	90.90	79.07	57.49	52.14
4000	370.06	203.10	148.15	121.19	105.42	76.65	69.52
5000	462.58	253.87	185.19	151.49	131.78	95.81	86.90
6000	555.09	304.65	222.22	181.79	158.13	114.97	104.28
7000	647.61	355.42	259.26	212.09	184.49	134.13	121.65
8000	740.12	406.20	296.30	242.38	210.84	153.29	139.03
9000	832.64	456.97	333.33	272.68	237.20	172.45	156.41
10000	925.15	507.74	370.37	302.98	263.55	191.61	173.79
11000	1017.67	558.52	407.40	333.28	289.91	210.77	191.17
12000	1110.18	609.29	444.44	363.57	316.26	229.93	208.55
13000	1202.70	660.06	481.48	393.87	342.62	249.09	225.93
14000	1295.21	710.84	518.51	424.17	368.97	268.25	243.30
15000	1387.73	761.61	555.55	454.46	395.33	287.41	260.68
16000	1480.24	812.39	592.59	484.76	421.68	306.57	278.06
17000	1572.76	863.16	629.62	515.06	448.04	325.73	295.44
18000	1665.27	913.93	666.66	545.36	474.39	344.89	312.82
19000	1757.79	964.71	703.70	575.65	500.75	364.05	330.20
20000	1850.30	1015.48	740.73	605.95	527.10	383.21	347.58
21000	1942.82	1066.25	777.77	636.25	553.46	402.37	364.95
22000	2035.33	1117.03	814.80	666.55	579.81	421.53	382.33
23000	2127.85	1167.80	851.84	696.84	606.17	440.69	399.71
24000	2220.36	1218.58	888.88	727.14	632.52	459.85	417.09
25000	2312.88	1269.35	925.91	757.44	658.88	479.01	434.47
26000	2405.39	1320.12	962.95	787.74	685.23	498.17	451.85
27000	2497.91	1370.90	999.99	818.03	711.59	517.33	469.23
28000	2590.42	1421.67	1037.02	848.33	737.94	536.49	486.60
29000	2682.94	1472.44	1074.06	878.63	764.30	555.65	503.98
30000	2775.45	1523.22	1111.09	908.92	790.65	574.81	521.36
31000	2867.97	1573.99	1148.13	939.22	817.01	593.97	538.74
32000	2960.48	1624.77	1185.17	969.52	843.36	613.13	556.12
33000	3053.00	1675.54	1222.20	999.82	869.72	632.29	573.50
34000	3145.51	1726.31	1259.24	1030.11	896.07	651.45	590.88
35000	3238.03	1777.09	1296.28	1060.41	922.43	670.61	608.25
36000	3330.54	1827.86	1333.31	1090.71	948.78	689.77	625.63
37000	3423.06	1878.63	1370.35	1121.01	975.14	708.93	643.01
38000	3515.57	1929.41	1407.39	1151.30	1001.49	728.09	660.39
39000	3608.09	1980.18	1444.42	1181.60	1027.85	747.25	677.77
40000	3700.60	2030.96	1481.46	1211.90	1054.20	766.41	695.15
45000	4163.18	2284.82	1666.64	1363.38	1185.98	862.21	782.04
50000	4625.75	2538.69	1851.82	1514.87	1317.75	958.01	868.93
55000	5088.32	2792.56	2037.00	1666.36	1449.53	1053.81	955.83
60000	5550.90	3046.43	2222.18	1817.84	1581.30	1149.61	1042.72
65000	6013.47	3300.30	2407.37	1969.33	1713.08	1245.41	1129.61
70000	6476.05	3554.17	2592.55	2120.82	1844.85	1341.21	1216.50
75000	6938.62	3808.04	2777.73	2272.30	1976.63	1437.01	1303.40
80000	7401.20	4061.91	2962.91	2423.79	2108.40	1532.81	1390.29
85000	7863.77	4315.77	3148.09	2575.28	2240.18	1628.61	1477.18
90000	8326.35	4569.64	3333.27	2726.76	2371.95	1724.41	1564.07
95000	8788.92	4823.51	3518.46	2878.25	2503.73	1820.21	1650.97
100000	9251.49	5077.38	3703.64	3029.74	2635.50	1916.02	1737.86

AMOUNT OF LOAN	NUMBER OF YEARS IN TERM						
	20	25	28	29	30	35	40
$ 25	.42	.42	.42	.42	.42	.42	.42
50	.84	.83	.83	.83	.83	.83	.83
75	1.26	1.25	1.24	1.24	1.24	1.24	1.24
100	1.68	1.66	1.66	1.66	1.66	1.65	1.65
200	3.36	3.32	3.31	3.31	3.31	3.30	3.30
300	5.04	4.98	4.96	4.96	4.96	4.95	4.94
400	6.72	6.64	6.62	6.61	6.61	6.60	6.59
500	8.40	8.30	8.27	8.26	8.26	8.24	8.24
600	10.08	9.95	9.92	9.91	9.91	9.89	9.88
700	11.76	11.61	11.57	11.57	11.56	11.54	11.53
800	13.44	13.27	13.23	13.22	13.21	13.19	13.18
900	15.12	14.93	14.88	14.87	14.86	14.83	14.82
1000	16.80	16.59	16.53	16.52	16.51	16.48	16.47
2000	33.59	33.17	33.06	33.03	33.01	32.96	32.93
2500	41.99	41.46	41.32	41.29	41.27	41.19	41.17
3000	50.38	49.75	49.59	49.55	49.52	49.43	49.40
4000	67.17	66.33	66.11	66.06	66.02	65.91	65.86
5000	83.97	82.92	82.64	82.58	82.53	82.38	82.33
6000	100.76	99.50	99.17	99.09	99.03	98.86	98.79
7000	117.55	116.08	115.69	115.61	115.54	115.33	115.26
8000	134.34	132.66	132.22	132.12	132.04	131.81	131.72
9000	151.14	149.24	148.75	148.64	148.55	148.29	148.19
10000	167.93	165.83	165.27	165.15	165.05	164.76	164.65
11000	184.72	182.41	181.80	181.67	181.56	181.24	181.12
12000	201.51	198.99	198.33	198.18	198.06	197.71	197.58
13000	218.30	215.57	214.85	214.70	214.56	214.19	214.05
14000	235.10	232.16	231.38	231.21	231.07	230.66	230.51
15000	251.89	248.74	247.91	247.72	247.57	247.14	246.98
16000	268.68	265.32	264.44	264.24	264.08	263.62	263.44
17000	285.47	281.90	280.96	280.75	280.58	280.09	279.91
18000	302.27	298.48	297.49	297.27	297.09	296.57	296.37
19000	319.06	315.07	314.02	313.78	313.59	313.04	312.84
20000	335.85	331.65	330.54	330.30	330.10	329.52	329.30
21000	352.64	348.23	347.07	346.81	346.60	345.99	345.77
22000	369.43	364.81	363.60	363.33	363.11	362.47	362.23
23000	386.23	381.39	380.12	379.84	379.61	378.95	378.70
24000	403.02	397.98	396.65	396.36	396.12	395.42	395.16
25000	419.81	414.56	413.18	412.87	412.62	411.90	411.63
26000	436.60	431.14	429.70	429.39	429.12	428.37	428.09
27000	453.40	447.72	446.23	445.90	445.63	444.85	444.56
28000	470.19	464.31	462.76	462.42	462.13	461.32	461.02
29000	486.98	480.89	479.29	478.93	478.64	477.80	477.49
30000	503.77	497.47	495.81	495.44	495.14	494.28	493.95
31000	520.56	514.05	512.34	511.96	511.65	510.75	510.42
32000	537.36	530.63	528.87	528.47	528.15	527.23	526.88
33000	554.15	547.22	545.39	544.99	544.66	543.70	543.34
34000	570.94	563.80	561.92	561.50	561.16	560.18	559.81
35000	587.73	580.38	578.45	578.02	577.67	576.65	576.27
36000	604.53	596.96	594.97	594.53	594.17	593.13	592.74
37000	621.32	613.54	611.50	611.05	610.68	609.61	609.20
38000	638.11	630.13	628.03	627.56	627.18	626.08	625.67
39000	654.90	646.71	644.55	644.08	643.68	642.56	642.13
40000	671.69	663.29	661.08	660.59	660.19	659.03	658.60
45000	755.66	746.20	743.72	743.16	742.71	741.41	740.92
50000	839.62	829.11	826.35	825.74	825.24	823.79	823.25
55000	923.58	912.02	908.98	908.31	907.76	906.17	905.57
60000	1007.54	994.93	991.62	990.88	990.28	988.55	987.90
65000	1091.50	1077.84	1074.25	1073.46	1072.80	1070.92	1070.22
70000	1175.46	1160.76	1156.89	1156.03	1155.33	1153.30	1152.54
75000	1259.42	1243.67	1239.52	1238.60	1237.85	1235.68	1234.87
80000	1343.38	1326.58	1322.16	1321.18	1320.37	1318.06	1317.19
85000	1427.34	1409.49	1404.79	1403.75	1402.90	1400.44	1399.52
90000	1511.31	1492.40	1487.43	1486.32	1485.42	1482.82	1481.84
95000	1595.27	1575.31	1570.06	1568.90	1567.94	1565.19	1564.17
100000	1679.23	1658.22	1652.69	1651.47	1650.47	1647.57	1646.49

20.00% MONTHLY AMORTIZING PAYMENTS

AMOUNT OF LOAN	NUMBER OF YEARS IN TERM						
	1	2	3	4	5	10	15
$ 25	2.32	1.28	.93	.77	.67	.49	.44
50	4.64	2.55	1.86	1.53	1.33	.97	.88
75	6.95	3.82	2.79	2.29	1.99	1.45	1.32
100	9.27	5.09	3.72	3.05	2.65	1.94	1.76
200	18.53	10.18	7.44	6.09	5.30	3.87	3.52
300	27.80	15.27	11.15	9.13	7.95	5.80	5.27
400	37.06	20.36	14.87	12.18	10.60	7.74	7.03
500	46.32	25.45	18.59	15.22	13.25	9.67	8.79
600	55.59	30.54	22.30	18.26	15.90	11.60	10.54
700	64.85	35.63	26.02	21.31	18.55	13.53	12.30
800	74.11	40.72	29.74	24.35	21.20	15.47	14.06
900	83.38	45.81	33.45	27.39	23.85	17.40	15.81
1000	92.64	50.90	37.17	30.44	26.50	19.33	17.57
2000	185.27	101.80	74.33	60.87	52.99	38.66	35.13
2500	231.59	127.24	92.91	76.08	66.24	48.32	43.91
3000	277.91	152.69	111.50	91.30	79.49	57.98	52.69
4000	370.54	203.59	148.66	121.73	105.98	77.31	70.26
5000	463.18	254.48	185.82	152.16	132.47	96.63	87.82
6000	555.81	305.38	222.99	182.59	158.97	115.96	105.38
7000	648.45	356.28	260.15	213.02	185.46	135.28	122.95
8000	741.08	407.17	297.31	243.45	211.96	154.61	140.51
9000	833.72	458.07	334.48	273.88	238.45	173.94	158.07
10000	926.35	508.96	371.64	304.31	264.94	193.26	175.63
11000	1018.98	559.86	408.80	334.74	291.44	212.59	193.20
12000	1111.62	610.75	445.97	365.17	317.93	231.91	210.76
13000	1204.25	661.65	483.13	395.60	344.43	251.24	228.32
14000	1296.89	712.55	520.30	426.03	370.92	270.56	245.89
15000	1389.52	763.44	557.46	456.46	397.41	289.89	263.45
16000	1482.16	814.34	594.62	486.89	423.91	309.21	281.01
17000	1574.79	865.23	631.79	517.32	450.40	328.54	298.58
18000	1667.43	916.13	668.95	547.75	476.89	347.87	316.14
19000	1760.06	967.03	706.11	578.18	503.39	367.19	333.70
20000	1852.70	1017.92	743.28	608.61	529.88	386.52	351.26
21000	1945.33	1068.82	780.44	639.04	556.38	405.84	368.83
22000	2037.96	1119.71	817.60	669.47	582.87	425.17	386.39
23000	2130.60	1170.61	854.77	699.90	609.36	444.49	403.95
24000	2223.23	1221.50	891.93	730.33	635.86	463.82	421.52
25000	2315.87	1272.40	929.09	760.76	662.35	483.14	439.08
26000	2408.50	1323.30	966.26	791.19	688.85	502.47	456.64
27000	2501.14	1374.19	1003.42	821.62	715.34	521.80	474.21
28000	2593.77	1425.09	1040.59	852.06	741.83	541.12	491.77
29000	2686.41	1475.98	1077.75	882.49	768.33	560.45	509.33
30000	2779.04	1526.88	1114.91	912.92	794.82	579.77	526.89
31000	2871.67	1577.77	1152.08	943.35	821.32	599.10	544.46
32000	2964.31	1628.67	1189.24	973.78	847.81	618.42	562.02
33000	3056.94	1679.57	1226.40	1004.21	874.30	637.75	579.58
34000	3149.58	1730.46	1263.57	1034.64	900.80	657.07	597.15
35000	3242.21	1781.36	1300.73	1065.07	927.29	676.40	614.71
36000	3334.85	1832.25	1337.89	1095.50	953.78	695.73	632.27
37000	3427.48	1883.15	1375.06	1125.93	980.28	715.05	649.83
38000	3520.12	1934.05	1412.22	1156.36	1006.77	734.38	667.40
39000	3612.75	1984.94	1449.38	1186.79	1033.27	753.70	684.96
40000	3705.39	2035.84	1486.55	1217.22	1059.76	773.03	702.52
45000	4168.56	2290.32	1672.37	1369.37	1192.23	869.66	790.34
50000	4631.73	2544.80	1858.18	1521.52	1324.70	966.28	878.15
55000	5094.90	2799.27	2044.00	1673.67	1457.17	1062.91	965.97
60000	5558.08	3053.75	2229.82	1825.83	1589.64	1159.54	1053.78
65000	6021.25	3308.23	2415.64	1977.98	1722.11	1256.17	1141.60
70000	6484.42	3562.71	2601.46	2130.13	1854.58	1352.79	1229.41
75000	6947.59	3817.19	2787.27	2282.28	1987.05	1449.42	1317.23
80000	7410.77	4071.67	2973.09	2434.43	2119.52	1546.05	1405.04
85000	7873.94	4326.15	3158.91	2586.59	2251.99	1642.68	1492.86
90000	8337.11	4580.63	3344.73	2738.74	2384.45	1739.31	1580.67
95000	8800.28	4835.11	3530.55	2890.89	2516.92	1835.93	1668.49
100000	9263.46	5089.59	3716.36	3043.04	2649.39	1932.56	1756.30

MONTHLY AMORTIZING PAYMENTS 20.00%

AMOUNT OF LOAN	NUMBER OF YEARS IN TERM						
	20	25	28	29	30	35	40
$ 25	.43	.42	.42	.42	.42	.42	.42
50	.85	.84	.84	.84	.84	.84	.84
75	1.28	1.26	1.26	1.26	1.26	1.26	1.26
100	1.70	1.68	1.68	1.68	1.68	1.67	1.67
200	3.40	3.36	3.35	3.35	3.35	3.34	3.34
300	5.10	5.04	5.02	5.02	5.02	5.01	5.01
400	6.80	6.72	6.70	6.69	6.69	6.68	6.67
500	8.50	8.40	8.37	8.36	8.36	8.35	8.34
600	10.20	10.08	10.04	10.04	10.03	10.01	10.01
700	11.90	11.75	11.72	11.71	11.70	11.68	11.68
800	13.60	13.43	13.39	13.38	13.37	13.35	13.34
900	15.29	15.11	15.06	15.05	15.04	15.02	15.01
1000	16.99	16.79	16.74	16.72	16.72	16.69	16.68
2000	33.98	33.57	33.47	33.44	33.43	33.37	33.35
2500	42.48	41.97	41.83	41.80	41.78	41.71	41.69
3000	50.97	50.36	50.20	50.16	50.14	50.05	50.02
4000	67.96	67.14	66.93	66.88	66.85	66.74	66.70
5000	84.95	83.93	83.66	83.60	83.56	83.42	83.37
6000	101.93	100.71	100.39	100.32	100.27	100.10	100.04
7000	118.92	117.50	117.13	117.04	116.98	116.78	116.71
8000	135.91	134.28	133.86	133.76	133.69	133.47	133.39
9000	152.90	151.07	150.59	150.48	150.40	150.15	150.06
10000	169.89	167.85	167.32	167.20	167.11	166.83	166.73
11000	186.88	184.63	184.05	183.92	183.82	183.52	183.40
12000	203.86	201.42	200.78	200.64	200.53	200.20	200.08
13000	220.85	218.20	217.51	217.36	217.24	216.88	216.75
14000	237.84	234.99	234.25	234.08	233.95	233.56	233.42
15000	254.83	251.77	250.98	250.80	250.66	250.25	250.09
16000	271.82	268.56	267.71	267.52	267.37	266.93	266.77
17000	288.81	285.34	284.44	284.24	284.08	283.61	283.44
18000	305.79	302.13	301.17	300.96	300.79	300.30	300.11
19000	322.78	318.91	317.90	317.68	317.50	316.98	316.79
20000	339.77	335.70	334.63	334.40	334.21	333.66	333.46
21000	356.76	352.48	351.37	351.12	350.92	350.34	350.13
22000	373.75	369.26	368.10	367.84	367.63	367.03	366.80
23000	390.73	386.05	384.83	384.56	384.34	383.71	383.48
24000	407.72	402.83	401.56	401.28	401.05	400.39	400.15
25000	424.71	419.62	418.29	418.00	417.76	417.07	416.82
26000	441.70	436.40	435.02	434.72	434.47	433.76	433.49
27000	458.69	453.19	451.75	451.44	451.18	450.44	450.17
28000	475.68	469.97	468.49	468.16	467.89	467.12	466.84
29000	492.66	486.76	485.22	484.88	484.60	483.81	483.51
30000	509.65	503.54	501.95	501.60	501.31	500.49	500.18
31000	526.64	520.33	518.68	518.32	518.02	517.17	516.86
32000	543.63	537.11	535.41	535.04	534.73	533.85	533.53
33000	560.62	553.89	552.14	551.76	551.44	550.54	550.20
34000	577.61	570.68	568.87	568.48	568.15	567.22	566.87
35000	594.59	587.46	585.61	585.20	584.86	583.90	583.55
36000	611.58	604.25	602.34	601.92	601.57	600.59	600.22
37000	628.57	621.03	619.07	618.64	618.28	617.27	616.89
38000	645.56	637.82	635.80	635.36	634.99	633.95	633.57
39000	662.55	654.60	652.53	652.08	651.70	650.63	650.24
40000	679.53	671.39	669.26	668.80	668.41	667.32	666.91
45000	764.48	755.31	752.92	752.39	751.96	750.73	750.27
50000	849.42	839.23	836.58	835.99	835.51	834.14	833.64
55000	934.36	923.15	920.24	919.59	919.07	917.56	917.00
60000	1019.30	1007.08	1003.89	1003.19	1002.62	1000.97	1000.36
65000	1104.24	1091.00	1087.55	1086.79	1086.17	1084.39	1083.73
70000	1189.18	1174.92	1171.21	1170.39	1169.72	1167.80	1167.09
75000	1274.12	1258.84	1254.86	1253.99	1253.27	1251.21	1250.45
80000	1359.06	1342.77	1338.52	1337.59	1336.82	1334.63	1333.82
85000	1444.01	1426.69	1422.18	1421.19	1420.37	1418.04	1417.18
90000	1528.95	1510.61	1505.84	1504.78	1503.92	1501.46	1500.54
95000	1613.89	1594.53	1589.49	1588.38	1587.47	1584.87	1583.91
100000	1698.83	1678.46	1673.15	1671.98	1671.02	1668.28	1667.27

91

21.00% MONTHLY AMORTIZING PAYMENTS

AMOUNT OF LOAN	NUMBER OF YEARS IN TERM						
	1	2	3	4	5	10	15
$ 25	2.33	1.29	.95	.78	.68	.50	.46
50	4.66	2.57	1.89	1.55	1.36	1.00	.92
75	6.99	3.86	2.83	2.33	2.03	1.50	1.38
100	9.32	5.14	3.77	3.10	2.71	2.00	1.84
200	18.63	10.28	7.54	6.20	5.42	4.00	3.67
300	27.94	15.42	11.31	9.29	8.12	6.00	5.50
400	37.25	20.56	15.08	12.39	10.83	8.00	7.33
500	46.56	25.70	18.84	15.49	13.53	10.00	9.16
600	55.87	30.84	22.61	18.58	16.24	12.00	10.99
700	65.18	35.97	26.38	21.68	18.94	14.00	12.82
800	74.50	41.11	30.15	24.78	21.65	16.00	14.65
900	83.81	46.25	33.91	27.87	24.35	18.00	16.48
1000	93.12	51.39	37.68	30.97	27.06	20.00	18.31
2000	186.23	102.78	75.36	61.94	54.11	39.99	36.62
2500	232.79	128.47	94.19	77.42	67.64	49.99	45.77
3000	279.35	154.16	113.03	92.90	81.17	59.98	54.92
4000	372.46	205.55	150.71	123.87	108.22	79.98	73.23
5000	465.57	256.93	188.38	154.83	135.27	99.97	91.54
6000	558.69	308.32	226.06	185.80	162.33	119.96	109.84
7000	651.80	359.70	263.73	216.76	189.38	139.96	128.15
8000	744.92	411.09	301.41	247.73	216.43	159.95	146.45
9000	838.03	462.48	339.08	278.70	243.49	179.94	164.76
10000	931.14	513.86	376.76	309.66	270.54	199.94	183.07
11000	1024.26	565.25	414.43	340.63	297.59	219.93	201.37
12000	1117.37	616.63	452.11	371.59	324.65	239.92	219.68
13000	1210.48	668.02	489.78	402.56	351.70	259.92	237.98
14000	1303.60	719.40	527.46	433.52	378.75	279.91	256.29
15000	1396.71	770.79	565.13	464.49	405.81	299.90	274.60
16000	1489.83	822.18	602.81	495.46	432.86	319.90	292.90
17000	1582.94	873.56	640.48	526.42	459.91	339.89	311.21
18000	1676.05	924.95	678.16	557.39	486.97	359.88	329.52
19000	1769.17	976.33	715.83	588.35	514.02	379.88	347.82
20000	1862.28	1027.72	753.51	619.32	541.07	399.87	366.13
21000	1955.39	1079.10	791.18	650.28	568.13	419.86	384.43
22000	2048.51	1130.49	828.86	681.25	595.18	439.85	402.74
23000	2141.62	1181.87	866.53	712.22	622.23	459.85	421.05
24000	2234.74	1233.26	904.21	743.18	649.29	479.84	439.35
25000	2327.85	1284.65	941.88	774.15	676.34	499.83	457.66
26000	2420.96	1336.03	979.56	805.11	703.39	519.83	475.96
27000	2514.08	1387.42	1017.23	836.08	730.45	539.82	494.27
28000	2607.19	1438.80	1054.91	867.04	757.50	559.81	512.58
29000	2700.30	1490.19	1092.58	898.01	784.55	579.81	530.88
30000	2793.42	1541.57	1130.26	928.98	811.61	599.80	549.19
31000	2886.53	1592.96	1167.93	959.94	838.66	619.79	567.49
32000	2979.65	1644.35	1205.61	990.91	865.71	639.79	585.80
33000	3072.76	1695.73	1243.28	1021.87	892.77	659.78	604.11
34000	3165.87	1747.12	1280.96	1052.84	919.82	679.77	622.41
35000	3258.99	1798.50	1318.63	1083.80	946.87	699.77	640.72
36000	3352.10	1849.89	1356.31	1114.77	973.93	719.76	659.03
37000	3445.21	1901.27	1393.98	1145.74	1000.98	739.75	677.33
38000	3538.33	1952.66	1431.66	1176.70	1028.03	759.75	695.64
39000	3631.44	2004.05	1469.33	1207.67	1055.09	779.74	713.94
40000	3724.56	2055.43	1507.01	1238.63	1082.14	799.73	732.25
45000	4190.12	2312.36	1695.38	1393.46	1217.41	899.70	823.78
50000	4655.69	2569.28	1883.76	1548.29	1352.67	999.66	915.31
55000	5121.26	2826.22	2072.13	1703.12	1487.94	1099.63	1006.84
60000	5586.83	3083.14	2260.51	1857.95	1623.21	1199.60	1098.37
65000	6052.40	3340.07	2448.88	2012.78	1758.47	1299.56	1189.90
70000	6517.97	3597.00	2637.26	2167.60	1893.74	1399.53	1281.43
75000	6983.54	3853.93	2825.64	2322.43	2029.01	1499.49	1372.96
80000	7449.11	4110.86	3014.01	2477.26	2164.27	1599.46	1464.49
85000	7914.68	4367.79	3202.39	2632.09	2299.54	1699.42	1556.03
90000	8380.24	4624.71	3390.76	2786.92	2434.81	1799.39	1647.56
95000	8845.81	4881.64	3579.14	2941.75	2570.07	1899.36	1739.09
100000	9311.38	5138.57	3767.51	3096.57	2705.34	1999.32	1830.62

MONTHLY AMORTIZING PAYMENTS 21.00%

AMOUNT OF LOAN	NUMBER OF YEARS IN TERM						
	20	25	28	29	30	35	40
$ 25	.45	.44	.44	.44	.44	.44	44
50	.89	.88	.88	.88	.88	.88	.88
75	1.34	1.32	1.32	1.32	1.32	1.32	1.32
100	1.78	1.76	1.76	1.76	1.76	1.76	1.76
200	3.56	3.52	3.52	3.51	3.51	3.51	3.51
300	5.34	5.28	5.27	5.27	5.27	5.26	5.26
400	7.12	7.04	7.03	7.02	7.02	7.01	7.01
500	8.89	8.80	8.78	8.78	8.77	8.76	8.76
600	10.67	10.56	10.54	10.53	10.53	10.51	10.51
700	12.45	12.32	12.29	12.28	12.28	12.26	12.26
800	14.23	14.08	14.05	14.04	14.03	14.01	14.01
900	16.00	15.84	15.80	15.79	15.79	15.77	15.76
1000	17.78	17.60	17.56	17.55	17.54	17.52	17.51
2000	35.56	35.20	35.11	35.09	35.07	35.03	35.01
2500	44.45	44.00	43.88	43.86	43.84	43.78	43.77
3000	53.33	52.79	52.66	52.63	52.61	52.54	52.52
4000	71.11	70.39	70.21	70.17	70.14	70.05	70.02
5000	88.89	87.99	87.76	87.71	87.68	87.56	87.53
6000	106.66	105.58	105.31	105.26	105.21	105.08	105.03
7000	124.44	123.18	122.87	122.80	122.74	122.59	122.53
8000	142.22	140.78	140.42	140.34	140.28	140.10	140.04
9000	159.99	158.37	157.97	157.88	157.81	157.61	157.54
10000	177.77	175.97	175.52	175.42	175.35	175.12	175.05
11000	195.55	193.57	193.07	192.97	192.88	192.64	192.55
12000	213.32	211.16	210.62	210.51	210.41	210.15	210.06
13000	231.10	228.76	228.18	228.05	227.95	227.66	227.56
14000	248.88	246.36	245.73	245.59	245.48	245.17	245.06
15000	266.65	263.95	263.28	263.13	263.02	262.68	262.57
16000	284.43	281.55	280.83	280.68	280.55	280.20	280.07
17000	302.20	299.15	298.38	298.22	298.08	297.71	297.58
18000	319.98	316.74	315.93	315.76	315.62	315.22	315.08
19000	337.76	334.34	333.49	333.30	333.15	332.73	332.59
20000	355.53	351.94	351.04	350.84	350.69	350.24	350.09
21000	373.31	369.53	368.59	368.38	368.22	367.76	367.59
22000	391.09	387.13	386.14	385.93	385.75	385.27	385.10
23000	408.86	404.73	403.69	403.47	403.29	402.78	402.60
24000	426.64	422.32	421.24	421.01	420.82	420.29	420.11
25000	444.42	439.92	438.80	438.55	438.36	437.80	437.61
26000	462.19	457.52	456.35	456.09	455.89	455.32	455.12
27000	479.97	475.11	473.90	473.64	473.42	472.83	472.62
28000	497.75	492.71	491.45	491.18	490.96	490.34	490.12
29000	515.52	510.31	509.00	508.72	508.49	507.85	507.63
30000	533.30	527.90	526.55	526.26	526.03	525.36	525.13
31000	551.07	545.50	544.10	543.80	543.56	542.88	542.64
32000	568.85	563.10	561.66	561.35	561.10	560.39	560.14
33000	586.63	580.69	579.21	578.89	578.63	577.90	577.64
34000	604.40	598.29	596.76	596.43	596.16	595.41	595.15
35000	622.18	615.89	614.31	613.97	613.70	612.92	612.65
36000	639.96	633.48	631.86	631.51	631.23	630.44	630.16
37000	657.73	651.08	649.41	649.05	648.76	647.95	647.66
38000	675.51	668.68	666.97	666.60	666.30	665.46	665.17
39000	693.29	686.27	684.52	684.14	683.83	682.97	682.67
40000	711.06	703.87	702.07	701.68	701.37	700.48	700.17
45000	799.94	791.85	789.83	789.39	789.04	788.04	787.70
50000	888.83	879.84	877.59	877.10	876.71	875.60	875.22
55000	977.71	967.82	965.34	964.81	964.38	963.16	962.74
60000	1066.59	1055.80	1053.10	1052.52	1052.05	1050.72	1050.26
65000	1155.47	1143.79	1140.86	1140.23	1139.72	1138.28	1137.78
70000	1244.36	1231.77	1228.62	1227.94	1227.39	1225.84	1225.30
75000	1333.24	1319.75	1316.38	1315.65	1315.06	1313.40	1312.82
80000	1422.12	1407.74	1404.13	1403.36	1402.73	1400.96	1400.34
85000	1511.00	1495.72	1491.89	1491.07	1490.40	1488.52	1487.86
90000	1599.88	1583.70	1579.65	1578.77	1578.07	1576.08	1575.39
95000	1688.77	1671.68	1667.41	1666.48	1665.74	1663.64	1662.91
100000	1777.65	1759.67	1755.17	1754.19	1753.41	1751.20	1750.43

93

22.00% MONTHLY AMORTIZING PAYMENTS

AMOUNT OF LOAN	NUMBER OF YEARS IN TERM						
	1	2	3	4	5	10	15
$ 25	2.34	1.30	.96	.79	.70	.52	.48
50	4.68	2.60	1.91	1.58	1.39	1.04	.96
75	7.02	3.90	2.87	2.37	2.08	1.56	1.43
100	9.36	5.19	3.82	3.16	2.77	2.07	1.91
200	18.72	10.38	7.64	6.31	5.53	4.14	3.82
300	28.08	15.57	11.46	9.46	8.29	6.21	5.72
400	37.44	20.76	15.28	12.61	11.05	8.27	7.63
500	46.80	25.94	19.10	15.76	13.81	10.34	9.53
600	56.16	31.13	22.92	18.91	16.58	12.41	11.44
700	65.52	36.32	26.74	22.06	19.34	14.47	13.35
800	74.88	41.51	30.56	25.21	22.10	16.54	15.25
900	84.24	46.70	34.38	28.36	24.86	18.61	17.16
1000	93.60	51.88	38.20	31.51	27.62	20.67	19.06
2000	187.19	103.76	76.39	63.02	55.24	41.34	38.12
2500	233.99	129.70	95.48	78.77	69.05	51.68	47.65
3000	280.79	155.64	114.58	94.52	82.86	62.01	57.18
4000	374.38	207.52	152.77	126.03	110.48	82.68	76.24
5000	467.98	259.40	190.96	157.54	138.10	103.35	95.29
6000	561.57	311.27	229.15	189.04	165.72	124.02	114.35
7000	655.17	363.15	267.34	220.55	193.34	144.69	133.41
8000	748.76	415.03	305.53	252.05	220.96	165.36	152.47
9000	842.35	466.91	343.72	283.56	248.58	186.03	171.52
10000	935.95	518.79	381.91	315.07	276.19	206.70	190.58
11000	1029.54	570.66	420.10	346.57	303.81	227.37	209.64
12000	1123.14	622.54	458.29	378.08	331.43	248.04	228.70
13000	1216.73	674.42	496.48	409.58	359.05	268.71	247.75
14000	1310.33	726.30	534.67	441.09	386.67	289.38	266.81
15000	1403.92	778.18	572.86	472.60	414.29	310.05	285.87
16000	1497.52	830.06	611.05	504.10	441.91	330.72	304.93
17000	1591.11	881.93	649.24	535.61	469.53	351.39	323.98
18000	1684.70	933.81	687.43	567.11	497.15	372.06	343.04
19000	1778.30	985.69	725.62	598.62	524.76	392.73	362.10
20000	1871.89	1037.57	763.81	630.13	552.38	413.40	381.16
21000	1965.49	1089.45	802.00	661.63	580.00	434.07	400.21
22000	2059.08	1141.32	840.19	693.14	607.62	454.74	419.27
23000	2152.68	1193.20	878.39	724.64	635.24	475.41	438.33
24000	2246.27	1245.08	916.58	756.15	662.86	496.08	457.39
25000	2339.86	1296.96	954.77	787.66	690.48	516.75	476.44
26000	2433.46	1348.84	992.96	819.16	718.10	537.42	495.50
27000	2527.05	1400.72	1031.15	850.67	745.72	558.09	514.56
28000	2620.65	1452.59	1069.34	882.18	773.33	578.76	533.62
29000	2714.24	1504.47	1107.53	913.68	800.95	599.43	552.67
30000	2807.84	1556.35	1145.72	945.19	828.57	620.10	571.73
31000	2901.43	1608.23	1183.91	976.69	856.19	640.77	590.79
32000	2995.03	1660.11	1222.10	1008.20	883.81	661.44	609.85
33000	3088.62	1711.98	1260.29	1039.71	911.43	682.10	628.90
34000	3182.21	1763.86	1298.48	1071.21	939.05	702.77	647.96
35000	3275.81	1815.74	1336.67	1102.72	966.67	723.44	667.02
36000	3369.40	1867.62	1374.86	1134.22	994.29	744.11	686.08
37000	3463.00	1919.50	1413.05	1165.73	1021.90	764.78	705.13
38000	3556.59	1971.37	1451.24	1197.24	1049.52	785.45	724.19
39000	3650.19	2023.25	1489.43	1228.74	1077.14	806.12	743.25
40000	3743.78	2075.13	1527.62	1260.25	1104.76	826.79	762.31
45000	4211.75	2334.52	1718.58	1417.78	1242.86	930.14	857.60
50000	4679.72	2593.91	1909.53	1575.31	1380.95	1033.49	952.88
55000	5147.70	2853.30	2100.48	1732.84	1519.05	1136.84	1048.17
60000	5615.67	3112.69	2291.43	1890.37	1657.14	1240.19	1143.46
65000	6083.64	3372.09	2482.38	2047.90	1795.23	1343.53	1238.75
70000	6551.61	3631.48	2673.34	2205.43	1933.33	1446.88	1334.03
75000	7019.58	3890.87	2864.29	2362.96	2071.42	1550.23	1429.32
80000	7487.56	4150.26	3055.24	2520.49	2209.52	1653.58	1524.61
85000	7955.53	4409.65	3246.19	2678.02	2347.61	1756.93	1619.90
90000	8423.50	4669.04	3437.15	2835.55	2485.71	1860.28	1715.19
95000	8891.47	4928.43	3628.10	2993.08	2623.80	1963.63	1810.47
100000	9359.44	5187.82	3819.05	3150.61	2761.90	2066.97	1905.76

MONTHLY AMORTIZING PAYMENTS 22.00%

AMOUNT OF LOAN	NUMBER OF YEARS IN TERM						
	20	25	28	29	30	35	40
$ 25	.47	.47	.46	.46	.46	.46	.46
50	.93	.93	.92	.92	.92	.92	.92
75	1.40	1.39	1.38	1.38	1.38	1.38	1.38
100	1.86	1.85	1.84	1.84	1.84	1.84	1.84
200	3.72	3.69	3.68	3.68	3.68	3.67	3.67
300	5.58	5.53	5.52	5.51	5.51	5.51	5.51
400	7.43	7.37	7.35	7.35	7.35	7.34	7.34
500	9.29	9.21	9.19	9.19	9.18	9.18	9.17
600	11.15	11.05	11.03	11.02	11.02	11.01	11.01
700	13.00	12.89	12.87	12.86	12.86	12.84	12.84
800	14.86	14.73	14.70	14.70	14.69	14.68	14.67
900	16.72	16.58	16.54	16.53	16.53	16.51	16.51
1000	18.58	18.42	18.38	18.37	18.36	18.35	18.34
2000	37.15	36.83	36.75	36.74	36.72	36.69	36.68
2500	46.43	46.04	45.94	45.92	45.90	45.86	45.85
3000	55.72	55.24	55.13	55.10	55.08	55.03	55.01
4000	74.29	73.65	73.50	73.47	73.44	73.37	73.35
5000	92.86	92.07	91.88	91.84	91.80	91.72	91.69
6000	111.43	110.48	110.25	110.20	110.16	110.06	110.02
7000	130.00	128.89	128.63	128.57	128.52	128.40	128.36
8000	148.57	147.30	147.00	146.94	146.88	146.74	146.70
9000	167.14	165.72	165.37	165.30	165.24	165.09	165.03
10000	185.71	184.13	183.75	183.67	183.60	183.43	183.37
11000	204.28	202.54	202.12	202.03	201.96	201.77	201.70
12000	222.85	220.95	220.50	220.40	220.32	220.11	220.04
13000	241.42	239.37	238.87	238.77	238.68	238.45	238.38
14000	259.99	257.78	257.25	257.13	257.04	256.80	256.71
15000	278.56	276.19	275.62	275.50	275.40	275.14	275.05
16000	297.13	294.60	293.99	293.87	293.76	293.48	293.39
17000	315.71	313.02	312.37	312.23	312.12	311.82	311.72
18000	334.28	331.43	330.74	330.60	330.48	330.17	330.06
19000	352.85	349.84	349.12	348.97	348.84	348.51	348.40
20000	371.42	368.25	367.49	367.33	367.20	366.85	366.73
21000	389.99	386.67	385.87	385.70	385.56	385.19	385.07
22000	408.56	405.08	404.24	404.06	403.92	403.53	403.40
23000	427.13	423.49	422.62	422.43	422.28	421.88	421.74
24000	445.70	441.90	440.99	440.80	440.64	440.22	440.08
25000	464.27	460.32	459.36	459.16	459.00	458.56	458.41
26000	482.84	478.73	477.74	477.53	477.36	476.90	476.75
27000	501.41	497.14	496.11	495.90	495.72	495.25	495.09
28000	519.98	515.55	514.49	514.26	514.08	513.59	513.42
29000	538.55	533.97	532.86	532.63	532.44	531.93	531.76
30000	557.12	552.38	551.24	550.99	550.80	550.27	550.09
31000	575.69	570.79	569.61	569.36	569.16	568.61	568.43
32000	594.26	589.20	587.98	587.73	587.52	586.96	586.77
33000	612.83	607.61	606.36	606.09	605.88	605.30	605.10
34000	631.41	626.03	624.73	624.46	624.24	623.64	623.44
35000	649.98	644.44	643.11	642.83	642.60	641.98	641.78
36000	668.55	662.85	661.48	661.19	660.96	660.33	660.11
37000	687.12	681.26	679.86	679.56	679.32	678.67	678.45
38000	705.69	699.68	698.23	697.93	697.68	697.01	696.79
39000	724.26	718.09	716.61	716.29	716.04	715.35	715.12
40000	742.83	736.50	734.98	734.66	734.40	733.69	733.46
45000	835.68	828.56	826.85	826.49	826.20	825.41	825.14
50000	928.53	920.63	918.72	918.32	918.00	917.12	916.82
55000	1021.39	1012.69	1010.60	1010.15	1009.80	1008.83	1008.50
60000	1114.24	1104.75	1102.47	1101.98	1101.60	1100.54	1100.18
65000	1207.09	1196.81	1194.34	1193.82	1193.40	1192.25	1191.87
70000	1299.95	1288.87	1286.21	1285.65	1285.19	1283.96	1283.55
75000	1392.80	1380.94	1378.08	1377.48	1376.99	1375.67	1375.23
80000	1485.65	1473.00	1469.95	1469.31	1468.79	1467.38	1466.91
85000	1578.51	1565.06	1561.83	1561.14	1560.59	1559.10	1558.59
90000	1671.36	1657.12	1653.70	1652.97	1652.39	1650.81	1650.27
95000	1764.21	1749.19	1745.57	1744.81	1744.19	1742.52	1741.96
100000	1857.06	1841.25	1837.44	1836.64	1835.99	1834.23	1833.64